BUSINESS STUDIES REVISION NOTES

FOR

JUNIOR CERTIFICATE

(4TH EDITION)

JOHN F. O'SULLIVAN

GILL & MACMILLAN

Gill & Macmillan Ltd
Hume Avenue
Park West
Dublin 12
with associated companies throughout the world
www.gillmacmillan.ie

978 07171 4122 7

Print origination by Carrigboy Typesetting Services

The paper used in this book is made from the wood pulp of managed forests. For every tree felled, at least one tree is planted, thereby renewing natural resources.

Contents

Section Three — Enterprise

Section Four — Information Technology

* **Higher level only**

Preface

The aim of this book is to provide students with a comprehensive summary of the Junior Certificate Business Studies course, both Ordinary and Higher level.

- All chapters updated reflecting recent Business Developments.
- It contains more than fifty fully worked solutions to past exam questions.
- A glossary of clearly defined business terms is included at the end of many chapters.
- Past examination papers are fully analysed with reference to specific questions outlined.
- The end of the book contains advice on how to approach the examination; exam format with specific information on description of questions, marks per question and time allocation is included.

I hope that this book will be of major assistance when revising business studies in the months prior to the Junior Certificate examination.

John F. O'Sullivan BComm HDE
Business Studies Department
St Peter's Community School
Passage West
Co. Cork

This book is dedicated to Claire, Breffni, Shane, Cillian and Jennifer.

SECTION ONE — THE BUSINESS OF LIVING

BUDGETING

Chapter 1 — Income

A. Income

Income is money we receive.

B. Regular Income

Regular income is received each week or month, e.g. wages, salary, unemployment benefit.

C. Additional Income

Additional income is received occasionally, e.g. overtime, bonus, commission.

D. Benefit in Kind — Perks

Official payments for work in forms other than money, e.g. company car, lunch vouchers.

Unofficial — private telephone calls, paper, pens.

E. Main Sources of Income

Employed	**Self-Employed**	**Unemployed**
Wage Salary Overtime Commission Bonus	Profit from business	Jobseeker's benefit
Student	**Pensioner**	
Pocket money Wage — part-time work Grant	State Pension Pension from work Wage — part-time work	

F. Gross Wage (Gross Pay)

Gross wage = basic pay + overtime + commission + bonus

G. Net Wage (Net Pay)

Net wage = gross pay – deductions

H. Deductions

There are two types of deduction: statutory deductions and non-statutory (voluntary) deductions.

1. Statutory Deductions

The two statutory deductions are PAYE and PRSI.

(1) **PAYE** (PAY AS YOU EARN)

This is income tax: every employee is liable to pay income tax, which is calculated using the 'Tax Credits' system as follows:

1. The employee is taxed on the full amount of their income, that is, income multiplied by the appropriate rate(s) of tax.
2. Employee's tax credit is deducted from tax liability to give net amount of income tax due.

Example — Tax Computation

John is single and earns €50,000 a year. He has single-person tax credit of €1,630 and a PAYE credit of €1,490. He pays tax on the first €32,000 at the rate of 20% and on the remainder of his salary at the rate of 42%.

Calculate: (i) John's net income tax due;
(ii) His net income for the year.

Solution

Wages/Salary			€50,000
Tax: 32,000 at 20%	6,400		
Tax: 18,000 at 42%	7,560		
Gross income tax		13,960	
Less tax credit			
Single-person tax credit	1,630		
PAYE tax credit	1,490	(3,120)	
Net income tax due			10,840
Net income for year			39,160

(2) **PRSI** (PAY-RELATED SOCIAL INSURANCE)

This is a contribution towards a social welfare benefit that may be claimed in the future, i.e. jobseeker's benefit, illness benefit and state pension.

PRSI is charged as a percentage of gross pay.

What income tax is used for	What PRSI is used for
It helps to pay for state services: Gardaí Army Health services Public services	It provides the following benefits: Jobseeker's benefit Maternity benefit State pension Illness benefit Deserted wife's benefit Widow's pension Dental/Optical benefit

J. Voluntary Deductions (NS Deductions)

These are deductions that the employee requests to be taken from his gross pay, e.g. union fees, Voluntary Health Insurance (VHI, BUPA), pension (superannuation), car insurance, savings. The employer deducts these and passes them on to the relevant organisation.

K. Summary

Gross pay = Basic pay + Overtime + Bonus + Commission
Net pay = Gross pay – Total deductions

L. Business Terms

Basic Wage Payment for working a normal week.
Bonus Income in addition to basic pay.
Budget A plan of future income and expenditure.
Commission A payment based on each item sold to encourage salespeople to sell more goods.
Deductions Money taken from an employee's pay before he receives it.
Gross Pay Total earnings before deductions.
Income Tax Money paid to the government, i.e. PAYE.
Net Pay Take-home pay.
Overtime The payment for working extra hours.
Payslip The document that an employee gets on payday, giving details of pay and deductions.
Statutory Deductions Deductions compulsory by law paid to the government, i.e. PAYE, PRSI.
Superannuation Contributions paid towards a pension.
Tax Credit Given each year to individual taxpayers for the purpose of reducing their tax liability, i.e. the amount to be paid in tax.

Calculation of Net Pay and Preparation of Payslip — Sample Question and Solution

Question

Ann O'Dowd works in Euro Biscuits Ltd. The wages are €8 per hour for a basic forty-hour week, time and a half for the first ten hours of overtime and double time thereafter. On her first week she worked fifty-four hours. Tax Credit was €100 per week, rate of tax 40%, PRSI 10% of gross; other deductions were union fee €5, VHI €10, pension 5% of gross.

Calculate her net wage and complete payslip. (15 marks)

WAGE SLIP											
Name	Basic	O/T	Gross	Tax-Free Allowance	PAYE	PRSI	Union	VHI	Pension	Total Dedu.	Net Pay

Source: Junior Certificate Higher Level.

Deductions (PAYE to Pension)

Solution

(a) Calculation of Gross Wage

Gross Wage = Basic Wage + Overtime

Basic Wage: 40 hours @ €8 per hour	€320
Overtime: 10 hours @ €12 per hour	€120
4 hours @ €16 per hour	€64
Gross Wage	= €504

(b) Calculation of PAYE

Gross Wage €504 × 40%	= €201.60
Less tax credit	= €100.00
PAYE	= €101.60

(c) Calculation of PRSI — **N.B.** PRSI is calculated on gross wage.

PRSI = 10% of €504 (Gross Wage) = €50.40

(d) Calculation of Pension

Pension = 5% of €504 (Gross Wage) = €25.20

(e) Find Total Deductions

	€
PAYE	101.60
PRSI	50.40
Union	5.00
VHI	10.00
Pension	25.20
Total Deductions	**192.20**

(f) Gross Wage – Deductions = Net Wage

€504 – €192.20 = €311.80

WAGE SLIP											
Name	Basic	O/T	Gross	Tax Credit	PAYE	PRSI	Union	VHI	Pension	Total Dedu.	Net Pay
Ann O'Dowd	320	184	504	100	101.60	50.40	5	10	25.20	192.20	311.80

Deductions

Chapter 2 — Expenditure

A. Types of Expenditure

(1) FIXED EXPENDITURE
A **fixed amount** must be paid out on a **fixed date**.

(2) IRREGULAR EXPENDITURE
Amount varies and/or the **payment date varies**.

(3) DISCRETIONARY EXPENDITURE
This is where the consumer has a **choice** after fixed and irregular expenditure has been paid.

B. Main Items of Household Expenditure

Fixed Expenditure	Irregular Expenditure	Discretionary
Mortgage	Telephone	Holidays
Rent	Electricity	Birthday presents
House insurance	Coal/Gas/Oil	Cinema/Theatre
Service charges	Groceries	Newspapers
TV licence	Clothes	Magazines
Car loan	School books	Meals out
Car tax	School uniforms	
Car insurance	Pocket money	
	Car service	
	Petrol/Diesel	

C. Filing Expenditure Records

Electricity bills, telephone bills and all other invoices, delivery notes and receipts should be carefully filed in a safe place so that they can be easily and quickly located when required.

D. Checking Bills — Invoices — Delivery Notes

All bills should be checked for accuracy before you pay them.

(1) ELECTRICITY BILL
This bill is made up of General Domestic (charge per unit used), Standing Charge (rental for service and meters) and Value Added Tax.

Example: Electricity Bill

Meter Reading		Units & Rate	Description	Amount
Present	**Previous**	**(Euro Cent)**		**€**
49,258	48,165	1,093 x 12.20	**General Domestic**	133.34
			Standing Charge	14.18
				147.52
			VAT @ 13.5% on 147.52	19.92
			Total due €	**167.44**

(2) TELEPHONE BILL

A **land line telephone bill** is made up of residence line rental, equipment rental, call charges and value added tax (VAT).

Example – Your Bimonthly Telephone Bill

Recurring & activity charges	168.51
Call charges	116.84
Charges for this period	285.35
VAT on i285.35 at 21.00%	59.92
Total bill	€345.27

A mobile phone bill is made up of a monthly service charge, call charges and value added tax (VAT).

Example: Mobile Phone Invoice

Light pay monthly option	16.53
Total calls	19.16
Subtotal	35.69
VAT @ 20%	7.49
Total	€43.18

(3) INVOICE = BILL

Sent by seller to buyer when goods are bought on credit. Shows quantity, description, unit price, VAT, total cost.

(4) DELIVERY NOTE

Sent when goods are delivered. Signed by buyer. Proof of delivery.

(5) RECEIPT

List of items. Proof of payment.

E. Business Terms

False Economies Short-term saving ⇛ long-term cost, i.e. buying a cheap pair of shoes for €30 — last two months; a good pair of shoes for €80 — last two years.

Impulse Buying Buying without thinking of the cost, buying on the spur of the moment. It results in overspending and buying things that are not required.

Opportunity Cost With limited income, we must make choices. When we choose one item, we must do without something else. This is called opportunity cost.

Priorities Spending on the most needed or most important items first.

Chapter 3 — Household Budgeting

A. Budget

A budget is a financial plan which forecasts future income, expenditure and savings. We must estimate or guess what these figures will be.

B. Reasons Why a Household Would Prepare a Budget

(1) To make sure that the family will have enough to cover future expenditure.
(2) To ensure that they will live within their means.
(3) To see which months they may have to arrange borrowings.
(4) To see which months they will have a surplus or deficit, so that they can plan for the future.
(5) To identify the amount to be spent on different areas, e.g. car, house.
(6) To identify areas of expenditure that they could cut back on.

C. Planning a Budget

(1) **Estimate future income** — include overtime, etc. and allow for expected pay increases.

(2) **Estimate future expenditure** — allow for increased costs, i.e. cost of living, and for possible future expenditure, e.g. holidays.

(3) **Compare estimated income with estimated expenditure.**

If estimated income > estimated expenditure → surplus (savings).
If estimated income < estimated expenditure → deficit (shortage).
If estimated income = estimated expenditure → breakeven.

(4) **Net cash = Total income – Total expenditure.**

(5) **Opening cash** is 'the amount of cash that the family have at the start of the month'.

(6) **Closing cash** is found by 'adding net cash to the opening cash' and is the amount of cash that the family **expect** to have at the end of the month.

(7) **Closing cash** of one month will be the opening cash of the next month.

D. Current Expenditure & Capital Expenditure, Accruals & Savings

(1) **Current expenditure** is spending on items necessary to run the house and family on a daily basis, e.g. food, entertainment, clothing, petrol.

(2) **Capital expenditure** is spending on items that will last a long period of time, e.g. house, car, television, video, cooker.

(3) **Accruals**
These are services that we do not pay for at the time of use, e.g. electricity, telephone. When we get the bill we pay the amount owed.

(4) Savings
This is putting money aside for the future, e.g. to buy a house or car, to finance children's education, holidays and emergencies.

E. Comparing Budget with Actual

Compare the actual income and expenditure with the budgeted income and expenditure. You will then see where the actual is different from the budgeted and be able to make whatever changes are necessary when drawing up the next budget.

F. If a Family Had a Deficit for the Year, What Possible Changes Could They Make in the Household Budget?

(1) Cut back on discretionary expenditure — birthdays, holidays, entertainment, presents, etc.
(2) Reduce household costs through better buying.
(3) Shop around for cheaper car and house insurance.
(4) Consider selling some investments.
(5) Do overtime or part-time work, or increase income in some other way.
(6) Cut back on household costs and car costs.

G. Business Terms

Breakeven Income equals expenditure.

Budget A plan of future income and expenditure.

Closing Cash Opening Cash + Net Cash.

Consumer Durables Goods that will last for a long period of time.

Deficit Expenditure greater than income.

Estimate A guess at the size of the income and expenditure.

Net Cash Total income minus total expenditure.

Surplus Income greater than expenditure.

Examination-Style Questions and Solutions

Question 1.
Answer (a), (b) and (c). This is a Household Budget Question.
The following is a budget for the Lydon household for the first four months of the year.
Opening Cash in Hand is €370.

Planned Income
- Richard Lydon earns €1,200 net, per month.
- Claire Lydon earns €1,350 net, per month.
- Child benefit is €60 per month.
- Richard expects to receive €250 interest on a building society investment in March.

Planned Expenditure

- House mortgage will be €450 per month.
- Repayments on Richard's car loan (to be fully paid by end of February) will cost €340 per month until then.
- Richard's annual car insurance €380 is due for payment in March.
- Claire's annual car insurance €520 is due for payment in April.
- House insurance premium, €240 per year, is payable monthly, starting in January.
- Household expenses are usually €630 per month.
- Car running costs are expected to be €90 per month for Richard and €50 per month for Claire.
- ESB bills for light and heat are expected to amount to €180 in January and €230 in March.
- A fill of heating oil, costing €360, will be needed in February.
- The telephone bill is expected to be €170 in February and €210 in April.
- Birthdays will cost €110 in January and €120 in April.
- Entertainment will cost €130 each month.
- The Lydon family have booked a holiday in February which will cost €1,500.

(a) Complete fully the blank household budget form (given at the end of the question) using all the above figures. (50)

(b) Work out the total cost of having two cars in the family for the four months and put this figure into the box at the end of the budget form. (5)

(c) Will the Lydon family have enough money to pay for their holiday in February? In the space provided at the end of the budget form, give **one** reason for your answer. (5)

(60 marks)

Source: Junior Certificate Ordinary Level.

For use with Question 1. Household Budget

1. (a) LYDON FAMILY	JAN.	FEB.	MARCH	APRIL	TOTAL
Planned Income	€	€	€	€	€
Richard Lydon — Salary					
Claire Lydon — Salary					
Child Benefit					
Interest from Building Society					
TOTAL INCOME					
PLANNED EXPENDITURE					
Fixed					
Mortgage					
Car Loan					
Car Insurance					
House Insurance					
Subtotal					
Irregular					
Household Expenses					
Car Running Costs					
Light and Heat					
Telephone					
Subtotal					
Discretionary					
Birthdays					
Entertainment					
Holidays					
Subtotal					
TOTAL EXPENDITURE					
Net Cash					
Opening Cash					
Closing Cash					

1. (b)	Total cost of having two cars in the family:	
1. (c)	Will they have enough money to pay for the holiday in February?	
	Reason:	

Solution to Question 1.

For use with Question 1. Household Budget					
1. (a) LYDON FAMILY	**JAN.**	**FEB.**	**MARCH**	**APRIL**	**TOTAL**
Planned Income	€	€	€	€	€
Richard Lydon — Salary	1,200	1,200	1,200	1,200	4,800
Claire Lydon — Salary	1,350	1,350	1,350	1,350	5,400
Child Benefit	60	60	60	60	240
Interest from Building Society			250		250
TOTAL INCOME	2,610	2,610	2,860	2,610	10,690
PLANNED EXPENDITURE					
Fixed					
Mortgage	450	450	450	450	1,800
Car Loan	340	340			680
Car Insurance			380	520	900
House Insurance	20	20	20	20	80
Subtotal	810	810	850	990	3,460
Irregular					
Household Expenses	630	630	630	630	2,520
Car Running Costs	140	140	140	140	560
Light and Heat	180	360	230		770
Telephone		170		210	380
Subtotal	950	1,300	1,000	980	4,230
Discretionary					
Birthdays	110			120	230
Entertainment	130	130	130	130	520
Holidays		1,500			1,500
Subtotal	240	1,630	130	250	2,250
TOTAL EXPENDITURE	2,000	3,740	1,980	2,220	9,940
Net Cash	610	–1,130	880	390	750
Opening Cash	370	980	–150	730	370
Closing Cash	980	–150	730	1,120	1,120

1. (b) Total cost of having two cars in the family:	€2,140
1. (c) Will they have enough money to pay for the holiday in February?	No.
Reason: *They will not have cash to pay for the holiday because total expenditure €3,740 exceeds total income €2,610. (They have a deficit of €1,130.)*	

Question 2.

Answer all sections. This is a Household Budget Question.

2. (a) At the end of the question is a partially completed budget for the McCarthy family for a six-month period, January to June.

You are required to complete this form by filling in the figures in the 'Total' column and also the missing figures in the Section at the end dealing with '**Net Cash, Opening Cash and Closing Cash**'. (13)

For use with Question 2.

2. (a) McCarthy Family Budget: January–June

	JAN. €	FEB. €	MAR. €	APRIL €	MAY €	JUNE €	TOTAL
Income							
Mr McCarthy — *Salary*	700	700	700	750	750	750	
Mrs McCarthy — *Salary*	700	700	700	700	700	700	
Child Benefit	40	40	40	40	40	40	
Other Income	—	—	—	60	—	—	
Total Income	1,440	1,440	1,440	1,550	1,490	1,490	
Expenditure							
Fixed							
Mortgage	400	400	400	400	400	400	
Personal Insurance	—	—	—	—	—	240	
Car Loan	350	350	350	350	350	350	
Car Tax	—	—	180	—	—	—	
Car Insurance	—	—	410	—	—	—	
House Insurance	—	—	180	—	—	—	
Irregular							
Housekeeping	370	370	370	380	380	380	
Car Service	—	60	—	—	80	—	
ESB	80	—	60	—	50	—	
Discretionary							
Birthdays	40	—	80	—	30	—	
Entertainment	60	60	60	60	60	60	
Total Expenditure	1,300	1,240	2,090	1,190	1,350	1,430	
Net Cash	140						
Opening Cash	20						
Closing Cash							

Answer the following questions in your Answerbook.

2. (b) What is the purpose of preparing a budget? (3)

2. (c) (i) How much income, in total, does the McCarthy family expect to receive in the six months?

(ii) What percentage of total expenditure will be spent, by the McCarthy family, on discretionary expenditure in this budget?

(iii) Give **one** example of **other income**. (9)

2. (d) (i) In what month is there a shortfall (deficit)?

(ii) Give a reason for the shortfall.

(iii) Suggest one way of overcoming this shortfall. (9)

2. (e) The McCarthys are considering saving for a family visit to America in five years time. Suggest a suitable place to invest their savings. Give a reason for your answer. (6)

Source: Junior Certificate Higher Level. **(40 marks)**

Solution to Question 2.

2. (a) McCarthy Family Budget: January–June

	JAN. €	FEB. €	MARCH €	APRIL €	MAY €	JUNE €	TOTAL €
Income							
Mr McCarthy — *Salary*	700	700	700	750	750	750	*4,350*
Mrs McCarthy — *Salary*	700	700	700	700	700	700	*4,200*
Child Benefit	40	40	40	40	40	40	*240*
Other Income	—	—	—	60	—	—	*60*
Total Income	1,440	1,440	1,440	1,550	1,490	1,490	*8,850*
Expenditure							
Fixed							
Mortgage	400	400	400	400	400	400	*2,400*
Personal Insurance	—	—	—	—	—	240	*240*
Car Loan	350	350	350	350	350	350	*2,100*
Car Tax	—	—	180	—	—	—	*180*
Car Insurance	—	—	410	—	—	—	*410*
House Insurance	—	—	180	—	—	—	*180*
Irregular							
Housekeeping	370	370	370	380	380	380	*2,250*
Car Service	—	60	—	—	80	—	*140*
ESB	80	—	60	—	50	—	*190*
Discretionary							
Birthdays	40	—	80	—	30	—	*150*
Entertainment	60	60	60	60	60	60	*360*
Total Expenditure	1,300	1,240	2,090	1,190	1,350	1,430	*8,600*
Net Cash	140	*200*	*(650)*	*360*	*140*	*60*	*250*
Opening Cash	20	*160*	*360*	*(290)*	*70*	*210*	*20*
Closing Cash	*160*	*360*	*(290)*	*70*	*210*	*270*	*270*

2. (b) *To allocate limited income, avoid debt. To plan savings. To ensure that one lives within one's means.*

2. (c) *(i) €8,850.*

(ii) 5.9% (€510 × 100/€8,600).

(iii) Bank Interest (Deposit)/Tax Refund.

2. (d) *(i) March.*

(ii) Car tax and insurance in the same month.

(iii) Pay motor insurance by instalment.

2. (e) *National Instalment Savings/safe/guaranteed return/tax-free.*

OR

Savings Certificates/safe/good return/tax-free.

Question 3.

Answer (a) and (b). This is a Household Budget Question.

3. (a) At the end of the question is a partially completed Personal Budget form for the Moran household.

You are required to complete this form for October, November, December, as well as all the 'Total' columns.

The following information should be taken into account.

- T. Moran expects to earn €150 a month in **extra** overtime in November and December.
- S. Moran will be getting a Christmas bonus of €100 in December.
- Child benefit is the same for each month.
- House mortgage is expected to increase by $2\frac{1}{2}$% beginning with the October payment.
- Car loan will be fully paid off by the end of November.
- Annual Car Insurance of €580 is due in full in December.
- Annual House Insurance premium of €260 is paid half-yearly in April and October.
- Household Costs (Groceries, etc.) are estimated as follows: October — €300; November — €330; December — €490.
- Car running costs are estimated at €50 per month, plus a car service in November costing a further €60.
- ESB is estimated at €50 per month for October and November and €65 for December.
- Telephone is estimated at €70 every two months.
- Entertainment expenses are estimated at €30 a month for October and November and €60 for December.
- Wallpapering of living room and hall will cost €280 in November and household decorating for Christmas will cost €100 in December.
- Christmas presents are expected to cost €150 in December. (36)

3. (b) Give two possible reasons why the ESB costs are expected to increase in December. (4)

Source: Junior Certificate Higher Level. **(40 marks)**

For use with Question 3.

3. (a) Personal Budget for the Moran household for six months — July to December

	July €	Aug. €	Sept. €	Oct. €	Nov. €	Dec. €	Total €
Expected Income							
T. Moran	600	600	600				
S. Moran	550	550	550				
Child Benefit	30	30	30				
TOTAL INCOME	1,180	1,180	1,180				
Planned Expenditure							
Fixed							
House Mortgage	360	360	360				
Car Loan	250	250	250				
Car Insurance	—	—	—				
House Insurance	—	—	—				
Subtotal	610	610	610				
Irregular							
Household Costs (incl. Groceries)	280	310	350				
Car Running Costs	50	50	50				
ESB	40	40	45				
Telephone	—	70	—				
Subtotal	370	470	445				
Discretionary							
Birthdays/Presents	—	60	—				
Entertainment	60	—	—				
Household Decoration	—	50	—				
Subtotal	60	110	—				
TOTAL EXPENDITURE	1,040	1,190	1,055				
Net Cash (Surplus/Deficit)	140	(–10)	125				
Opening Cash	80	220	210	335			
Closing Cash	220	210	335				

3. (b) (i)

(ii)

Solution to Question 3.

3. (a)

	JULY €	AUG. €	SEPT. €	OCT. €	NOV. €	DEC. €	TOTAL €
Income							
T. Moran	600	600	600	600	750	750	3,900
S. Moran	550	550	550	550	550	650	3,400
Child Benefit	30	30	30	30	30	30	180
TOTAL INCOME	1,180	1,180	1,180	1,180	1,330	1,430	7,480
Expenditure							
Fixed							
House Mortgage	360	360	360	369	369	369	2,187
Car Loan	250	250	250	250	250	—	1,250
Car Insurance	—	—	—	—	—	580	580
House Insurance	—	—	—	130	—	—	130
Subtotal	610	610	610	749	619	949	4,147
Irregular							
Household Costs (incl. Groceries)	280	310	350	300	330	490	2,060
Car Running Costs	50	50	50	50	110	50	360
ESB	40	40	45	50	50	65	290
Telephone	—	70	—	70	—	70	210
Subtotal	370	470	445	470	490	675	2,920
Discretionary							
Birthdays/Presents	—	60	—	—	—	150	210
Entertainment	60	—	—	30	30	60	180
Household Decoration	—	50	—	—	280	100	430
Subtotal	60	110	—	30	310	310	820
TOTAL EXPENDITURE	1,040	1,190	1,055	1,249	1,419	1,934	7,887
Net Cash (Surplus/Deficit)	140	(–10)	125	(69)	(89)	(504)	(407)
Opening Cash	80	220	210	335	266	177	80
Closing Cash	220	210	335	266	177	(327)	(327)

3. (b) (i) *Greater usage in winter.*

(ii) *Christmas cooking and holidays etc.*

Question 4.
Answer (a) and (b).
This is a Household Budget Question.

4. (a) At the end of the question is a partially completed Personal Budget form for the Reidy family.

You are required to complete this form by filling in the figures for the 'Estimate April to December' column and the 'Total for Year' column. The following information should be taken into account.

- John Reidy is due a salary increase of 5% from 1 July.
- Mary Reidy expects a special bonus of €320 in December.
- Child benefit will continue each month as for the first three months of the year.
- House mortgage is expected to increase by €40 a month from 1 August.
- House insurance, per month, will continue as for the first three months of the year.
- Household costs, per month, are expected to remain the same for each month until September and to increase by €30 a month beginning in October.
- Car running costs are expected to remain at €80 a month, with an additional car service cost of €90 in September.
- ESB for the twelve months (January–December) is estimated at €1,150.
- Christmas presents are expected to cost €200 in December.
- Entertainment is expected to cost €600 for the twelve months (January–December).
- The family holiday in July is expected to cost €1,400. (35)

4. (b) Explain what is meant by the term 'Discretionary' expenditure. (5)
(Write your answer in the box at the end of the budget form.)

Source: Junior Certificate Higher Level. **(40 marks)**

For use with Question 4.
Personal Budget for the Reidy household

4. (a)	JAN.	FEB.	MAR.	TOTAL JAN.–MAR.	ESTIMATE APR.–DEC.	TOTAL FOR YEAR JAN.–DEC.
Planned Income	€	€	€	€	€	€
Salaries						
John Reidy	660	660	660	1,980		
Mary Reidy	700	700	700	2,100		
Child Benefit	30	30	30	90		
TOTAL INCOME	1,390	1,390	1,390	4,170		
Planned Expenditure						
Fixed						
Mortgage	280	280	280	840		
Annual Car Tax	240	—	—	240		
Annual Car Insurance	—	—	650	650		
House Insurance	18	18	18	54		
Subtotal	538	298	948	1,784		
Irregular						
Household Costs	490	490	490	1,470		
Car Running Costs	80	80	80	240		
ESB	190	—	160	350		
Subtotal	760	570	730	2,060		
Discretionary						
Presents	—	40	—	40		
Entertainment	45	60	55	160		
Holidays	—	—	—	—		
Subtotal	45	100	55	200		
TOTAL EXPENDITURE	1,343	968	1,733	4,044		
Net Cash (Surplus/Deficit)	47	422	–343	126		
Opening Cash	75	122	544	75	201	75
Closing Cash	122	544	201	201		

WORKINGS

4. (b) Discretionary Expenditure ....
....
....
....

Solution to Question 4.
Personal Budget for the Reidy household

4. (a)	JAN.	FEB.	MAR.	TOTAL JAN.–MAR.	ESTIMATE APR.–DEC.	TOTAL FOR YEAR JAN.–DEC.
Planned Income	€	€	€	€	€	€
Salaries						
John Reidy	660	660	660	1,980	6,138	8,118
Mary Reidy	700	700	700	2,100	6,620	8,720
Child Benefit	30	30	30	90	270	360
TOTAL INCOME	1,390	1,390	1,390	4,170	13,028	17,198
Planned Expenditure						
Fixed						
Mortgage	280	280	280	840	2,720	3,560
Annual Car Tax	240	—	—	240	—	240
Annual Car Insurance	—	—	650	650	—	650
House Insurance	18	18	18	54	162	216
Subtotal	538	298	948	1,784	2,882	4,666
Irregular						
Household Costs	490	490	490	1,470	4,500	5,970
Car Running Costs	80	80	80	240	810	1,050
ESB	190	—	160	350	800	1,150
Subtotal	760	570	730	2,060	6,110	8,170
Discretionary						
Presents	—	40	—	40	200	240
Entertainment	45	60	55	160	440	600
Holidays	—	—	—	—	1,400	1,400
Subtotal	45	100	55	200	2,040	2,240
TOTAL EXPENDITURE	1,343	968	1,733	4,044	11,032	15,076
Net Cash (Surplus/Deficit)	47	422	–343	126	1,996	2,122
Opening Cash	75	122	544	75	201	75
Closing Cash	122	544	201	201	2,197	2,197

WORKINGS

4. (b) Discretionary Expenditure

Where the consumer has a choice after fixed and irregular expenditure have been paid.

Comparing budget with actual

1. Sometimes the Actual Budget may differ from the Planned Budget for a variety of reasons, e.g. redundancy, expected overtime was not available, unexpected family expenses, increased telephone bill, repairs, increased insurance permiums.
2. Comparisons must be made between the budget and the actual income and expenditure (from analysed cash book) and make whatever adjustments are necessary.

Example and solution

The following budget comparison statement shows the budget figures and the actual figures for the Murphy family. Show the difference between the 'actual' and the 'budget' figures by completing the column marked 'difference'.
NOTE: Use plus sign(+) if 'actual' is greater than 'budget' figure.
Use minus (–) if 'actual' is less than 'budget' figure.

	Budget	Actual	Difference
Income	€	€	€
Salaries	1,600	1,900	**+300**
Deposit Interest	50	30	**–20**
Dividends	30	140	**+110**
Child Benefit	20	30	**+10**
	1,700	2,100	**+400**
Expenditure			
Fixed	500	600	**+100**
Irregular	600	400	**–200**
Discretionary	200	500	**+300**
Total Expenditure	1,300	1,500	**+200**
Net Cash	+400	+600	+200

A. Budget was off target by €200. Expected Net Cash Surplus was €400 but the actual was €600.
B. Income was up by €400 but Expenditure was up by €200.

Chapter 4 — Household Accounts

A. Analysed Cash Book

Used to record actual income and expenditure of the household.

Most people keep some cash on them and make cash payments. Many people keep a bank account and pay for goods and services by cheque. In the Analysed Cash Book we have two columns on each side, one for Cash and one for Bank.

An Analysed Cash Book is laid out as follows:

Debit Receipts (Money in) ANALYSED CASH BOOK Credit Payments (Money out)

Date	Details	Cash	Bank	Date	Details	Cheque Nos.	Cash	Bank	Analysis Columns

Explanation

(1) The debit side (left side) records opening cash and money coming in/received.
(2) The credit side (right side) records money owed to the bank and money going out/paid out.

B. Rule for Analysed Cash Book

DEBIT ALL MONEY RECEIVED
CREDIT ALL MONEY PAID OUT

C. Balancing Analysed Cash Book

- Balance only Cash and Bank columns.
- Add both columns.
- Find difference = balance.
- Put balance on smaller side.
- Total both sides.
- Bring down balance (B/d) on opposite side.
- Bank DR ⇛ asset – money in bank.
  CR ⇛ overdraft.
- Total analysis columns.

D. Contra Entry

Affects both sides of Cash Book.

TYPES

(1) Lodged Cash in Bank ⇛ Money into Bank ⇛ Debit
Money out of Cash ⇛ Credit

(2) Withdrew from Bank ⇛ Money out of Bank ⇛ Credit
Money into Cash ⇛ Debit

E. 'Did Household Budget Live Within Its Means?'

Every household should try to live within its means for the week/month. However, this isn't always possible. To answer this question you find total income for the period and compare it with total expenditure for the period. If income was greater than expenditure — the family lived within its means. If expenditure was greater than income — the family did not live within its means.

F. Business Terms

Balance The difference between the two sides of an account.
Contra Entry Where money is switched between the Cash A/C and Bank A/C.
Credit Right-hand side of Analysed Cash Book.
Debit Left-hand side of Analysed Cash Book.

Examination-Style Question and Solution

Question 1.
Answer (a), (b) and (c). This is a Household Analysed Cash Book Question.

Tom Roche, 14 Forest Drive, Galway, opened a current account in the local branch of Bank of Ireland on 1 May 2013. His account number is 57364217. He was given a cheque book, cheque card and a Pass card.

He made his first lodgment of €580 on the same date. It was made up as follows: Salary Cheque €500 and €80 in notes won in a local raffle.

During the first two weeks of May he had the following Bank transactions:

		€
May 2	Paid for groceries by cheque (no. 901)	60
May 3	Paid telephone by cheque (no. 902)	133
May 5	Withdrew cash by Pass card for entertainment	25
May 9	Paid ESB by cheque (no. 903)	64
May 10	Paid for groceries by cheque (no. 904)	59
May 11	Lodged cash from sale of old furniture	150
May 13	Paid for home heating by cheque (no. 905)	104
May 14	Paid monthly mortgage repayment by standing order	150

1. (a) Assuming you are Tom Roche, complete the lodgment form fully for 1 May 2013. (Use the blank document supplied at the end of the question.) (10)

1. (b) Write up the Analysed Cash Book, using the following money column headings.
Receipt side: Bank
Payments side: Bank; Groceries; Light & Heat; Entertainment; Other. (22)

1. (c) Based on the figures in Tom's Analysed Cash Book, do you think he was living within his means in May? Explain your answer briefly. (8)

Lodgment Record Subject to Verification | **LODGMENT** **Bank of Ireland**

Name

Current Account Number

Please specify Account:
Current ☐ Savings ☐
Other ☐ ....

€	

Name

Address

Date

Please specify Account:
Current ☐ Savings ☐ Other ☐ ....

Customer's Account Number

Notes	€ .....
Coin	—
Total Cash	€ .....
Cheques	€ .....
Other	—
Total	€ .....

Source: Junior Certificate Higher Level. **(40 marks)**

Solution to Question 1.
1. (a)

Lodgment Record Subject to Verification | **LODGMENT** **Bank of Ireland**

Name *Tom Roche*

Current Account Number

5	7	3	6	4	2	1	7

Please specify Account:
Current ☑ Savings ☐
Other ☐ ....

€ 580	00

Name *Tom Roche*

Address *14 Forest Drive*
Galway Date *1-5-13*

Please specify Account:
Current ☑ Savings ☐ Other ☐ ....

Customer's Account Number

5	7	3	6	4	2	1	7

Notes	€80
Coin	—
Total Cash	€80
Cheques	€500
Other	—
Total	€580

1. (b) Household Account (Bank)

Date	Details	€ Bank	Date	Details	Cheque No.	€ Bank	€ Groceries & Heat	€ Light	€ Entertainment	€ Other
1/5/13	Lodgment	580	2/5/13	Groceries	901	60	60			
11/5/13	Lodgment	150	3/5/13	Telephone	902	133				133
			5/5/13	Cash withdrawal	ATM	25			25	
			9/5/13	ESB	903	64		64		
			10/5/13	Groceries	904	59	59			
			13/5/13	Oil	905	104		104		
			14/5/13	Mortgage	SO	150				150
						595	119	168	25	283
				Balance C/d	135					
			730			730				
Balance B/d		135								

1. (c) *NO — Expenditure was €595 for the month, while regular income is only €500 p.m. Additional once-off income in May was €80 raffle / €150 sale of furniture.*

OR

YES — He had €135 left over.

Chapter 5 — The Informed Consumer

A. Consumer

A consumer is a person who buys goods and services, e.g. food, clothes, cars, entertainment, newspapers, etc.

B. The Informed Consumer

(1) Is aware of legal rights.
(2) Is aware of organisations that protect him.
(3) Is able to make a complaint.
(4) Does not buy impulsively.
(5) Makes enquiries, shops around, checks prices.
(6) Prepares a budget.
(7) Keeps receipts.
(8) Keeps the guarantee.
(9) Checks for value/quality.

C. Ordering Goods and Services

(1) By letter – keep a copy of the order-letter for future reference.
(2) By telephone – keep a written record and get the name of the person who took the order.
(3) Personal call – find out exact cost, and view the goods.

D. Paying for Goods

When you order the goods, you may be asked to pay a deposit — a small payment that is part of the purchase price and is made to ensure that the customer will return to collect the goods and pay the balance due.

E. Receipts

When you pay for the goods, you should receive a receipt — this is written proof that payment was made, and it may be required if there are any problems with the goods at a later date.

F. Symbols on Goods

Guaranteed Irish — symbol of quality — operated by Guaranteed Irish

Approved Quality Symbol — used on products that have reached a high standard

Pure New Wool

[***] will keep in freezer for three months

G. Bar Code

➢ Series of parallel lines, thirteen digits.
➢ Shows country of origin, product number, company number, check digit.
➢ Records price — receipt is produced.
➢ Stock record reduced by one.

H. Business Terms

Loss Leader A product sold at a very low price to attract customers.
Price War Where shops selling similar products undercut each other to attract customers.

Chapter 6 — Consumer Rights and Protection

A. Why Do Consumers Need Protection?

To ensure that the standards of goods and services available to the public are reasonable and acceptable.

B. How Is the Consumer Protected?

- ➢ The government protects the consumer by passing **laws.**
- ➢ **Agencies** have been set up to inform and protect individual consumers.

C. Laws

WHAT ARE MY RIGHTS WHEN BUYING GOODS?

When you buy goods or services, you enter into a contract with the seller. You pay your money, and in return the seller is obliged to provide goods and services that meet certain conditions.

SALE OF GOODS AND SUPPLY OF SERVICES ACT 1980

This sets out the conditions with which goods and services must comply, which are as follows:

(1) Goods should be of **merchantable quality**.
(2) Goods should be **fit for their purpose**.
(3) Goods should be **as described**.
(4) If goods are bought by **sample**, they should correspond with sample.
(5) Suppliers of services should:

(a) Have the **necessary skill** to provide the service, e.g. car mechanic.
(b) Provide the service with **proper care and diligence**.
(c) Ensure that **materials and parts** used in the service will be of **merchantable quality**.

(6) It is the **seller** who is responsible for putting things right.
(7) A **guarantee** is a bonus in addition to your normal legal rights. If you have a valid complaint, it may be easier to claim under the guarantee. A guarantee is where the manufacturer/supplier undertakes to repair or replace any defective part without charge during the period of the guarantee, which is usually one year.
(8) If you buy goods in a **sale**, they should be of merchantable quality, fit for purpose and as described.
(9) It does not matter whether you pay **cash**, buy on **credit**, **rent**, or buy on **hire purchase**, the goods must be of merchantable quality, fit for purpose and as described.
(10) If you buy a **motor car**, it should be of merchantable quality, fit for purpose and as described. You have a right to expect that the car is safe — free from any fault that would make it a danger to the public or to anyone in the car.

(11) Illegal Shop Notices:

NO MONEY REFUNDED
CREDIT NOTES ONLY
NO LIABILITY ACCEPTED FOR FAULTY GOODS
GOODS WILL NOT BE EXCHANGED

These notices are illegal and should not be displayed. You are not bound to accept a credit note. If your complaint is valid, you can refuse all offers of a credit note and insist on a cash refund.

CONSUMER INFORMATION ACT 1978

The purpose of this Act is to protect consumers against false or misleading claims about goods, services and prices. It makes the following stipulations:

(1) It is an offence for a supplier to give a false or misleading **description of goods**.
(2) It is an offence for a **supplier of services** to make false or misleading claims about the services it offers.
(3) It is an offence to publish an **advertisement** that will mislead the public.
(4) All statements about **prices** must be accurate. The following are offences:

(a) Charging extra for items that appear to be included in the price.
(b) Giving a false price reduction, e.g. goods advertised in a sale reduced from €79 to €49 should have been on sale for €79 for at least twenty-eight consecutive days in the previous three months.
(c) Displaying a price excluding VAT.

(5) The Consumer Information Act also established the **Office of Director of Consumer Affairs and Fair Trade**, which is responsible for enforcing the provisions of the Act.

EC LEGISLATION ON LABELLING AND PRICE

FOOD LABELS — WHAT THE LABELS SHOULD SHOW

(1) Name of food.
(2) List of ingredients in descending order of weight.
(3) Quantity.
(4) 'Best before date' for almost all food.
(5) Storage conditions or conditions of use.
(6) Name and address of manufacturer or seller.
(7) Particulars of place of origin.
(8) Instructions for use where necessary.

PRICING OF FOOD

(1) All foodstuffs must display a selling price.
(2) Food sold in bulk or loose must display a unit price.

D. Agencies that Protect the Consumer

(1) CONSUMER ASSOCIATION OF IRELAND

(a) It is a voluntary organisation set up to protect the interests of consumers in Ireland.

(b) It provides information and advice to members about goods, services and consumer law, and publishes an information magazine, *Consumer Choice.*

(c) It helps consumers to solve complaints.

(2) OFFICE OF DIRECTOR OF CONSUMER AFFAIRS

(a) Enforces the Consumer Information Act 1978.

(b) Promotes better standards of advertising.

(c) Informs consumers about their rights.

(d) A consumer can lodge a complaint regarding false advertising and pricing, and the Director will investigate it and have it rectified.

(3) OFFICE OF THE OMBUDSMAN

(a) The Ombudsman

The main duty of the Ombudsman is to investigate complaints made by members of the public about how they have been treated by public bodies in Ireland.

People can make a complaint if they are unhappy with the services provided by any of the following bodies:

- Government Departments
- Local authorities
- Health Boards
- An Post (the post office)

(b) The Financial Services Ombudsman

The Financial Services Ombudsman deals independently with unresolved complaints from consumers about their individual dealings with all financial services providers. The Ombudsman is therefore the arbitrator of unresolved disputes and is impartial. This arbitration is provided as a free service to the complainant.

The following financial service providers may be subject to investigation by the Ombudsman:

- Banks
- Building societies
- Insurance companies
- Credit unions
- Mortgage, insurance and other credit intermediaries
- Stockbrokers
- Pawnbrokers
- Moneylenders
- Bureaux de change
- Hire purchase providers
- Health insurance companies

(4) TRADE ASSOCIATIONS

Most retailers and suppliers of services are members of Trade Associations that lay down standards, e.g. Irish Travel Agents Association, Society of Irish Motor

Industry. Consumers can complain to the relevant association if standards are not being met.

(5) ADVERTISING STANDARDS AUTHORITY

(a) Promotes better standards of advertising.
(b) Ensures advertisements are decent and fair.

(6) SMALL CLAIMS COURT

- If a consumer has a claim against a trader for faulty goods/services up to €2,000, he/she can have the claim processed in the Small Claims Court.
- It is quick and cheap, as no solicitors are required.
- The court is managed by an official called the registrar.
- The claimant must pay a fee of €15, which is refundable if he/she wins the case.
- The claimant must have made every effort to settle the dispute with the seller before appealing to the court.

(7) MEDIA

Television and radio programmes, as well as newspapers and magazines, provide useful information to consumers. Here are some examples:

- *Prime Time*
- *Business News*
- Radio financial reports
- *Consumer Choice*
- *Which?* magazine

(8) NATIONAL CONSUMER AGENCY

The National Consumer Agency (NCA) was established to ensure that the rights of the Irish consumer are respected. The NCA ensures that the interests of consumers are brought to the forefront of national and local decision-making in Ireland. The National Consumer Agency seeks to make sure that all consumers are aware of their rights.

(9) NATIONAL STANDARDS AUTHORITY OF IRELAND

Monitors the safety standards of products sold in Ireland.

(10) FINANCIAL REGULATOR

Financial documents should be clear. The Financial Regulator promotes consumers' interests by regulating financial services firms in Ireland.

Chapter 7 — Consumer Complaints
Caveat Emptor — Let the Buyer Beware

A. Genuine Complaints

If goods are not of merchantable quality, or not as described, or not fit for their purpose, you then have a valid complaint and are entitled to some remedy, such as **cash refund**, **replacement** or **repair**.

B. Non-Valid Complaint

A complaint is not valid, and the consumer has no rights, if

(1) You change your mind about the goods after buying them.
(2) A fault arises due to misuse.
(3) A fault was pointed out at the time of purchase.

C. Where to Complain

(1) Complain firstly to the **supplier**.
(2) If negotiations fail, there may be a third party such as a **trade association**.
(3) Complain to the **Consumer Association of Ireland**.
(4) Complain to the **Office of Director of Consumer Affairs**.
(5) Approach the **Media** — make your complaint public.
(6) If all the above fail, you may have to consider taking **legal action**.

D. How to Complain

(1) Inform shop in writing or in person as soon as possible.
(2) Bring back the product and show evidence of purchase, i.e. receipt or credit card receipt.
(3) State your complaint clearly.
(4) State clearly what you want: refund/replacement/repair.
(5) If no agreement, consult a third party.

E. Written Complaints

(1) Write clearly.
(2) Give details and **evidence** of purchase. Enclose copy of receipt.
(3) State complaint clearly.
(4) State clearly what you want done about it: refund/replacement/repair.
(5) Give details of when and where you may be contacted.
(6) Keep a copy of letter for future reference.

F. Compensation

A consumer who has a valid complaint may be entitled to:

(1) Full **cash refund**.
(2) **Replacement** of the goods.
(3) **Repair** — where problem is of a minor nature.

WHAT ABOUT A CREDIT NOTE?

A consumer may be offered a credit note instead of a cash refund. This allows him to buy something else in the same shop to the value of the credit note. You are not bound to accept a credit note.

WHAT ABOUT A REPAIR?

A repair may be an acceptable solution if the problem is of a minor nature.

G. Business Terms

Caveat Emptor 'Let the buyer beware' — goods should be carefully examined before purchase.

Redress Some form of compensation (remedy).

H. Examples of Consumer Complaints

COMPLAINT	PROBLEM	CONSUMER RIGHTS
New car battery will not start car	Battery not of **merchantable quality**	Replacement or refund
Stain remover does not remove stain	Stain remover **not fit for purpose**	Replacement or refund
Shoe polish described as black on box but navy when applied	Polish **not as described**	Replacement
Lawnmower breaks down after service	**Service not provided by person with necessary skill**	Proper service and compensation for inconvenience
Car described as never crashed but it was	**False description of goods**	Refund
Photographs developed in one hour — but takes one day	**False description of services**	No rights, but consumer should inform Director of Consumer Affairs

Examination-Style Questions and Solutions

Question 1.

Answer (a) and (b). This is a Consumer Question and a Letter of Complaint.

Mary Noonan bought a new jacket in Angels Boutique on a recent holiday. She paid €145 for it. On her return home she noticed that the stitching on one sleeve was ripped and also that one shoulder was larger than the other. She was very disappointed. As the boutique is over seventy miles from where she lives, she has decided to write to them about it and return the jacket. She is not sure whether or not she should return the receipt. She is looking for a full cash refund.

1. (a) Using your knowledge of consumer legislation, answer the following questions:

(i) What is the legal basis for Mary's complaint? Explain it briefly. (7)

(ii) Do you think Mary is entitled to a full refund? Give a reason for your answer. (7)

(iii) If the boutique owner offered Mary a credit note for the full amount, should she accept it? Explain your answer. (7)

(iv) What advice would you give Mary on whether or not she should include the receipt with her letter? (4)

1. (b) Assuming you are Mary Noonan, write the letter of complaint to the Manager of Angels Boutique. (You may choose any addresses, date, etc. that are required yourself.) (15)

Source: Junior Certificate Higher Level. **(40 marks)**

Solution to Question 1.

1. (a) (i) Goods sold should be of merchantable quality — Sale of Goods and Supply of Services Act 1980.

(ii) YES as the faults were significant — one shoulder larger than the other.

(iii) NO.

➢ She is entitled to a full refund and should not be restricted to buying an alternative in that shop only.

➢ She lives seventy miles away from the boutique — she may never go back again.

OR

YES if she is satisfied that she will use it in the same shop within a reasonable time.

(iv) Send a copy or its reference number with the letter, hold the original receipt as evidence of purchase.

1. (b) Letter of Complaint to Angels Boutique

76 North Main Street
Macroom
Co. Cork

10 August 2014

For the attention of Mary Doherty

The Manager
Angels Boutique
Patrick Street
Limerick

Re: Faulty Jacket

Dear Ms Doherty,

On Saturday 5 August 2014, I bought a new jacket in your shop for €145 (copy of receipt enclosed). On bringing it home I noticed that the stitching on one sleeve was ripped and also that one shoulder was larger than the other.

I am very disappointed and wish to return the jacket. I would be very grateful if you would give me a full cash refund of €145.

I await your reply.

Yours sincerely

Mary Noonan

Mary Noonan

Enc (2)

Question 2.

Answer (a), (b) and (c). This is a Consumer Question.

Using your knowledge of consumer law, you are asked to read the following consumer problems and to answer the questions that follow.

2. (a) A two-week-old vacuum cleaner keeps breaking down — sometimes the suction power picks up all the dirt and other times it is very poor and hardly picks up anything.

The shop where it was bought refuses to help, saying that it is the manufacturer's fault, and tells the customer to write directly to the manufacturer.

Answer the following questions (give one reason in each case in support of your opinion).

(i) Is the shop liable?
(ii) Is the manufacturer liable?
(iii) What remedy do you think the customer is entitled to?
(iv) What advice would you give the shopkeeper in dealing with complaints of this kind? (20)

2. (b) A friend of yours recently bought an expensive coat, which the shop assistant clearly said was 100% 'pure new wool'.

A week later your friend discovered a small label on the inside of the sleeve which said 80% nylon. Your friend is very disappointed.

Answer the following questions (give one reason in each case in support of your opinion).

(i) What principle of consumer law has been broken in this situation?
(ii) In your opinion is your friend entitled to either a full refund or a credit note? (12)

2. (c) The following sign was recently seen hanging at the check-out of a large department store:

SORRY
IT IS COMPANY POLICY
NOT TO GIVE CASH REFUNDS

You are asked to comment briefly on what this sign says. (8)

Source: Junior Certificate Higher Level. **(40 marks)**

Solution to Question 2.

2. (a) (i) YES. Contract is with the shop — shop is liable to the consumer — shop will have recourse to manufacturer for faulty product.

(ii) YES. Goods not of merchantable quality, not fit for purpose. Manufacturer directly liable to shopkeeper and indirectly liable to consumer.

(iii) Three possible answers here:
Replacement — It is very new and it is a basic fault, not a minor one.

OR

Repair — Maybe a minor adjustment will get it working properly. Repair may be acceptable.

OR

Refund — Probably best remedy.
Vacuum cleaner not fit for purpose — it is a basic fault and customer perhaps has no confidence in it and is entitled to a full cash refund.

(iv) ➢ *Listen with courtesy to complaint.*
➢ *Investigate complaint — examine product.*
➢ *Advise customer what he proposes as a solution.*
➢ *Get customer agreement if possible.*

2. (b) *(i) Misleading claim about coat/false description — Consumer Information Act 1978.*
(ii) Full refund — the product was not as it was represented to be.

2. (c) *This sign is illegal — retailers may not take away a consumer's rights by displaying such a sign. It cuts across a consumer's basic right where a refund is the appropriate and correct solution.*

Chapter 8 — Money and Banking

1. FORMS OF MONEY

A. Barter

Before money was introduced, people had a system of barter or exchanging one product for another.

B. Money

The problems with barter led to the introduction of money, which had a standard value. Gold and silver were chosen and minted into coins.

C. Paper Money

People gave their gold and silver to a goldsmith for safe keeping. The goldsmith gave the person a receipt. These receipts were then used to buy goods and services. The person in possession of these receipts returned to the goldsmith and collected the gold.

D. Characteristics of Money

Money has to be:
(1) **Portable** — easy to carry.
(2) **Valuable** — acceptable in exchange for goods and services.
(3) **Scarce** — be in short supply.
(4) **Divisible** — can be broken down into small denominations.
(5) **Durable** — last a long time.

E. Functions of Money

(1) **Medium of exchange**
(2) **Measure of value**
(3) **Store of value**
(4) **Standard of deferred payment.**

F. Forms of Money Today

(1) Notes and coins (Euro and Cent)
(2) Cheques
(3) Plastic cards — Credit cards, Laser cards, smart cards, ATM cards, store cards, charge cards.

G. The Euro

The euro is the currency of twelve European Union countries stretching from the Mediterranean to the Arctic Circle (namely Belgium, Germany, Greece, Spain, France, Ireland, Italy, Luxembourg, the Netherlands, Austria, Portugal and

Finland). Euro notes and coins have been in circulation since January 2002 and are now a part of daily life for over 300 million Europeans living in the Euro area.

BENEFITS OF THE EURO

There are a number of clear benefits to having a single European currency:

(1) **Practical benefits for citizens**: tourism has increased, as citizens can travel more easily with the Euro. No currency conversion is required for travel within the Euro zone.

(2) **Single market**: consumers and enterprises can reap the full benefits of the European Union's single market.

(3) **Single financial market**: since the Euro is a major international currency, both savers and investors benefit from increased opportunities in a larger financial market.

(4) **Price comparisons**: all goods and services are priced in euro.

(5) **Reduced business costs**: there are no bank charges on foreign currency transactions.

H. Business Terms

Cheque Written instruction by a current account holder to his bank to pay a stated amount of money to a named person.

Credit Card Plastic money: buy now — pay later with interest.

Token Money Coins that do not contain their actual value in metal.

2. SAVING

A. Saving

SAVING MEANS NOT SPENDING

REASONS FOR SAVING

(1) Future purchases, e.g. house, car.

(2) Unforeseen events, illness, accident.

(3) Children's education.

(4) Income for the future.

(5) Holidays.

B. Investing

Investing means making your savings work so that they will earn interest.

WHY INVEST YOUR SAVINGS?

(1) To earn interest.

(2) For safety reasons.

C. Factors to be Considered Before Deciding Where to Invest

The wise investor will consider the following:

(1) **Safety** — will savings be safe?
(2) **Interest** — will savings earn interest?
(3) **Liquidity** — will it be easy to withdraw savings?
(4) **Tax** — will the investor have to pay Deposit Interest Retention Tax (DIRT)?
(5) **Future benefits**
(6) **Convenience**

D. Financial Institutions for Investing Your Savings

(1) COMMERCIAL BANK

(a) Deposit account or savings account

- **Interest** is paid and is subject to **Deposit Interest Retention Tax** (DIRT).
- Money is **safe** and can be **withdrawn on demand.**

(b) Cash save account

- Similar to deposit account with the advantage of being able to withdraw money at any Automated Teller Machine (ATM).

(2) BUILDING SOCIETY

(a) Deposit account

- A competitive interest rate is paid on deposits.
- Interest is subject to **DIRT.**
- **Savings record** — you can apply for a mortgage (House Loan).
- Many branches around country with convenient opening hours.

(3) CREDIT UNION

(a) Savings account

- Interest on savings comes in the form of a dividend.
- Members can obtain loans at reasonable rates of interest.
- Local and convenient.

(4) AN POST

All savings invested with An Post are very safe. They are state-guaranteed.

(a) Deposit account

- **Interest** is paid on deposits.
- Interest is subject to **DIRT**.
- Withdrawals can be made at any branch of An Post.

(b) National instalment saving

- Save a **fixed amount** every month for twelve months.
- The money is then **left on deposit** for a period of one to five years.
- Guaranteed minimum rate of interest **after five years**.
- Interest is **tax-free.**

(c) Savings certificates
- Sold in units of a fixed amount.
- Guaranteed minimum return after five years and six months.
- Interest is **tax-free**.

(d) Savings bonds
- Sold in units of a fixed amount.
- Guaranteed minimum return after three years.
- Interest is tax-free.

(e) Prize bonds
- State-guaranteed, risk-free investment.
- No interest, but all numbers are entered in a weekly draw.
- There are over 2000 tax-free cash prizes to win each week, with a jackpot prize each month.

(5) STOCKS AND SHARES

People could invest their savings in **shares in companies**. The investor would
- Get a **dividend**.
- Make a **capital gain** if share price increases.

(6) INSURANCE COMPANIES
- A person could save by taking out an **endowment policy**.

E. Calculating Interest on a Deposit Account

Interest on a deposit account is calculated on a simple interest or compound interest basis.

(1) SIMPLE INTEREST

The interest is calculated on a fixed principal over a period of time.
Formula:

$$\text{Interest} = \frac{\text{Principal} \times \text{Rate} \times \text{Time}}{100}$$

(2) COMPOUND INTEREST

The interest earned in one year is added on to the principal, and the next year interest is calculated on this new principal.

CAR (Compound Annual Rate) is used to compare various deposits and investments in financial institutions.

F. Deposit Interest Retention Tax (DIRT)

(1) A **tax on interest** earned in a Deposit Account.
(2) It is **deducted at 20%** rate by the financial institution and sent to the Revenue Commissioners.

Example

Gross interest earned	€400
Less DIRT 20%	€ 80
Interest received	€320

G. Summary of Investment Institutions

	Safety	Interest	Liquidity	Tax	Future Benefits	Convenience
Commercial Bank	Safe	Yes	On Demand	DIRT	Mortgages Other Loans & Services	Extended Opening Hours ATM — All Time
Building Society	Safe	Yes	Limit — Societies Differ	DIRT	Mortgages Other Loans & Services	Extended Opening Hours ATM — All Time
Credit Union	Safe	Yes	On Demand	None	Loans	Normal Day
An Post Deposit A/C	Safe	Yes	On Demand	DIRT	Loans	Normal Day
NIS	Safe	Yes	On Demand	None	Loans	Normal Day
Saving Certs	Safe	Yes	Notice	None	Loans	Normal Day
Saving Bonds	Safe	Yes	Notice	None	Loans	Normal Day
Prize Bonds	Safe	No	On Demand	None		Normal Day
Stocks and Shares	Risky	Dividend	May sell at any time	Income Tax		
Insurance Companies	Safe	No	Difficult	Lump Sum Tax-Free		

Examination-Style Question and Solution

Question 1.

Answer all sections. This question deals with a Treasurer — investing money, interest calculations and foreign exchange.

You have been appointed treasurer of the organising committee for next year's school tour to France. There are thirty students travelling and the total cost per student is €170. Students have been saving €10 each per week for the five weeks up to 31 May. This money was kept in the school safe until 31 May. As treasurer, you are responsible for collecting this money and investing it wisely.

1. (a) Suggest **three** possible places where this money could be invested, giving one advantage for **each** place mentioned. (9)
1. (b) Calculate how much money has been saved by 31 May. (4)
1. (c) A deposit of €500 is sent to the tour company on 31 May. The balance is invested on 1 June. Assuming a rate of interest of 8% per annum, how much money would be in the investment account on 1 September? (Ignore tax.) Show your workings. (8)
1. (d) All the students pay the balance due on their return to school on 1 September.
(i) Calculate how much money the students pay on 1 September. (4)
(ii) If this money is added to the same investment account on 1 September, calculate how much money would be in this account, in total, on 1 December. (Rate of interest 8% per annum; ignore tax.) Show your workings. (10)

(35 marks)

Source: Junior Certificate Higher Level.

Solution to Question 1.

1. (a) *(i) Commercial Bank.*
- *Withdrawal on demand.*
- *Money is safe.*
- *Money earns interest.*

(ii) Building Society
- *Competitive interest rates.*
- *Can get mortgage in future.*
- *Money earns interest.*

(iii) Credit Union
- *Local and convenient.*
- *Can avail of low interest rate loans in future.*

(iv) An Post
- *Money state-guaranteed.*
- *Convenient/good opening hours.*
- *Competitive rates of interest.*

1. (b) *30 students x €10 ea. = €300 x 5 weeks = €1,500*
1. (c) *31 May amount saved €1,500*
Deposit sent to tour company €500
Balance to invest €1,000

Money invested @8% for 3 months (1/4 of yr) — June, July, August.
Calculations €1,000 @8% 1 yr = €80
1/4 of year = €20
Answer = Principal €1,000 + Interest €20 = €1,020

1. (d) *(i) Students have already paid €10 ea. x 5 weeks = €50*
Cost of tour €170
Saved already €50
Balance to pay 1 Sept. €120 ea. x 30 students = €3,600

OR

Alternatively, students must pay only €3,600 – €20 (interest earned) = €3,580

(ii)	*September balance*	*€1,020*
	Lodgment	*€3,600.00*
		€4,620.00
	3 months interest @8% =	*€92.40*
	Answer	*€4,712.40*

Workings

$$€4{,}620 \times \frac{8}{100} \times \frac{1}{4} = €92.40$$

3. MONEY TRANSMISSION

Money transmission is transferring money from one person to another.

Methods of transferring money within Ireland:

A. Cash — Registered Mail

Notes may be sent through the post, but the letter should be registered to ensure its safe transfer.

B. Cheque Payments

(1) CHEQUES

A person with a current account can make payments by cheque.

(2) BANK DRAFT

A bank draft is a cheque drawn by a bank on its own bank account. Very safe.

C. Direct Bank Payments

(1) STANDING ORDER

This is an instruction to a bank to pay a fixed amount from the account at regular intervals to a specified firm or creditor, e.g. rent, mortgage.

(2) DIRECT DEBIT

This is permission granted by an account-holder to a creditor to withdraw fixed or variable amounts from the account at any time, e.g. an ESB bill.

(3) CREDIT TRANSFER (BANK GIRO)

This is a way of transferring money directly into another person's or firm's bank account.

(4) PAY PATH

An employee's wages or salary can be paid directly into his bank account. Safe, convenient and cheaper for the employer than paying by cheque.

D. Card Payments

(1) AUTOMATED TELLER MACHINE (ATM) — CASH DISPENSERS

(a) Customer is given an ATM card and a personal identification number, PIN.
(b) Customer goes to ATM at any bank, inserts card in machine, keys in PIN.
(c) Customer can lodge, withdraw, check the balance, order a statement, order a cheque book, pay a bill.

(2) CREDIT CARD

(a) Customer is given a card and a credit limit.
(b) Goods and services can be purchased or bills paid up to this limit.
(c) Customer receives a monthly statement. Failure to clear the account results in high interest charges.
(d) Examples are Mastercard and Visa.
(e) Widely accepted in shops, garages, hotels, restaurants.
(f) Best way to use a credit card is to settle account in full each month — no interest is incurred.
(g) Bookings can be made over the telephone and Internet using the card.

(3) CHARGE CARD

(a) Similar to credit card.
(b) When statement is received, customer must pay amount due.
(c) Examples are American Express and Diners.

(4) STORE CARD/FUEL CARD

(a) Department stores and oil companies give their customers store/fuel cards.
(b) Customers are given a credit limit.
(c) Examples include Esso, Shell, Texaco, Brown Thomas, Marks and Spencer.

(5) LASER CARD/DEBIT CARD

(a) Can be used by current account holders to pay for goods or services.
(b) Laser card is 'swiped' through terminal at cash desk. Amount of money is keyed in.
(c) If there are sufficient funds in the account, a receipt is given to customer for signature.
(d) Money is deducted from customer's account and credited to retailer's account.
(e) A 'cash back' facility is also available at the checkout.

E. An Post — Sending Money Home or Abroad

An Post offers a variety of secure methods for sending money nationally and internationally. A person can send money nationally by postal order and internationally by eurogiro, sterling draft and Western Union.

(1) SENDING MONEY NATIONALLY

Postal Money Order

You can pay bills, shop by mail order, donate to charity and send monetary gifts by post. Just go to your local post office to carry out the transaction.

(2) SENDING MONEY INTERNATIONALLY

(a) Eurogiro
Suitable if you are sending money to Europe. You transfer the money into the currency of the receiving country. It is paid to the recipient in cash or lodged into a bank account. It is cost-effective, and the service is carried out at most post offices. Transfers are usually completed within four working days.

(b) Sterling Draft Service
Suitable for making sterling draft payments to many countries worldwide. The sterling draft is lodged to the recipient's bank account.

(c) Western Union Money Transfer
Suitable if you need to send money quickly. Recipients pick up their money in local currency in minutes. Global coverage – no bank account is required. The recipient picks up the money at a local Western Union branch. The service is carried out at selected post offices nationwide.

F. Foreign Exchange

(1) BANK DRAFT — FOREIGN DRAFT

A bank draft can also be purchased and made out in a foreign currency, e.g. US dollars. Very acceptable way of making foreign payments.

(2) TRAVELLER'S CHEQUES

(a) If you are going abroad you can buy traveller's cheques in exchange for cash. They are available in different currencies.
(b) They have to be signed twice, once in the presence of the bank cashier issuing them and again in the presence of the person you are paying. The signatures must correspond. Usually a passport is required as proof of identity.

(3) CREDIT CARDS

Mastercard and Visa can be used as a means of paying for goods and services abroad.

(4) LASER CARD

A laser card with Cirrus facility enables a person to withdraw cash from ATM machines displaying the Cirrus symbol worldwide.

Examination-Style Question and Solution

Question 1.
Answer (a) and (b). This is a Banking Question.

1. (a) State a method of payment provided by Banks, which you would recommend, in **each** case below.

(i) A tenant wishes to pay rent of €80 monthly, directly from her own bank current account to the landlord's bank account.

Answer: Standing Order.

(ii) A student, who does not have a bank account, wishes to pay exam fees directly into the bank account of the Department of Education.

Answer: Credit Transfer.

(iii) A student wishes to send £26.78 sterling to a London publisher for a book.

Answer: *Sterling Bank Draft.*

(iv) Mrs O'Connell wants to have her telephone bill paid in future directly by her bank from her current account.

Answer: *Direct Debit.* (24)

1. (b) Eithne Dunne, Ahamore, Castlecomer, Co. Kilkenny, has a current account No. 42367898 at the Castlecomer branch of the Bank of Ireland.

On 20 May 2014 Eithne visited her bank with €40 notes and €10 coins to send, by credit transfer, to her niece, Maura O'Gorman.

Maura O'Gorman keeps her account, No. 10864219, with the Allied Irish Banks Ltd, Rathmines branch, Dublin.

Assuming you are Eithne Dunne, complete fully the Credit Transfer form, using the blank document supplied at the end of the question, from the information supplied. (16)

Credit Transfer
SUBJECT TO VERIFICATION
Destination Branch Code 90 – 04 – 07
BANK GIRO CREDIT TRANSFER

To Bank
Branch
A/c
Account Number

€

Brand Initials

TO BANK Date
Branch
CREDIT ACCOUNT
Account Number
Ref. No. | | | | | | | | | Tx

Brand/Initials

CASH. LODG.		99
NO. REMS.		98
CASH WITHDR.		97

A/C/N

Paid in by
Address

Notes		
Coin		
Total Cash		
Cheques (See over)		
TOTAL €		

Credit Transfer
SUBJECT TO VERIFICATION
Destination Branch Code 90 – 04 – 07
BANK GIRO CREDIT TRANSFER

To Bank *AIB*
Branch *Rathmines*
A/c *Maura O'Gorman*
Account Number
1	*0*	*8*	*6*	*4*	*2*	*1*	*9*

€ *50* | *—*

Brand Initials

TO BANK *Allied Irish Banks* Date
Branch *Rathmines*
CREDIT ACCOUNT *Maura O'Gorman*
Account Number
Ref. No. | *1* | *0* | *8* | *6* | *4* | *2* | *1* | *9* | Tx

Brand/Initials

CASH. LODG.		99
NO. REMS.		98
CASH WITHDR.		97

A/C/N

Paid in by *Eithne Dunne*
Address *Ahamore*
Castlecomer
Co. Kilkenny

Notes	*40*	*—*
Coin	*10*	*—*
Total Cash	*50*	*—*
Cheques (See over)	*—*	
TOTAL €	*50*	*—*

Source: Junior Certificate Higher Level. **(40 marks)**

4. BANK ACCOUNTS

A. Deposit Account — Savings Account

A Deposit Account is a savings account. Money invested earns interest and can be withdrawn on demand at any bank.

B. Cashsave Account

This is similar to a Deposit Account except that you can lodge or withdraw using an ATM.

C. How to Open Deposit/Cashsave Account

- Application form — name, address, occupation.
- Show proof of identity — passport/driving licence/utility bill, e.g. ESB bill.
- Given Deposit Book and ATM card.

D. Lodging Money to a Deposit Account

- Complete lodgment slip.
- Present slip, cash and deposit book to cashier — balance will be updated and account credited.

E. Withdrawing Money from Deposit Account

- Complete withdrawal slip.

OR

- Use your ATM card if Cashsave Account.

F. Current Account

If you want to use a cheque book to make payments you must open a Current Account. Money in a Current Account does not earn interest.

G. How to Open a Current Account

- Application form — name, address, occupation.
- Show proof of identity — passport/driving licence/utility bill, e.g. ESB bill.
- Submit reference if not known to bank.
- Give specimen signature.
- Lodge money.
- You are given A/C number, cheque book, cheque card, ATM card and PIN.

H. Advantages of Having a Current Account

Account holders:

- Have access to their money at all times.
- May get an overdraft or loan.
- Can arrange to have payments made by standing order or direct debit.
- Can avail of credit transfers.

- Can benefit from PayPath.
- Can have Internet and telephone banking.
- Can make cheque payments.

I. Lodging Money to a Current Account

- Lodgment slip

OR

- ATM lodgment

OR

- Credit Transfer.

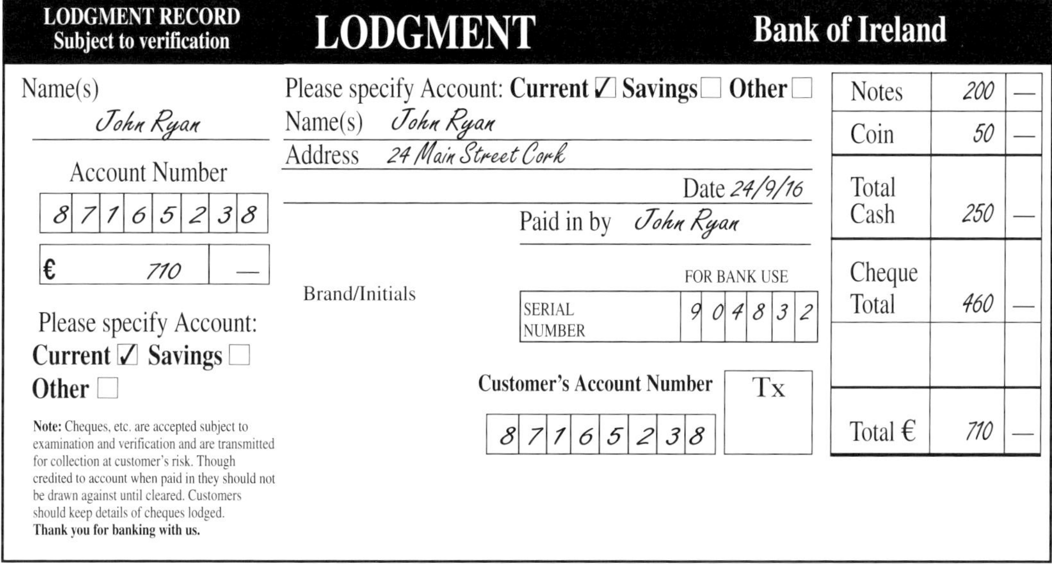

LODGMENT RECORD
Subject to verification

LODGMENT

Bank of Ireland

Name(s) *John Ryan*

Account Number

8 7 1 6 5 2 3 8

€ 710 —

Please specify Account:
Current ☑ Savings ☐
Other ☐

Note: Cheques, etc. are accepted subject to examination and verification and are transmitted for collection at customer's risk. Though credited to account when paid in they should not be drawn against until cleared. Customers should keep details of cheques lodged.
Thank you for banking with us.

Please specify Account: **Current** ☑ **Savings** ☐ **Other** ☐

Name(s) *John Ryan*

Address *24 Main Street Cork*

Date *24/9/16*

Paid in by *John Ryan*

Brand/Initials

FOR BANK USE

SERIAL NUMBER 9 0 4 8 3 2

Customer's Account Number 8 7 1 6 5 2 3 8

Tx

Notes	200	—
Coin	50	—
Total Cash	250	—
Cheque Total	460	—
Total €	710	—

J. Withdrawing Money from a Current Account

- Withdrawal slip at bank counter

OR

- Write a cheque

OR

- ATM withdrawal

OR

- Standing order or direct debit

OR

- Laser card/Debit card

WITHDRAWAL RECORD | **WITHDRAWAL** | **Bank of Ireland**

Name(s) *John Ryan*
24 Main St., Cork
Account Number
8 7 1 6 5 2 3 8
€ 200 —
Please specify Account:
Current ☑ Savings ☐
Other ☐ . . . .
. . . .
Thank you for banking with us.

Please specify Account: **Current** ☑ **Savings** ☐ **Other** ☐
Received the sum of (words) *Two hundred Euro*
Date *15/10/16*
Name of Account Holder(s) *John Ryan*
Signature(s) *John Ryan*

JOINT SAVINGS ACCOUNT
I certify that all parties in the Account are alive at this date.
Signed:

Brand/Initials
SERIAL NUMBER
9 0 4 8 3 2
Customer's Account Number
8 7 1 6 5 2 3 8

Address *24 Main St*
Cork
Tx
€ 200 —

K. Bank Overdraft

(1) Bank overdraft is where a person writes cheques or withdraws more money than the amount held in the account.
(2) An agreed limit is set by bank.
(3) Interest on overdrawn amounts on reducing balance.
(4) An overdraft can be repaid at any time in variable amounts and should be cleared in one year.

L. Conditions that Must Be Met Before a Current Account Can Be Overdrawn

(1) Established customer.
(2) Creditworthy.
(3) Is able to repay.
(4) Agrees to keep within the overdraft limit.
(5) The account must be cleared of the agreed overdraft limit within the time specified or within one year.

M. Preparation of Bank Account

All Current Account customers should keep their own personal bank accounts to record:

(1) Opening Balance.
(2) Lodgments to the account.
(3) Withdrawals or **payments** made from the account.
(4) Closing Balance.

BANK ACCOUNT — FORMAT

The bank account can be laid out using a **T Account Ledger** format or in the **continuous balancing ledger format.**

NB Ordinary level students can use either format. Higher level students must be able to use **both** formats.

N. Bank Statement

Current account holders receive regular bank statements. It is a copy of the customer's account from the **bank's point of view**. It shows transactions known to the bank.

A bank statement shows:

(1) Opening balance — Balance column.
(2) Lodgments into the account — Credit column.
(3) Payments from the account — Debit column.
(4) Closing balance in the account on a particular date.

O. Comparing Bank Account and Bank Statements

When you receive a bank statement, the final figure shows what the bank says you have in your account. This figure may be different from the figure in your own personal bank account.

REASONS FOR DIFFERENCE

(1) Cheques written — not yet cashed.
(2) Lodgments made — but not shown on statement.
(3) Certain items will appear in the **bank statement** that the **account holder will not know about until the statement arrives**, e.g. standing orders, direct debits, current account fees, interest charged, government duty on cheque books, credit transfers into the account.

When the balance shown in the bank statement does not agree with the balance in the customer's own bank account, **a bank reconciliation statement** must be prepared.

HOW TO RECONCILE THE TWO BALANCES

(1) CORRECT OR UPDATE THE BANK ACCOUNT

Look at bank statement and at bank account. **Identify items known to bank.**

Credit bank account with items that were taken out of the account, e.g. bank interest, standing orders, direct debits, current account fees, government duty on cheque books.

Debit the bank account with items that went into the account, e.g. credit transfers, salary paid direct to account.

The bank account is now correct.

(2) PREPARE A BANK RECONCILIATION STATEMENT

Start with balance as per bank statement.

Add lodgments not credited.

Subtract cheques not presented for payment.

Your answer will be balance as per corrected bank account.

Example: Bank A/C — Bank Statement — Bank Reconciliation Statement
(a) Bank Account is prepared by the customer

DR +		Bank A/C					CR –
			€			Ch. No.	€
1/1/16	Balance	B/d	500✓	1/1/16	Giggs	Ch. 1	400✓
1/1/16	Cantona		500✓	1/1/16	Wages		100✗
1/1/16	Cole		10✗	1/1/16	Sharp	Ch. 2	400✓
				1/1/16	Balance C/d		110
			1,010				1,010
1/1/16	Balance	B/d	110				
					(Customer has €110 in bank)		

(b) Bank Statement is prepared by Bank

	Bank Statement	–	+	
Date	**Details**	**Debit €**	**Credit €**	**Balance €**
1/1/16	Balance			500 ✓
1/1/16	Cheque No. 1	400 ✓		100
1/1/16	Lodgment		500 ✓	600
1/1/16	Bank Charges	20 ✗		580
1/1/16	Cheque No. 2	400 ✓		180

According to the bank the customer has €180 in bank.

(c) Corrected Bank Account

Items that are in the Bank Statement but not in Bank A/C

		Corrected Bank A/C					
			€				€
1/1/16	Balance	B/d	110	1/1/16	Bank Charges		20
				1/1/16	Balance	C/d	90
			110				110
1/1/16	Balance	B/d	90				

(d) Bank Reconciliation Statement (To reconcile the difference)

	€
Balance as per Bank Statement	**180**
Add Lodgment not Credited — Cole (DR in bank not in bank statement)	**10**
	190
Less Cheque not Presented — Wages (CR in bank not in bank statement)	**100**
Balance as per Bank Account	**90**

P. Reasons Why a Bank Reconciliation Statement Is Prepared

(1) To identify any errors in the bank's records.
(2) To identify any errors or omissions in the customer's records.
(3) To identify:
- Cheques drawn but not presented
- Lodgments not credited
- Bank charges/interest charges

(4) To see the correct balance in the account.
(5) To clarify if the updated cash book is in agreement with the bank statement.

Q. Business Terms

Bank Reconciliation Statement Prepared to reconcile bank account and bank statement.

Bank Statement Contains details of all transactions in a customer's current account.

Current Account Customer receives cheque book — no interest paid on account.

Deposit Account Savings account where interest is earned on money invested.

Government Duty on Cheques Tax collected by the government on cheques.

Overdraft Accommodation Permission granted by banks to current account holders allowing them to overdraw their accounts by a stated amount.

Examination-Style Question and Solution

Question 1.
Answer all sections. This is a Banking Question.

Michael Lynch has a current account with Bank of Ireland.
He received this bank statement on 30 March 2014.

Bank of Ireland

CURRENT ACCOUNT

Post to

Michael Lynch
13 Woodlands Park,
Palmerstown,
Dublin 20

90–07–72
Branch Code

70
Statement Number

30 March 2014
Date of Statement

74107628
Account Number

Date	Details		Debit	Credit	Balance
			€	€	€
28 FEB	BALANCE FORWARD			1,081	
8 MAR	CHEQUE	393	126		955
10 MAR	CHEQUE	392	54		901
11 MAR	CREDIT TRANSFER			100	1,001
13 MAR	ATM		150		851
20 MAR	FIRST NBS	SO	160		691
22 MAR	IRISH LIFE	DD	68		623
27 MAR	CHEQUE	395	120		503
29 MAR	CURRENT ACC.	Fees	6		497

Study this bank statement and answer the following questions:

1. (a) On what date was the statement issued? (3)

1. (b) On 28 February did M. Lynch have an overdraft or have money in the bank? (3)

1. (c) Why are the cheque numbers not in sequence (order)? Explain your answer. (4)

1. (d) List two possible items that could be included in the heading 'Current Account Fees' on 29 March. (4)

1. (e) Explain the main difference between a direct debit (DD) and a standing order (SO) as a means of making payments. (6)

1. (f) The following is Michael Lynch's own account of his bank transactions. Compare this Account with the Bank Statement he received from the bank. Make whatever adjustments that are necessary to Michael's own records in your answer-book, and then prepare a Bank Reconciliation Statement at 31 March 2014. (20)

(M. Lynch's own records)

BANK ACCOUNT

		F	€			F	Cheq. No.	€
Feb. 28	Balance	B/d	1,081	Mar. 1	ESB		392	54
Mar. 30	Lodgment		355	6	ELF Garage		393	126
				13	Cash ATM		—	150
				20	First Nat. Bld. Soc.		SO	160
				22	Irish Life Assur.		DD	68
				27	Shopwell Ltd		394	75
				28	Mulligans Hardware		395	120
				30	Balance	C/d		683
			1,436					1,436
Mar. 31	Balance	B/d	683					

(40 marks)

Source: Junior Certificate Higher Level.

Solution to Question 1.

1. (a) *30 March 2014.*

1. (b) *Money in the bank.*

1. (c) *The cheques may have been presented for payment in a random fashion.*

1. (d) *Withdrawal charges, standing order charges, direct debit charges, credit transfer fees, charges for ordering cheque books.*

1. (e) *Direct debit — for regular payments of varying amounts, e.g. ESB, telephone. Standing order — for regular payments of fixed amounts, e.g. fixed mortgage, insurance premiums, hire purchase payments.*

1. (f) *Adjustments to Michael's own records.*

Bank Account — T Account Presentation

			€			€
Mar. 31	Balance	B/d	683	Current Account	Fees	6
	Credit Transfer		100	Balance	C/d	777
			783			783
	Balance	B/d	777			

OR

Bank Account Continuous Balancing Format				
Date	**Details**	**Debit €**	**Credit €**	**Balance €**
Mar. 31	Balance		683	
	Credit Transfer	100		783
	Current Account Fees		6	777

Bank Reconciliation Statement	
	€
Balance as per Bank Statement	497
ADD Lodgment Not Credited	355
	852
DEDUCT Cheque 394 not presented for payment	75
Balance as per corrected bank account	777

5. CHEQUES

A. Definition of Cheque

A cheque is a written instruction from the holder of a current account to his bank to pay a stated sum of money out of the holder's account to the person named in the cheque or to the bearer.

B. Parties to a Cheque

(1) Drawer — Person who writes the cheque.
(2) Drawee — Bank where drawer holds his account.
(3) Payee — Person to whom the cheque is payable.

C. Cheque

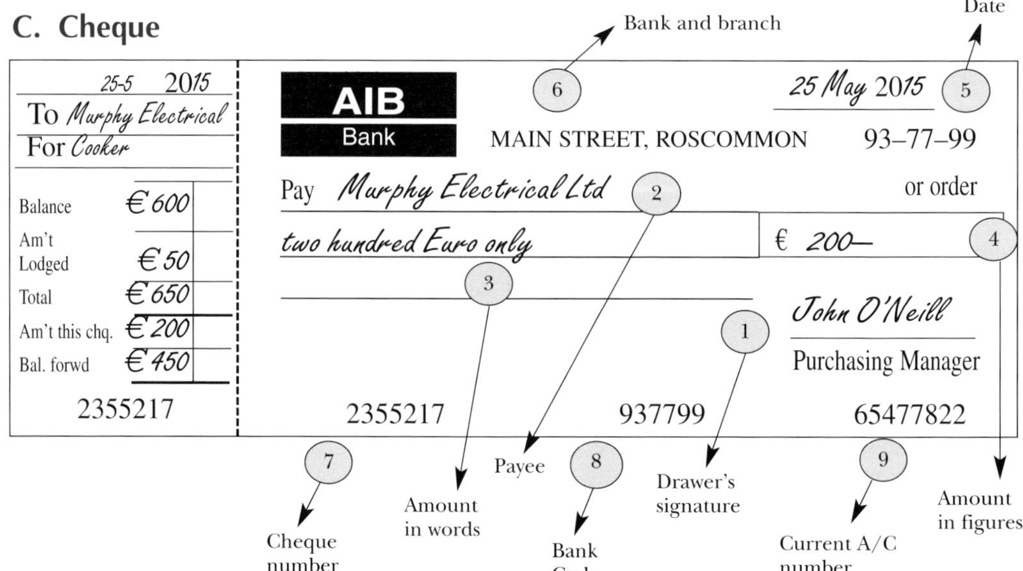

D. Counterfoil of Cheque (Stub)

The purpose of the counterfoil is to record the amount of the cheque, the name of the person paid and the date that the cheque was written. The amount left in the account after the cheque is also recorded. The account holder uses completed counterfoils to write up his own bank records.

E. Rules for Completing a Cheque

- Keep words close together.
- Keep figures close to € sign.
- Complete stub.
- Initial corrections.
- Cross cheque.

F. Cheque Card/Banker's Card

(1) An identity card given to creditworthy current account holders.
(2) Guarantees cheque up to a certain limit.
(3) Many banks now have a combined ATM/cheque card and photograph.
(4) Cheques can be cashed at outlets where you are not personally known.
(5) Details of the card include card number, expiry date and cardholder's signature.

Steps to be followed when accepting a personal cheque with a cheque card.

(i) The cheque must be signed in the presence of the Payee/Seller.
(ii) The Drawer's signature must match that on the card.
(iii) The cheque book code number must match that on the card.
(iv) The card must not be out of date.
(v) Write the card number on the back of the cheque.
(vi) The amount of the cheque must be for less than the cheque card limit.

G. Crossing a Cheque

Draw two parallel lines across the face of the cheque. This makes the cheque safe, as it must be paid into the bank account of the payee.

Types of Crossing

(1) General Crossing

& Co.

(2) Special Crossing

Cheque can be paid only into payee account.

A/c payee only

H. Endorsing/Negotiating a Cheque

The payee signs the back of the cheque and passes it on to a third party.

I. Different Types of Cheque

(1) **Or Order cheques** — have 'or order' printed on them. The cheque may be endorsed and passed on.
(2) **Stale cheque** — one that was drawn over six months ago. You must get the drawer to re-date it or issue a new one before you can cash it.
(3) **Postdated cheque** — date in the future.
(4) **Antedated cheque** — has a date before the date of issue.
(5) **Blank cheque** — vital information is missing.
(6) **Open cheque** — not crossed.
(7) **Receipt cheque** — a cheque that must be signed by the payee before cashing.
(8) **Dishonoured cheques/Bounced cheques** — cheques which the bank refuses to pay. The cheques will be returned to the payee marked R/D — Refer to Drawer.
(9) **Stopped cheque** — One where the drawer informs the bank not to honour it.

J. Why Banks Refuse to Cash a Cheque

(1) If the cheque is stale.
(2) If drawer dies or becomes bankrupt.
(3) If drawer has not enough money in the account.
(4) If amount in words does not match figures.
(5) If forgery is suspected.
(6) If signature does not match specimen signature.
(7) If cheque is not signed.

K. Cashing a Cheque

When you receive a cheque you can:
(1) Lodge it in your bank account.
(2) Endorse it and give it to someone else.
(3) Cash it in a shop where you are known.

6. OTHER BANKING SERVICES

A. Term Loan

(1) Given for a fixed term, usually from two to seven years.
(2) Given for a specific purpose.
(3) Repaid in fixed monthly instalments.
(4) Must be negotiated with the bank manager.

B. Mortgages — House Loans

Banks give house loans. The deeds of the premises will be given as collateral — security. Costs involved in House Purchase include — solicitor's fees, stamp duty, administration fees, registration fees.

C. Strongroom Facilities

For storage of valuables and jewellery, or deeds of premises.

D. Purchase and Sale of Shares

Banks provide the facility for purchasing and selling shares in companies quoted on the stock exchange.

E. Financial Advice

To individuals, the farming community and business community.

F. Telephone Banking

Customers can access a range of services over the telephone 24 hours a day, including checking accounts, paying bills, money transmission, applying for loans, ordering foreign currency.

G. Trustee or Executor

Banks act as trustee or executor for their customers in relation to wills.

H. Income Tax and Life Assurance

Banks provide advice in relation to income tax and life assurance.

I. Night Safe

A facility where money can be lodged in the bank after banking hours through a chute located in the bank wall; a numbered leather wallet and key are provided. The account is credited the following day.

J. Foreign Exchange

All banks provide a foreign exchange service. This is the exchanging of one currency for another.

K. Banking on the Internet

Most banks have websites on which they give information about their products and services.

L. Business Terms

Electronic Funds Transfer at Point of Sale (EFTPOS) The use of Laser cards and smart cards to pay for goods and services.

Executor A person appointed by another person to ensure that his/her estate is distributed according to his/her will.

Life Assurance Policy providing money for family after death of main earner in family.

Mortgage House loan, deeds of house are given as security.

Share Part-ownership of a company.

Stock Exchange A market where shares are bought and sold.

Strongroom A safe for storage of valuables and important documents.

Trustee A person appointed by another person to manage funds.

7. MAIN FINANCIAL INSTITUTIONS AND THEIR SERVICES

	Names	Main Services
COMMERCIAL BANKS	Allied Irish Banks (AIB) Bank of Ireland Ulster Bank ATM = Service till National Irish Bank Permanent TSB	Savings, Lending Money Transmission Foreign Exchange Specialised Financial Services Specialised Advice
BUILDING SOCIETIES	Permanent TSB Educational Building Society First National Building Society Irish Nationwide Building Society ICS Building Society	Savings, Lending Money Transmission Foreign Exchange Specialised Financial Services Specialised Advice
CREDIT UNION	There are about 500 Credit Unions in Ireland, e.g. ASTI, TUI, Credit Unions	Savings, Lending at reasonable interest rates
AN POST	There are about 400 Post Offices nationwide	Savings, Lending — Post Loan Money Transmission Foreign Exchange

Chapter 9 — Credit and Borrowing

1. CREDIT

A. How We Can Buy Goods and Services

Goods and services can be bought by:
(1) Cash
(2) Credit
(3) Borrowing.

B. Credit

(1) When we buy goods on credit, we get the goods immediately and pay later.
(2) Before a person is given credit, a business will make sure that he is creditworthy, i.e. check to see if he will repay the money.
(3) Ways of checking creditworthiness/credit status:
- ➢ Bank can be asked for information on your financial position.
- ➢ Reference from other firms that you deal with.
- ➢ Credit Status Enquiry Agency.
- ➢ Get sales representatives to make enquiries.
- ➢ Look up *Stubbs Gazette.*

REASONS FOR SELLING GOODS ON CREDIT
(1) To attract new customers.
(2) To increase sales and profit.
(3) To help genuine customers short of cash temporarily.
(4) To compete with other firms offering credit.

HOW A BUSINESS CAN REDUCE ITS LOSSES CAUSED BY BAD DEBTS
(1) Offer discounts for prompt payment.
(2) Have a good credit control system and good accounting system.
(3) Retain ownership of goods until payment is received.
(4) Sell for cash only.

C. Types of Credit

(1) CONSUMER CREDIT
This is where consumers buy goods and use services and pay the seller/supplier at a later date, e.g. milk, electricity, telephone, local shop.

(2) CREDIT CARD
When a consumer buys goods and services using a credit card, the bill is paid by the credit card company and the consumer then pays the credit card company within the agreed credit period. Examples include Visa, Mastercard.

(3) HIRE PURCHASE

➢ Hire purchase is a system of buying goods on credit by paying an initial deposit and paying the balance owed by regular instalments over an agreed period of time.

The buyer obtains **the immediate use of the goods** but does not become the legal owner until the **last instalment is paid**. It is expensive, as hire purchase companies charge a flat rate of interest.

Parties Involved in Hire Purchase

(a) Consumer/Buyer
(b) Retailer/Seller
(c) HP Company.

Example of a Hire Purchase Transaction

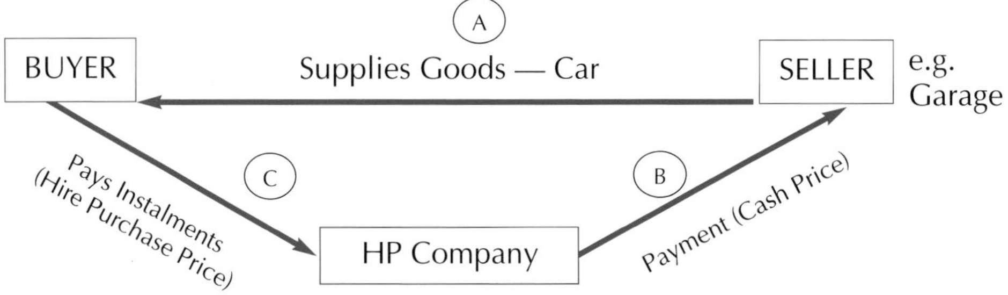

Consumer Protection in Relation to Hire Purchase

Consumers are protected by the Hire Purchase Acts 1946 and 1960, which state the following:

(a) A hire purchase **agreement** must be prepared and signed by both parties.
(b) This agreement must show:

➢ Cash price of goods.
➢ Hire purchase price.
➢ APR — Annual Percentage Rate.
➢ Number of instalments.
➢ Amount of each instalment.
➢ Description of the goods.

(c) The agreement must also **contain the right of the hirer to terminate** the agreement.

➢ If at least **half of the hire purchase** is paid, the goods are then returned to the hire purchase company.

(d) The agreement also contains the following restrictions on the hire purchase company's right to recover the goods:

➢ Without hirer's consent, the hire purchase company has no authority to enter the hirer's premises to take back the goods.
➢ If one-third or more of the hire purchase price is paid, the hire purchase company cannot take back the goods without a court order.

(e) A copy of the agreement must be sent to the hirer within fourteen days.

Advantages to the Consumer of Buying on a Hire Purchase

(a) Immediate possession and use.
(b) Consumer has the use of item while paying for it.
(c) HP finance is easily available.
(d) Security is not required.

Disadvantages to the Consumer of Buying a Hire Purchase

(a) Expensive – a flat rate of interest is charged.
(b) Ownership acquired only after paying final instalment.
(c) Could encourage overspending.

(4) LEASING/RENTING

(a) When you lease/rent something, you have the **use** of the item, e.g. television, car, video, but you will never **own** it.
(b) A regular payment is made for the use of the item.
(c) Leasing/renting makes financial sense only if you need the item for just a short period of time or have no ambition to own it, e.g. video cassette.

(5) DEFERRED PAYMENT/BUDGET ACCOUNT

This is where an item is purchased, e.g. suite of furniture, with a deposit being paid and the balance paid in instalments. **Ownership of the goods passes to the buyer when the deposit is paid.** If the buyer defaults in payment, the goods cannot be repossessed but the seller can sue the buyer for the balance outstanding.

D. Summary of Methods of Purchasing Goods/Services

	Method	**Possession**	**Ownership**	**Examples of goods that can be bought**
1.	Cash	Immediate	Immediate	Anything
2.	Consumer Credit	Immediate	Immediate	Groceries, ESB, telephone, gas, milk, etc.
3.	Credit Card	Immediate	Immediate	Most items, e.g. petrol, groceries, holidays, etc.
4.	Hire Purchase	Immediate	On payment of last instalment	Cars, TVs, electrical equipment, computers, etc.
5.	Leasing/ Renting	Immediate	Never own goods	Cars, TVs, houses, videos, dress suits, etc.
6.	Deferred Payment	Immediate	Immediate	Furniture, carpets, electrical goods, TVs, etc.

Examination-Style Question and Solution

Question 1.

Answer all sections. This is a Hire Purchase Question.

Eoin and Úna Murphy purchased a video after seeing the following advertisement in a shop.

All the repayments were made on time until Eoin lost his job $1^{1}/_{2}$ years later. As a result they failed to make one of the repayments. A week later a hire purchase company representative entered their house, without permission, and took the video away.

1. (a) The above advertisement is illegal, as it does not include certain information required by law. Identify **two** additional items of information that a legal advertisement for hire purchase credit should include. (12)

1. (b) What was illegal about the behaviour of the hire purchase company representative? (4)

1. (c) Who was the lawful owner of the video at the time it was repossessed by the hire purchase company? (4)

1. (d) What is the main disadvantage of buying on hire purchase? (4)

1. (e) If Eoin and Úna had made all their repayments, what would be the total cost of the video? (4)

1. (f) Name **two** other ways they could have financed the purchase of the video other than by hire purchase credit. (12)

Source: Junior Certificate Higher Level. **(40 marks)**

Solution to Question 1.

1. (a) *Cash Price, APR, Total Credit Price.*

1. (b) *The hire purchase representative should have a court order to*
(i) enter the dwelling house;
(ii) repossess the goods when more than one-third has been paid. He didn't have the court order and permission.

1. (c) *Hire purchase company.*

1. (d) *(i) It is expensive. Hire purchase companies charge a flat rate of interest, which results in a very high APR.*
(ii) Consumers may spend more than they can afford.
(iii) A lot of future earnings may be spent on hire purchase.

1. (e) *€15 per month × 24 months + €60 deposit*
= €360 + €60 = €420

1. (f) *(i) Bank loan, credit union loan, or loan from building society.*
(ii) Buy it out of personal savings.
(iii) Deferred payment.

2. BORROWING

A. Borrowing

Borrow the money and repay the lending agency in the future with interest (cost).

B. Factors to be Considered Before Borrowing

Before borrowing, we must ask ourselves a number of questions:

(1) Do we need the goods or services?
(2) Can we meet the repayments?
— Ability to repay.
(3) What security/collateral can we offer the lender?
(4) Rate of Interest — APR.
(5) Length of repayments.
(6) Amount required.
(7) Job security.
(8) Which financial institution best meets our requirements?

C. Collateral/Security

Lender will require collateral or security. This means that you hand over/sign over some valuable asset. The lender will hold this asset until the loan is repaid. It may be liquidated by the lender if the borrower fails to repay.

ACCEPTABLE FORMS OF SECURITY/COLLATERAL

➢ Deeds of premises or property.
➢ Life Assurance Policy.
➢ Share Certificates.
➢ Guarantor.

D. Advantages of Borrowing

(1) Enables people to buy goods without saving for a long time.
(2) Increases standard of living.
(3) Helps people in difficult financial situations.

E. Disadvantages of Borrowing

(1) Carries a high cost — rate of interest.
(2) Commits borrower to repayments in the future.
(3) High borrowings cause many social problems.

F. Applying for a Loan

➢ Fill out loan application form.
➢ Meet lender.
➢ Agree terms of repayment.

G. Information Required by Lender on Application Form

➢ Name, address, age, occupation, employment, income.
➢ Amount of loan.
➢ Purpose of loan.

- ➢ Length of time required to repay.
- ➢ Security available.
- ➢ Track record.
- ➢ Other commitments.

H. Factors Taken into Consideration by Bank Before Lending

(1) Current financial position of borrower.
(2) Creditworthiness of borrower/Previous record/Credit rating.
(3) Collateral/security available.
(4) Purpose of loan.
(5) Duration of loan.
(6) Ability to repay/Job security/Occupation.

I. Cost of Borrowing

The cost of borrowing is the rate of interest charged by the lender.

(1) FLAT RATE OF INTEREST

Interest is charged on the original loan amount over the full duration of the loan. No credit is given for repayments made.

(2) TRUE RATE OF INTEREST/APR

Interest is charged on the **reducing balance of the loan**, i.e. it is calculated on the amount outstanding after each instalment is paid. Another name for true rate is APR, **Annual Percentage Rate**, and it includes other costs in taking out a loan, e.g. administration fees, stamp duty and insurance. All lending institutions must by law show the annual percentage rate on any advertisement for a loan. This allows consumers to make comparisons between lending agencies.

J. Advertising Credit Facilities to Consumers

All borrowers have a right to know:

- ➢ Cash price.
- ➢ Credit price.
- ➢ APR.
- ➢ Amount of instalments.
- ➢ Number of instalments.

K. Rights of Borrower

The rights of the borrower are protected by legislation, including:
(1) Hire Purchase Acts 1946 and 1960.
(2) Sale of Goods and Supply of Services Act 1980.

L. Responsibilities of Borrower

(1) To provide true and accurate information to the lender.
(2) To pay the monthly instalments on time.
(3) To repay the loan in full.

M. Bankruptcy

If a person borrows and is unwilling or unable to repay his debts, he can be declared bankrupt by the High Court.

N. Duration of Loans

Loans can be for the short term, up to one year; medium term, one to five years; or long term, five to twenty years. Here are some of the most **common reasons** for borrowing matched with the **sources available** and the **duration of the borrowing**.

	REASONS	SOURCES AVAILABLE	DURATION
1.	Christmas expenses	Bank overdraft, credit card, credit union, moneylender	Short-term
2.	Temporary shortage of cash	Bank overdraft	Short-term
3.	Furniture	Short-term bank loan, credit union	Short-term
4.	Holidays	Bank overdraft, credit card, credit union	Short-term
5.	Telephone bill/ESB bill	Moneylender, credit card, bank overdraft	Short-term
6.	Communion, Confirmation expenses	Credit card, credit union, bank overdraft	Short-term
7.	College expenses	Credit union/Short-term loan	Short-term
8.	Car	Bank term loan, credit union, hire purchase	Medium-term
9.	Computer	Bank term loan, credit union, hire purchase	Medium-term
10.	House improvements	Bank term loan, credit union	Medium-term
11.	Conservatory	Bank term loan, credit union	Medium-term
12.	House purchase	Building society mortgage, bank mortgage	Long-term
13.	House extension	Building society loan, bank loan	Long-term

O. Lending Agencies

(1) COMMERCIAL BANK

Commercial banks operate lending in a number of ways:

(a) Term loan: a loan given for a stated reason, for a specified period of time.
(b) Bank overdraft: where the bank manager gives permission to a current account holder to overdraw up to a certain limit.
(c) Mortgage: a home loan given by the bank for the purchase of a house.
(d) Bridging loan: short-term finance given to people who have a mortgage approved but are awaiting receipt of a building society loan.

(2) BUILDING SOCIETIES

Building societies provide home loans and other financial services.

(3) CREDIT UNION

You must be a member of a credit union with a savings record to qualify for a loan. The credit union will lend a multiple of the amount saved (two or three times). Loans are given for many purposes, including cars, furniture, holidays and electrical goods.

(4) HIRE PURCHASE

This was dealt with earlier in the chapter (see p. 62).

(5) MONEYLENDERS

People will borrow from moneylenders if they have difficulty in borrowing from other financial institutions. Moneylenders charge extremely high rates of interest. Licensed moneylenders have a licence from the Revenue Commissioners to operate. APR must be quoted on all loans. An unlicensed moneylender lends without a licence.

(6) PAWNBROKERS

A pawnbroker will lend money on the security of something valuable, e.g. jewellery. If the loan is not repaid, the security can be sold to repay the loan.

P. Business Terms

Bankruptcy A person can be declared bankrupt if he cannot pay what he owes.
Bridging Loan Short-term loan given to person awaiting receipt of building society loan.
Collateral Security given against a loan.
Creditor Person who is owed money.
Flat Rate of Interest Interest calculated on the full amount borrowed for the full period of the loan.
Guarantor A person who undertakes to repay the loan if the borrower cannot.
Moneylender A person who lends money at very high rates of interest.
Mortgage A home loan where the deeds of the house are given as security.
Overdraft Writing cheques for or withdrawing more than the amount in a current account.
Pawnbroker A person who lends on the security of valuables.
Share Certificate A certificate stating that you own part of a company.

Examination-Style Question and Solution

Question

Answer all sections. This is a Cost of Borrowing Question.

On 1 January T. McKenna obtained the following information in respect of a Solara 20" colour television set (list price €499). An investigation into the position reveals her options to be:

Rental Only: €4.25 per week (one month's rental payable in advance). A minimum of a one-year contract must be taken out, and it can thereafter be ended by one month's notice in writing by either side.

Rental Purchase: A €50 deposit plus €15 per month for four years. At the end of that period the set could be purchased outright on payment of a further €10.

Cash Purchase: 20" Solara €449.

McKenna has saved €50 but has been told by the bank manager that she can borrow up to €400 on term loan. The term loan would be at the rate of €3.50 per month (including interest) for each €100 borrowed.

You are asked to:

1. (a) Calculate the cost of each of the three methods above for the period to 31 December. (18)

1. (b) Recommend with reasons a particular method to T. McKenna. (16)

1. (c) Give three possible additional costs of T. McKenna having a TV set. (6)

Source: Junior Certificate Higher Level. **(40 marks)**

Solution to Question.

(a) *Cost of each of the three methods*

Rental Only	*52 weeks @ €4.25 = €221 x 4 yrs =*	*€884*
Rental Purchase	*Deposit €50*	
	€15 x 12 months = 180 x 4 yrs = €720	*€770*
Cash Purchase	*Cash price €449 Saved €50 Borrowing €400*	
	Cost of Borrowing €400 for 4 years @ €3.50 per €100	
	48 months x €3.50 = €168 x 4 = €672 + Deposit €50	
		€722

(b) *I would recommend that T. McKenna borrow the €400 and use the cash purchase method because:*

(i) It is the cheapest method.

(ii) It will give T. McKenna immediate ownership of the TV.

(c) *Three possible additional costs of having a TV set:*

(i) Increased insurance cover.

(ii) Television licence.

(iii) Service contract.

(iv) Increased ESB charges.

(v) Cost of cable and aerial.

Examination-Style Question and Solution

Question

Answer (A), (B) and (C). This is a question on Borrowing.
To be completed on blank loan application form.

Rhona King, who is single, lives at 56 Banks Road, Cork, in a house which she purchased in 1990 with the help of a mortgage of €40,000 from the Startup Building Society and to whom she repays €200 per month. Her telephone number is 021–134567.

Rhona is employed as a legal secretary with Smart & Keane, Solicitors, Airport Road, Cork, where she started work in 1986. She earns a Gross Salary of €1,900 per month, out of which she pays income tax and PRSI totalling €650 per month.

Rhona wishes to buy a new car for her next birthday. She was 35 years old on 14 August 2000.

In order to buy the car, she needs to borrow €10,000, which she hopes to repay in monthly instalments of €230 over the next four years. She is already paying the Cork Credit Union €50 per month for a loan of €1,000, which she obtained in 1999.

She gets a Loan Application Form from her local branch of AIB Bank.

(A) Complete Rhona's Loan Application Form on today's date. (40)
(B) If the bank grants Rhona the loan for the car at €230 per month, how much interest will she have paid after four years? Show your workings. (8)
(C) Explain **three** of the following terms

Hire Purchase
Collateral
Mortgage
Debtor
Bankruptcy (12)

(60 marks)

Source: Junior Certificate Ordinary Level.

For use with question on borrowing

(A) LOAN APPLICATION FORM					
PERSONAL DETAILS					
Name				Mr, Mrs, Ms.	
Address					
Number of years at this address				Owner or Rented	
Telephone					**AIB Bank**
Date of birth					
Mortgage amount (if any)					
Annual repayments on mortgage					
Mortgage borrowed from					
EMPLOYMENT DETAILS					
Occupation					
Employer's Name & Address					
Net salary per month					
No. of years in your present employment					
LOAN REQUIRED					
Amount					
Purpose					
How long do you want the loan for?					
How much can you repay each month?					
Details of other existing loans					
Lender		Amount		Annual repayments	
SIGNATURE			DATE		

Don't forget Parts (B) and (C) of this question.

Solution to question on borrowing

A

LOAN APPLICATION FORM					
PERSONAL DETAILS					
Name	*Rhona King*			Mr, Mrs, Ms.	*Ms*
Address	*56 Banks Rd*				
	Cork				
Number of years at this address	*10*		Owner or Rented	*Owner*	
Telephone	*021-134567*			**AIB Bank**	
Date of birth	*14/8/1965*				
Mortgage amount (if any)	*€40,000*				
Annual repayments on mortgage	*€2,400*				
Mortgage borrowed from	*Startup Building Society*				
EMPLOYMENT DETAILS					
Occupation	*Legal secretary*				
Employer's Name & Address	*Smart & Keane Solicitors, Airport Rd, Cork*				
Net salary per month	*€1,250*				
No. of years in your present employment	*14*				
LOAN REQUIRED					
Amount	*€10,000*				
Purpose	*To buy a car*				
How long do you want the loan for?	*4 years*				
How much can you repay each month?	*€230*				
Details of other existing loans					
Lender	*Cork Credit Union*	Amount	*€1,000*	Annual repayments	*€600*
SIGNATURE	*Rhona King*		DATE	*14/6/–*	

B *Total repaid €230 x 48 months =* *€11,040*

Less amount borrowed = *€10,000*

Interest paid = *€1,040*

C

- *Hire purchase: the customer buys a product from a retailer, the retailer is paid by the HP company, the customer repays the HP company plus interest. The customer does not own the goods until after the last repayment is made.*
- *Collateral: this is the security a borrower must give when taking out a loan.*
- *Mortgage: this is a long-term loan used to buy a house. The house is used as security, and the loan and interest are repaid usually over 20 years.*
- *Debtor: a person or a business who owes us money.*
- *Bankruptcy: this occurs when a person cannot pay his debts and his creditors go to court to have him declared bankrupt.*

Chapter 10 — Insurance

A. What Is Insurance?

Insurance is protection against a possible loss that we hope will not happen, e.g. a house going on fire or a car accident. A fee called a premium is paid to the insurance company for this cover.

B. How Insurance Works

It is based on the idea of many people paying premiums into an insurance company fund and any person who suffers a loss being able to claim compensation.

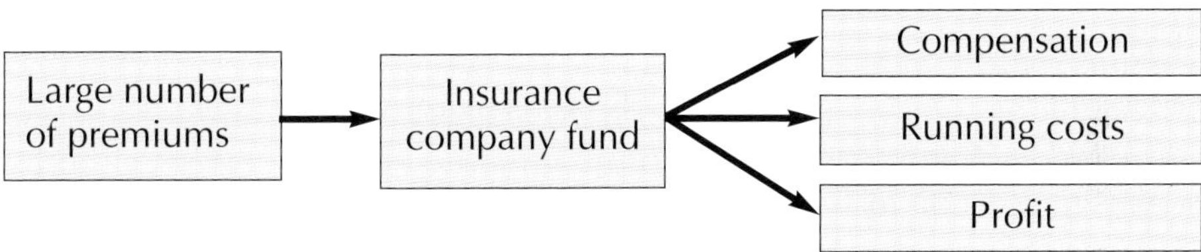

C. Risks

INSURABLE RISKS AND NON-INSURABLE RISKS

(1) Insurable risks are risks that can be insured against, e.g. house against fire and theft.

(2) Uninsurable risks are risks that cannot be insured against, e.g. damage caused by war or earthquakes, losses due to bad management.

D. Need for Adequate Insurance

Any insurance taken out by an individual or household should be adequate, that is, it should cover **all relevant risks** insured for the correct amount. Failure to insure risks for the correct amounts leads to underinsurance and reduction in compensation paid.

E. Basic Principles of Insurance

Insurance operates under a set of basic rules called the basic principles of insurance. They are:

(1) Insurable interest
(2) Utmost good faith
(3) Indemnity
(4) Subrogation
(5) Contribution

(1) INSURABLE INTEREST

In order to insure something you must have an **insurable interest** in the item. You must benefit by its existence and suffer financially by its loss, e.g. you can insure your house but not your neighbour's house.

(2) UTMOST GOOD FAITH

When completing a proposal form for insurance, you must answer all the questions truthfully and disclose all material facts/relevant information.

(3) INDEMNITY

You cannot make a profit out of insurance. Compensation is limited to the value of the damage suffered irrespective of the level of cover. The aim of insurance is to place the insured in the same position financially as before the loss and not in a better position.

(4) SUBROGATION

When an insurance company compensates the insured for the loss, it can proceed to claim compensation from the person who caused the loss; once compensation has been paid, the damaged item becomes the property of the insurance company.

(5) CONTRIBUTION

If a person has the same risk insured with two companies, he cannot claim the full amount from each company. Each company will contribute towards the loss in proportion to the sum insured with it.

F. Taking Out Insurance

Insurance is costly, so it is in a person's interest to get the best possible quotation. You can do this in a number of ways:

(i) You can contact insurance companies directly.

(ii) You can contact an insurance broker who will get quotations from many companies. The broker is an insurance expert who arranges insurance, will give impartial advice and is free to sell any firm's policies.

(iii) You can contact an insurance agent who is employed by a particular insurance company to sell insurance policies on its behalf.

(1) PROPOSAL FORM

This is an application form for insurance. All questions must be truthfully and accurately answered giving all relevant details — the principle of utmost good faith.

(2) ACTUARY

An actuary will assess the risk and calculate the premium.

(3) PREMIUM

The annual cost of the insurance paid by the insured.

(4) POLICY

This is written evidence of the contract of insurance. It contains details of what risks are covered.

(5) COVER NOTE

Sometimes there may be a delay in the preparation of the policy. In the meantime the insurance company will issue a cover note. This provides evidence that insurance cover exists.

(6) CERTIFICATE OF INSURANCE

In motor insurance, a certificate of insurance is issued. This is proof of the existence of insurance. A portion of this document called the insurance disc is detached and displayed on the windscreen of the car to show that the car is insured.

(7) RENEWAL NOTICE

This is notice to remind you that the next premium is due.

(8) DAYS OF GRACE

These are additional days given by the insurance company to pay the renewal premium from the due date. There are no days of grace in motor insurance.

G. Making a Claim

When a loss occurs and you want to claim compensation:

(1) Notify your insurance company and give them your policy number.
(2) The insurance company will send you a **claim form** to return giving details of the loss suffered.
(3) Obtain estimates and quotations for repairing the damage or replacing the loss.
(4) The insurance company will check your policy to make sure that the loss suffered was as a direct result of the insured risk. This is known as **proximate cause**.
(5) An **assessor** is then sent to examine the damage or loss and assess how much compensation should be paid for the loss suffered.
(6) Claim may be settled by
   - ➢ Cash.
   - ➢ Replacement of item insured.
   - ➢ Repair.
   - ➢ Reinstatement.

H. Overinsured/Underinsured/Average Clause

(1) OVERINSURED

If you have overinsured, you will receive only compensation amounting to market value of the item.

(2) UNDERINSURED

If you are underinsured and the item is completely destroyed, you will receive only compensation amounting to the value for which the item is insured.

(3) AVERAGE CLAUSE — PARTIAL LOSS

Average clause applies in the case of a **partial** loss where the insurance cover is for less than the market value of the item lost, i.e. you are underinsured.

Example — Average Clause

House valued at €200,000 insured for €160,000.
Fire causes €20,000 worth of damage.

Q. How much compensation will be paid?

A. House is only eight-tenths, i.e. four-fifths, insured so the amount of compensation will be four-fifths of €20,000, which is €16,000.

N.B. If you are only partly insured, you will receive only partial compensation.

I. Types of Insurance

There are four main categories of insurance for the household and the individual. They are:

Personal	Property	Motor	Life
Salary protection insurance	Fire insurance	Third party insurance	Whole life assurance
Voluntary Health Insurance	Burglary insurance	Third party fire and theft	Endowment assurance
Personal accident insurance	All risks policy	Comprehensive insurance	Term assurance
Sports injuries insurance			Mortgage protection plan
Pay-Related Social Insurance			
Travel/Holiday insurance			
Wedding insurance			

PERSONAL INSURANCE

(1) Salary Protection
Provides a payment of three-quarters of salary if you have to give up work because of accident or illness.

(2) Voluntary Health Insurance (VHI or BUPA)
Covers the cost of consultants and hospital bills.

(3) Personal Accident Insurance
Insures you against accidents.

(4) Sports Injuries Insurance
Covers loss of income and the cost of medical bills if you are injured while involved in sport.

(5) Pay-Related Social Insurance (PRSI)
Covers loss of income due to illness or unemployment.

(6) Travel/Holiday Insurance
Covers goods and luggage stolen while travelling on holidays and medical bills.

(7) Wedding Insurance
Covers the risk of the hotel being overbooked, or the wedding being cancelled, or the photographs or video not developing for some reason.

PROPERTY INSURANCE

(1) Fire Insurance
Covers building and contents against fire, or flooding or storm damage.

(2) Burglary Insurance
Covers theft or damage to contents as a result of a break-in.

(3) All Risks Policy

Householders can also take out an all risks policy which covers fire, burglary, public liability, as well as other risks such as storm damage, flooding, etc.

MOTOR INSURANCE

Car insurance is compulsory under the Road Traffic Act 1933.

(1) Third Party Insurance

This policy will pay compensation to victims for damage to them and their property (car) that arises as a result of an accident for which insured is responsible. It does not cover damage to insured's own vehicle or insured's medical bills.

(2) Third Party, Fire and Theft Insurance

Compensation is paid to the victims for damage to them and their property by the insured while driving a car. It does not cover the insured person or his/her car for damage caused by the insured — compensation is paid only when damage results from a fire or theft of the car.

(3) Comprehensive Insurance

Comprehensive insurance will pay compensation to victims for damage to them or their property by the insured while driving a car. It also covers the insured person's car against all risks.

Factors that Would Influence the Size of Premium for Car Insurance Cover

- Type of driving licence held.
- Age of insured.
- Driving history.
- Occupation of insured.
- Value of car/make.
- Purpose/use of car.

LIFE ASSURANCE

Life assurance is there to help families who lose the income earner through death. Life assurance covers risks that definitely happen — death.

(1) Whole life assurance

The assured pays premiums for the rest of his life. When the assured dies, a lump sum is paid to his dependants.

(2) Endowment policy

The assured pays premiums up to a certain age, e.g. sixty years. The lump sum is paid on the assured reaching this age or on death of assured, whichever comes first.

(3) Term assurance

This is where a policy is taken out for a specified period of time, e.g. ten years. If the assured dies within the ten years, his dependants will receive the lump sum. If the assured lives past the ten years, no payment is made. This type of policy is often used as security for a term loan.

(4) Mortgage protection policy

This policy is taken out by all mortgage holders. If the mortgage holder dies before the mortgage is paid, the policy will clear the mortgage and the house will become the property of the mortgage holder's dependants.

SURRENDER VALUE

This arises where a policy holder decides to stop paying the premiums on a life assurance policy. The policy can be cancelled, usually after about two years, and a sum of money known as surrender value will be paid to the policy holder. However, it will be much less than the value of the premiums paid.

J. Calculating Insurance Premiums

The premium to be paid for insurance cover will be calculated by an actuary. The amount of the premium will depend on many things.

(i) Value of item.
(ii) The risk involved.
(iii) Age of insured.
(iv) The loadings on the policy.
(v) The amount of no claims bonus (car insurance).

(1) MOTOR INSURANCE PREMIUMS

The **basic premium** is based on type of cover required, value and age of car, cubic capacity of engine.

Loadings are added because of greater risk of the insured event occuring in the following cases: provisional licence, first insurance, being under twenty-five, urban address, use of car for business, accident record.

Deductions of the basic premium plus loading may be made for: non-drinker, no claims bonus, full licence.

Premium = basic + loadings – deductions

Question — Calculation of Motor Insurance Premium

The Allied United Insurance Company quotes the following for car insurance: third party €30 per €1,000 car value; fire and theft €5 per €1,000; comprehensive €70 per €1,000.

Loadings: Provisional licence 20%; first insurance 30%; urban address 20%; being under twenty-five 25%; use of car for business 25%.

Deductions: Non-drinker 10%; no claims bonus 20%; full licence 10%.

John Kelly is seeking his first insurance. He is a travelling salesman living in Galway. He is twenty-four years old. He drives a car valued at €10,000. He has a full licence and an accident-free record. He is a non-drinker and has a full no claims bonus. He requires comprehensive insurance. Calculate his motor insurance premium.

Solution	Basic premium €70 x 10		**€700**
	Loadings: Use of car for business 700 x 25%	€175	
	Urban address 700 x 20%	€140	
	Under twenty-five years 700 x 25%	€175	
	First insurance 700 x 30%	€210	€700
			€1,400
	Less Deductions: Non-drinker €1,400 x 10%	€140	
	No claims bonus €1,400 x 20%	€280	
	Full licence €1,400 x 10%	€140	€560
	TOTAL PREMIUM DUE		**€840**

Loading: An amount added on to the premium because of an additional risk, e.g. previous claims, age, type of work, etc.

No Claims Bonus: A reduction/discount off the premium for not having sought compensation and for having accident-free driving.

(2) HOUSE INSURANCE PREMIUMS

Basic premium is based on the value of the house and its contents.
Loadings may be added for residing in an urban area.
Deductions may be made for having a burglar alarm, for having a smoke detector, and for being part of a community alert scheme.

Question — Calculation of House Insurance Premium

The Western Insurance Company quotes the following for house insurance:
Buildings €4 per €1,000
Contents €6 per €1,000

Loadings: Urban area 20%.
Deductions: Approved alarm 10%; smoke detector 5%; residing in community alert area 5%.

Joe and Maria Kelleher wish to insure their house for €70,000 and contents for €30,000. They live in Cork city. They have an approved alarm fitted and a smoke detector. Calculate their insurance premium.

Solution	Buildings €70,000 x €4 per €1,000	€280	
	Contents €30,000 x €6 per €1,000	€180	€460
	Loadings: Urban area 460 x 20%		€92
			€552
	Deductions: Alarm system €552 x 10% =	€55.20	
	Smoke detector €552 x 5% =	€27.60	€82.80
	TOTAL PREMIUM DUE		€469.20

HOW TO REDUCE COST OF HOUSEHOLD INSURANCE
(1) Fit a burglar alarm/fire alarm.
(2) Install a smoke detector.
(3) Become part of a community alert scheme.

(3) LIFE ASSURANCE PREMIUMS

Basic premium is calculated by referring to a ready reckoner which will give a figure per €1,000 lump sum payable on death.

The figure will depend on age, gender, whether you are a smoker/non-smoker.

Loadings: Premium may be loaded for medical history, dangerous occupation, dangerous hobbies and sporting interests.

Question — Calculation of Life Assurance Premium

Irish Assurance Company quotes the following: male aged thirty-five years, non-smoker — €9.72 per €1,000, lump sum payable in twenty years' time.

Loadings: Medical condition 10%, dangerous occupation 10%, dangerous hobbies 5%.

Denis is a bomb disposal expert. He is aged thirty-five and a non-smoker. He wants to take out an endowment life assurance policy for €200,000 payable in twenty years' time. He had a bypass heart operation two years ago. In his spare time he likes parachuting. Calculate his life assurance premium.

Solution	Basic premium €9.72 x 200	=	€1,944
	Loadings: Medical condition 10%	€194.40	
	Dangerous occupation 10%	€194.40	
	Dangerous hobby 5%	€97.20	€486
	TOTAL PREMIUMS DUE	=	€2,430 p.a.

K. Benefits of Insurance

(1) Life assurance provides a lump sum payment to the assured's dependants on death of assured.
(2) Life assurance is a form of saving.
(3) A life assurance policy can be used as security for a loan.
(4) Insurance gives everyone protection against loss or damage.

L. Insurance Companies Operating in Ireland

(1) Irish Life Assurance
(2) New Ireland Assurance Company
(3) Hibernian Insurance Company
(4) First Call Direct
(5) AXA Insurance
(6) Quinn Direct
(7) Eagle Star
(8) FBD Insurance
(9) Allianz
(10) Royal & SunAlliance

Examination-Style Questions and Solutions

Question 1.

Answer all sections. This is an Insurance Question.

The Noonan family purchased their first house recently with the help of a building society mortgage. They paid €45,000 for their home, and they have spent €15,000 on furniture and fittings.

Tom and Mary are now wondering about insurance and ask for your advice. They want to know the following.

1. (a) Are they required by law to insure the family property? (Give an explanation for your answer.) (4)

1. (b) Tom and Mary want you to calculate the total premium they would have to pay using the following information. It costs €1 for each €100 of buildings insured and €2 for each €100 of contents insured. (Show your workings.) (10)

1. (c) The Noonans think that the premium is very high, especially for the contents. They are now thinking of insuring the contents for just €10,000. They do not see the point of insuring the contents for the full value.

Show what compensation they would get if they had the contents insured for just €10,000 and if, as a result of a small fire, €3,000 worth of contents were destroyed. (16)

1. (d) Tom and Mary are also considering taking out life assurance, but they know very little about it. Explain briefly for them the following:

(i) The difference between insurance and assurance;

(ii) The difference between a Whole Life Assurance policy and an Endowment policy. (10)

Source: Junior Certificate Higher Level. **(40 marks)**

Solution to Question 1.

1. (a) *No. The only insurance that is compulsory by law is motor vehicle insurance. Property insurance is optional.*

1. (b) *Building valued at €45,000*

€45,000 ÷ 100 = 450 x €1 =	*€450*
Furniture and fittings valued at €15,000	
€15,000 ÷ 100 = 150 x €2 =	*€300*
Total premium =	*€750*

1. (c) *Contents are insured for only two-thirds of their value*

$$\left(\frac{€10,000}{€15,000} = 2/3\right)$$

2/3 of €3,000 = €2,000

Compensation paid will be €2,000.

1. (d) *(i) Insurance — is protection against events which might happen, e.g. fire.*
Assurance — is protection against something that will happen, e.g. death.
(ii) Whole Life Assurance — pay premiums for rest of life, lump sum is payable on death only.
Endowment policy — sum of money is paid after agreed number of years or on death, whichever comes first.

Question 2.

Answer all sections. This is an Insurance Question.

2. (a) Explain the difference between insurable and non-insurable risks. (Give **one** example of each.) (10)

2. (b) Before taking out insurance, a person must complete a proposal form. State **three** pieces of information that must be answered in the proposal form for house insurance. (12)

2. (c) What do insurance companies mean by the term '**insurable interest**'? Explain briefly. (6)

2. (d) John and Mary O'Brien live in their own house, have a family car and are both employed in full-time jobs.

(i) What insurance cover, if any, are they required to have by law? (6)

(ii) State two other insurance/assurance policies which you would recommend to them. (6)

Source: Junior Certificate Higher Level. **(40 marks)**

Solution to Question 2.

2. (a) *Insurable risk — a risk that you can get insurance cover for, e.g. fire, burglary, accident.*
Non-insurable risk — a risk that you cannot get insurance cover for. The insurance companies will not take on the risk proposed, e.g. losses due to bad management.

2. (b) *Proposal Form*

(i) Personal details (name, address, etc.).
(ii) Details of risk required to be covered.
(iii) Sum insured.
(iv) Any previous claims.
(v) Signature of applicant.

2. (c) *Insurable Interest*
You must have a financial interest in the item that is to be insured. You must gain by its existence and suffer by its loss.

2. (d) *(i) Third party car insurance and PRSI.*
(ii) House buildings insurance, house contents insurance, life assurance, VHI, personal accident insurance, salary protection insurance, serious illness insurance.

SECTION TWO — ECONOMIC AWARENESS

NATIONAL BUSINESS

Chapter 11 — Economic Framework

A. Needs and Wants

An individual or family has three **basic needs** to survive: food, shelter and clothing. Once these needs are satisfied, people **want** other things, like cars, TVs, videos, big houses.

B. Scarcity and Choice

To produce the goods that people need and want, four things are required: **land**, **money**, **workers** and someone with the **idea**. It is not possible to produce everything we need and want because resources are scarce. Thus choices must be made about which goods and services are to be produced.

C. Economics

Economics is the study of how scarce resources are used to produce the goods and services that people need and want.

D. Ireland's Economic Resources/Factors of Production

There are four main resources in the country used to produce goods and services. These resources are called factors of production and are **land**, **labour**, **capital** and **enterprise**.

FACTORS OF PRODUCTION

Factors of Production	Explanation of Factors of Production	Payment for Use of Factor/Reward
1. Land	All things supplied by nature for producing goods, i.e. land, sea, rivers, mines, gas fields, forests. From these we get raw materials which are made into finished goods.	Anyone with land is paid **rent** for the use of the land.
2. Labour	People employed to produce the goods or provide the service.	People are paid **wages** for the work they do.
3. Capital	Money invested to run a business. This money is used to buy or build factories, equipment, machinery needed to convert raw materials into finished goods.	People who provide money are paid **interest** for the use of their money.
4. Enterprise	Someone who has a business idea and is willing to take the risk of setting up a business is called an entrepreneur.	If the business is successful, the person gets a **profit** as payment for taking the risk of running a business.

E. Opportunity Cost/Making a Choice

Because resources are scarce, choices have to be made when producing goods. When it is decided to produce one product, the opportunity cost is the other products that cannot be produced.

F. Economic Systems

Each country wants to make best use of its scarce resources so choices must be made:

(i) What goods and services are to be produced?
(ii) Who will produce the goods and services?

The amount of choice that individuals or businesspeople have depends on the economic system that the country has.

There are three main economic systems:

(1) FREE ENTERPRISE ECONOMY

Consumers decide what they want to buy. Producers will supply the goods that people demand. Most choices are made by individuals and entrepreneurs, and there is little government involvement, e.g. USA.

(2) CENTRALLY PLANNED ECONOMY

Government decides what goods are to be produced, and individuals are given no say, e.g. China.

(3) MIXED ECONOMY

Mixed economy countries have a large amount of government intervention and a large amount of private enterprise. Many decisions are made by the government, and individuals are free to choose the goods and services they require, e.g. Ireland.

G. Economic Growth

The total amount of goods and services produced in a country in a year is called Gross National Product (GNP).

If this total amount of goods and services produced (GNP) increases relative to the previous year, the country has economic growth.

FORMULA FOR CALCULATING ECONOMIC GROWTH

$$\text{Economic growth} = \frac{\text{Increase in production (GNP)} \times 100\%}{\text{Last year's production (GNP)}}$$

Example

Total production of goods and services 2014 = €600 million
Total production of goods and services 2015 = €660 million

$$\text{Economic growth} = \frac{\text{€60m} \times 100\%}{\text{€600m}} = 10\%$$

Economic growth can sometimes be negative. When this happens, the country is said to be in a **recession**.

Ireland's economy has been growing at a fast rate in recent years. The boom in the economy is known as the 'Celtic tiger'.

HOW CAN A COUNTRY ACHIEVE ECONOMIC GROWTH?

(1) Keep inflation down.
(2) Keep interest rates down.
(3) Keep government borrowing down.
(4) Increase exports.

ADVANTAGES/CONSEQUENCES OF ECONOMIC GROWTH

(1) Higher standard of living for people.
(2) More employment will be created and workers will earn more.
(3) More tax revenue for the government.
(4) Better social services.
(5) More public utilities.
(6) Improved infrastructure.
(7) Higher house prices.

H. Inflation

(1) Inflation is the increase in the price of goods and services in general over a period of time.
(2) Rising prices mean that the cost of living is increasing, i.e. cost of food, clothes, fuel is increasing.
(3) An increase in the cost of living is measured by the Consumer Price Index (CPI). This is a list of goods and their prices that is compared from one period to the next.

FORMULA FOR CALCULATING RATE OF INFLATION

$$\text{Rate of inflation} = \frac{\text{Increase in price} \times 100\%}{\text{Previous price}}$$

Example Cost of living 2014 €9,000
Cost of living 2015 €9,600

$$\text{Rate of inflation} = \frac{€600 \times 100\%}{€9{,}000} = 6.6\%$$

CAUSES OF INFLATION

(1) **Demand Pull Inflation** = Excessive demand in the market. Demand > Supply ⇛ Prices rise.
(2) **Cost Push Inflation** = An increase in any of the following: taxes, wages, interest, oil, imports, material costs, service charges.

ADVANTAGES OF LOW INFLATION TO A COUNTRY

(1) Economic growth is aided.
(2) Goods can be produced much more cheaply so it will be easier to sell them abroad.

BENEFITS OF LOW INFLATION TO THE CONSUMER

(a) Prices in shops are stable.
(b) Purchasing power of money is protected.
(c) Value of savings is protected.
(d) Wage demands are lower.
(e) Value of money is maintained.

Interest rates

The rate of interest is the price paid for the use of money. Interest rates of Euro countries are set at the same level and are controlled by the European Central Bank.

Benefits of low interest rates to the economy/general public

1. Mortgages and loans will be cheaper.
2. Encourages new investment and enterprise.
3. Increased consumer spending.
4. Boosts economic activity and employment.
5. Reduces the cost of servicing the national debt.
6. Reduces business costs.
7. Gives people more disposable income.

Disadvantages of high interest rates to economy/general public

1. Discourages new investment.
2. Reduces consumer demand.
3. Increases business costs.
4. Increase cost of living — leading to wage demands.

I. Business Terms

Basic Needs Things necessary for survival: food, clothes, shelter.
Centrally Planned Economy Government decides what goods are produced.
Cost Push Inflation Increased costs push up price.
CPI Consumer Price Index. Shows changes in the cost of living.
Deflation Falling prices.
Demand Pull Inflation Excess demand pulls up price.
Economic Goods Products that people want and are prepared to pay money for.
Economic Growth An increase in Gross National Product from one year to the next.
Economist A person who studies economics.
Economising Making maximum use of one's resources/income, eliminating waste and encouraging efficiency.
Entrepreneur A person with a business idea who is willing to take the risk of setting up a business.
Factors of Production Land, labour, capital, enterprise.
Free Enterprise Choices made by individuals and entrepreneurs — little government involvement.
GNP — Gross National Product Total goods and services produced by a country in a year.

Inflation Rising prices.
Mixed Economy Some private enterprise and some government intervention.
National Economy Whole country.
Opportunity Cost When one product is chosen, another product must be sacrificed.
Profit The reward for enterprise.
Recession Where GNP declines from one period to the next.
Resources Things used to produce goods and services.
Third World Countries Poor/underdeveloped countries, e.g. India.
Wants Things that people would like to buy.
Wealth Stock of goods owned by an individual or country.

Examination-Style Question and Solution

Question 1.
Answer all sections. This is a Question on Inflation.
The Bar Graph below refers to the inflation rate of a country called SOMBIA.

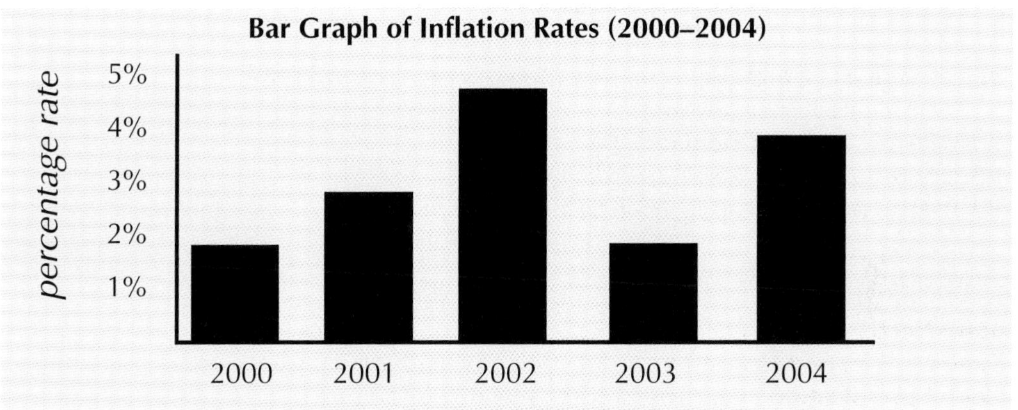

1. **(a)** Explain what is meant by the term **inflation.** (4)
1. **(b)** Calculate the average rate of inflation for the five years shown in the graph above. (4)
1. **(c)** What change occurred in the rate of inflation in 2003 compared to 2002? (4)
1. **(d)** Give **one** economic benefit to Ireland of having its inflation rate lower than that of its main trading competitors. (4)

Source: Junior Certificate Higher Level.

Solution to Question 1.

1. (a) *An increase in the general level of prices from one period to the next.*

OR

An increase in the cost of living from one year to the next.

1. (b) *3.2%.*

1. (c) *Fell by 3%.*

1. (d) *(i) Irish goods will be more competitive on the Irish market and on foreign markets.*
(ii) Lower wage demands.
(iii) More employment.
(iv) More foreign investment.
(v) Better balance of payments.

Chapter 12 — National Budgeting

A. National Budget

(1) A national budget is a **plan** of government **income** and **expenditure** for the country.
(2) The government plans where the income will come from and how the money will be spent (expenditure).
(3) Each government department **estimates** how much money it will need to run the department for the year.
(4) The **Department of Finance** decides how much each department can spend for the year ahead.
(5) The Department of Finance also decides how it is going to find this money.
(6) The **Minister for Finance** makes the budget speech in the Dáil in December each year telling the nation about the budget.

B. Government Budgets

The government must prepare two budgets:
(1) **Current Budget:** This outlines the expenditure needed to run the country on a day-to-day basis and where income to finance this will come from.
(2) **Capital Budget:** This outlines the expenditure on capital projects (long-term projects) and where the income to finance these projects will come from.

C. Current Budget

(1) CURRENT EXPENDITURE

This is expenditure on the day-to-day running of the country.
(a) **Wages and salaries** of civil servants, teachers, gardaí, army, prison officers.
(b) **Social welfare benefits**, e.g. unemployment benefit, old age pensions, children's allowances, etc.
(c) **Running costs of government departments**, e.g. telephone, stationery, heating and lighting.
(d) **Interest on borrowings**, i.e. national debt. Interest must be paid on money borrowed by the government over the years.

(2) CURRENT INCOME

This is income received by the government on a regular basis (monthly/annually) and it is used to cover current expenditure. The main sources of current income are set out below, the principal one being taxation.

TAXATION REVENUE

(a) **Income Tax:** Tax paid by all workers through the PAYE system.
(b) **Value Added Tax (VAT):** Tax on goods and services.
(c) **Customs Duties:** Tax on goods entering a country. It acts as a deterrent to imports.

(d) Excise Duties: Tax on certain goods produced in the country, e.g. whiskey, petrol, cigarettes, beer.
(e) Corporation Tax: Tax on the profits of companies paid to the government.
(f) Deposit Interest Retention Tax (DIRT): Tax on interest earned in a deposit account.

NON-TAX REVENUE

(a) Profit from state firms.
(b) Lottery receipts.

D. Balancing Current Budget

(1) BALANCED BUDGET

Current expenditure	=	Current income
e.g. €10,600m		€10,600m

(2) BUDGET SURPLUS

Current expenditure	<	Current income
e.g. €10,200m		€10,600m

Budget surplus = €400m

WHAT CAN THE GOVERNMENT DO WITH A BUDGET SURPLUS?

(a) Reduce taxation.
(b) Increase social welfare.
(c) Pay off some of the national debt.
(d) Put some of the surplus towards capital expenditure, thus reducing borrowing.
(e) Increase spending in some departments to give a better service, e.g. health and education.

(3) BUDGET DEFICIT

Current expenditure	>	Current income
e.g. €10,200m		€10,000m

Budget deficit €200m

HOW CAN THE GOVERNMENT ELIMINATE A BUDGET DEFICIT?

(a) Increase taxation.
(b) Reduce expenditure by cutting back on some services.
(c) Borrow the amount of the shortfall.

E. Capital Budget

(1) CAPITAL EXPENDITURE

This is money spent on long-term projects, e.g. new roads, new schools, new hospitals, airports, railway stations. These items are called the **infrastructure** of the state.

Public utilities

Much of the government spending is on services that are essential for the efficient running of the state, e.g. roads, railways, airports, harbours, ports, telephone, electricity, gas, water, sewerage, postal service, schools, hospitals.

(2) CAPITAL INCOME

This is income received 'once only' and is used for capital expenditure. **Borrowing** is the main source of capital income. Capital income has also been received by the government from the **sale of state companies** to private shareholders, called **privatisation**, e.g. Eircom, and from **EU Grants**.

F. Balancing Capital Budget

The capital budget will always balance because the amount of capital expenditure will be matched by capital income and borrowing.

G. National Debt

National debt is the **total amount of money that has been borrowed** by the government over the years. Interest has to be paid on this debt, and it is very high.

H. Local Authorities

County councils and corporations provide many services in the local area, e.g. water supply, sewerage schemes, refuse collection. They get most of their income from central government, but they also charge for their services. These charges are known as service charges, e.g. service charges for water supply and refuse collection.

I. Business Terms

Balanced Budget Government income is equal to government expenditure.

Book of Estimates Book published by government showing how much each government department needs to spend for the year.

Budget Deficit Government expenditure is greater than government income.

Budget Surplus Government income is greater than government expenditure.

Capital Expenditure Government expenditure on long-term projects, i.e. roads, schools, etc.

Capital Income Income received by the government on a once-off basis.

Corporation Tax Tax on the profits of companies paid to the government.

Current Expenditure Expenditure on day-to-day running of the country.

Current Income Income received by the government on a regular basis.

Debt Servicing Interest payments on the national debt paid by the goverment to its lenders.

Department of Finance The department in charge of government money.

Excise Duty Tax on certain home-produced goods, e.g. whiskey.

Local Authorities The bodies that provide essential services in local areas.

Minister for Finance The person in charge of Department of Finance.

National Debt Total amount of money borrowed by government.

Opportunity Cost When the government decides to spend on a particular project, some other project has to do without funds. The project sacrificed is the opportunity cost.
Public Utilities Essential services provided by the government, e.g. roads, harbours, water supply.
Rates Tax on business property paid to local authority.
Scarce Resources The government, like everybody, has limited income. It does not possess an endless fund and cannot satisfy all the demands made on it.
VAT Tax on goods and services.

Examination-Style Questions and Solutions

Question 1.

1. (a) Prepare the National Budget for 2014 from the following details:

Income: Income Tax €3,200m; EC and Other Receipts €2,100m; VAT €2,100m; Customs and Excise €1,900m; Corporation Tax €500m; Capital Tax €100m; Other Receipts €1,000m.

Expenditure: Security €800m; Social Welfare €3,000m; Education €1,368m; Health €1,400m; Agriculture €400m; Debt Service €2,432m; Miscellaneous €2,000m. (8)

1. (b) Was this budget a surplus or a deficit budget? (3)
1. (c) (i) What was the main source of government income?
(ii) What percentage of total expenditure was spent on education?
(iii) Give two examples of expenditure on security. (6)
1. (d) If you were Minister for Finance, suggest two changes you might make to the above budget. Give your reasons. (6)
1. (e) If inflation increased total expenditure by 5% and VAT was down by 10%, what effect would these have on the budget outcome? (Show your workings.) (8)
1. (f) Explain two effects of the decreasing level of unemployment on the national budget. (9)

Source: Junior Certificate Higher Level. **(40 marks)**

Solution to Question 1.

1. (a) **National Budget for 2014**

Income	€m	Expenditure	€m
Income Tax	3,200	Security	800
EC and Other Receipts	2,100	Social Welfare	3,000
VAT	2,100	Education	1,368
Customs and Excise	1,900	Health	1,400
Corporation Tax	500	Agriculture	400
Capital Tax	100	Debt Service	2,432
Other Receipts	1,000	Miscellaneous	2,000
Total Income	10,900	Total Expenditure	11,400

INCOME – EXPENDITURE
10,900 – 11,400 = (€500m)

1. (b) *This was a deficit budget.*

1. (c) *(i) Main source of income was income tax.*

(ii) Percentage spent on education:

$$\text{Formula} = \frac{\text{Education spending} \times 100\%}{\text{Total expenditure}}$$

$$\frac{€1,368m \times 100\%}{€11,400m} = 12\%$$

(iii) Security spending: gardai, army, navy.

1. (d)

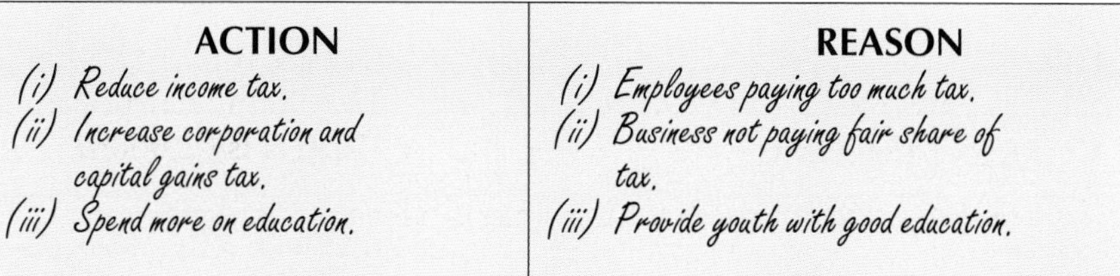

ACTION	REASON
(i) Reduce income tax.	*(i) Employees paying too much tax.*
(ii) Increase corporation and capital gains tax.	*(ii) Business not paying fair share of tax.*
(iii) Spend more on education.	*(iii) Provide youth with good education.*

1. (e) *Inflation increased total expenditure by 5%.*

Inflation 5% of €11,400m	*€570m*
Expenditure increased by	*€570m*
New expenditure figure would be	*€11,970*
VAT reduction by 10%.	
10% of €2,100m	*€210m*
Income reduced by	*€210m*
New income total	*€10,690m*

New budget deficit would be €1,280m (€10,690m – €11,970m).

1. (f) *Two effects of increasing level of unemployment:*

(i) Income from income tax will increase.

(ii) Expenditure on social welfare will decrease.

Question 2.

Answer all sections. This is a Government Income and Expenditure Question.

The estimated government current budget for 2013 is as follows:

Government current income €9,796

Government current expenditure €10,366

Answer the following questions:

2. (a) What is the amount of the difference in the two figures given, and what is the economic term used to describe this difference? (8)

2. (b) Which government department prepares the National Budget? (4)

2. (c) Give **two** examples of government **current income** and **two** examples of government **current expenditure.** (8)
2. (d) State **three ways** in which a government could use a current budget surplus. (12)
2. (e) Give **one** example of government **capital expenditure** and **one** example of government **capital income.** (8)

Source: Junior Certificate Higher Level. **(40 marks)**

Solution to Question 2.

2. (a) €570 million — budget deficit.
2. (b) Department of Finance.
2. (c)

CURRENT INCOME	CURRENT EXPENDITURE
(i) Income tax. (ii) VAT, DIRT. (iii) Profit from state companies. (iv) Lottery surplus. (v) Other indirect taxes.	(i) Salaries of teachers, nurses, gardaí, etc. (ii) Social welfare payments. (iii) Interest on government borrowings. (iv) Heating and maintenance of government buildings.

2. (d) Ways in which a government could use a current budget surplus:
(i) Reduce taxation.
(ii) Increase current expenditure.
(iii) Finance capital expenditure.
(iv) A mixture of all three above.

2. (e)

CAPITAL EXPENDITURE	CAPITAL INCOME
(i) New roads. (ii) New hospitals. (iii) New schools. (iv) New equipment.	(i) Sale of state companies. (ii) Borrowing.

Chapter 13 — Foreign Trade

A. Foreign Trade

Foreign trade occurs when Ireland buys goods and services from other countries or sells goods and services to other countries.

B. Importing

(1) VISIBLE IMPORTS

These are **goods** that Ireland buys from other countries, e.g. cars, oil, fruit, coffee, wine, clothes.

(2) INVISIBLE IMPORTS

These are **services** that Ireland buys from other countries. Examples include:

- Irish students going abroad on a school tour — Irish money goes to a foreign country.
- Irish people going on holidays abroad.
- Irish people buying services from foreign businesses, e.g. insurance, transport, entertainment.

(3) WHY DOES IRELAND IMPORT GOODS AND SERVICES?

(a) **Unsuitable climate**, e.g. oranges, bananas, tea.
(b) **Raw materials** required for production, e.g. oil, coal, steel.
(c) Irish consumers want **variety.**
(d) Certain countries have **natural skills**, e.g. French wines.
(e) Availability of products we cannot produce.

(4) SOURCES AND TYPES OF IMPORTS

PRINCIPAL SOURCES OF IMPORTS	VISIBLE IMPORTS (GOODS)	INVISIBLE IMPORTS (SERVICES)
UK USA Japan Germany France	Food, fruit, coffee Oil, petrol, coal Chemicals Clothes and footwear Electrical goods Timber Computers/Transport equipment Machinery, communication equipment Cars Wine	Foreign entertainers on tour in Ireland Irish students on foreign school tours Irish people holidaying abroad Irish people travelling on foreign ships or airlines Irish people borrowing from a foreign bank Irish people getting insurance from a foreign insurance company

N.B. Irish money goes to a foreign country.

C. Exporting

(1) VISIBLE EXPORTS

These are **goods** that Ireland sells to other countries, e.g. meat, dairy products, live animals, chemicals.

(2) INVISIBLE EXPORTS

These are **services** that Ireland sells to other countries, e.g. Spanish students coming to Ireland to learn English during the summer. Foreign money comes into Ireland.

(3) WHY DOES IRELAND EXPORT GOODS AND SERVICES?

(a) To **earn essential foreign money** to pay for imports.
(b) The Irish market is too small.
(c) Surplus production, e.g. beef.
(d) Demand for Irish products by consumers abroad, e.g. Kerrygold butter.
(e) Maintains jobs in Ireland.
(f) Ireland's ability to export encourages foreign firms to establish in Ireland.
(g) Helps balance of payments.

(4) DIFFICULTIES THAT AN IRISH FIRM WOULD EXPERIENCE WHEN EXPORTING GOODS

(a) Different languages.
(b) Different currency.
(c) Transport costs.
(d) Insurance costs.
(e) Cultural differences.
(f) Regulations to be adhered to.
(g) Standards to be met.

(5) DESTINATIONS AND TYPES OF EXPORTS

PRINCIPAL DESTINATIONS OF EXPORTS	VISIBLE EXPORTS (GOODS)	INVISIBLE EXPORTS (SERVICES)
UK Germany USA France Netherlands	Live animals Meat Dairy products Food products Chemical and pharmaceuticals Engineering products Computer equipment Scientific equipment	Irish entertainers giving concerts abroad A foreigner taking out insurance with an Irish company Foreigners borrowing money from an Irish bank Irish people working abroad and sending money to Ireland Foreign travellers using Irish airlines or Irish ferries

N.B. Foreign money comes into Ireland.

(6) STATE INVOLVEMENT IN EXPORTING

The state organisation Enterprise Ireland assists Irish exports in the following ways:

(a) Provides information on foreign markets, shipping and transport.
(b) Arranges meetings with foreign buyers.
(c) Provides information on trade regulations, packaging and language.
(d) Organises trade fairs and exhibitions abroad.
(e) Arranges training courses for salespeople.

D. European Union

The EEC was established in 1957 with the aim of eliminating **trade barriers between member states**. This means there is **'free trade'** between the members. Ireland joined in 1973. The EU is now a group of twenty-seven member countries.

E. Aims of EU

(1) **Free trade** between member countries.
(2) **Free movement of people** between member countries.
(3) **Free movement of money** between member states.
(4) **Common currency**.
(5) To provide **financial assistance** to the less prosperous regions of the EU.

F. Single European Act

The Single European Act came into effect on 1 January 1993, and all trade barriers were removed.

The act had the following effects:

(1) Irish people can look for work in any EU country.
(2) Less delay at border checkpoints, and customs documents will not be required.
(3) Irish people will be able to save/borrow money from any bank in any EU state.
(4) Irish people will be able to take out insurance in any member state.
(5) Taxes throughout the EU will be the same.
(6) Businesses can set up wherever they wish within the EU.

G. Benefits of EU Membership to Ireland

(1) Access to a European market — 500 million people.
(2) EU finance for farmers and industry.
(3) EU finance for infrastructure, i.e. roads, communications, etc.
(4) Increased consumer choice — goods imported from EU.
(5) Irish people can work in any EU member state (freedom of movement within EU).

H. European Union, Countries, Currency, Language

COUNTRY	CURRENCY	LANGUAGE
Lithuania	Litas	Lithuanian
France	Euro	French
Germany	Euro	German
Italy	Euro	Italian
Belgium	Euro	French/Flemish
Netherlands	Euro	Dutch
Luxembourg	Euro	French/German
United Kingdom	Pound Sterling (£)	English
Ireland	Euro	English/Irish
Denmark	Krone	Danish
Greece	Euro	Greek
Spain	Euro	Spanish
Portugal	Euro	Portuguese
Austria	Euro	German
Finland	Euro	Finnish/Swedish
Sweden	Krona	Swedish
Cyprus	Cyprus Punt	Greek/Turkish
Czech Republic	Czech Crown	Czech
Estonia	Estonian Crown	Estonian
Hungary	Florint	Hungarian
Latvia	Lats	Latvian
Malta	Maltese Lira	Maltese/English
Poland	Zloty	Polish
Slovakia	Slovak Koruna	Slovak
Slovenia	Euro	Slovene
Romania	Leu	Romanian/German/Hungarian
Bulgaria	Lev	Bulgarian/Turkish

I. Rate of Exchange

Every country has its own currency. If you want to buy goods or services from another country or travel to another country, you must convert your € (Euro) into that currency. Foreign currency can be bought at banks, building societies and Bureaux de Change. The cost of this currency is the rate of exchange.

BUYING FOREIGN CURRENCY

Use 'Sell at' rate.

Example

John touring USA wishes to convert €200 into US Dollars.

'Sell at' rate: 2.60, 'Buy at' rate: 2.74.

This means that for every €1 John will get US $2.60.

Formula: Converting € to foreign currency
Multiply € by bank sell rate

Answer: €200 × US $2.60 = US $520.

SELLING FOREIGN CURRENCY

Use 'Buy at' rate.

Example

John has US $25 left on returning from USA. He wishes to convert it back to Euro. 'Sell at' rate: 2.60, 'Buy at' rate: 2.74.

This means that for US $2.74 John will get €1.

Formula: Converting currency into €
Divide foreign currency by bank buy rate

Answer: US $25 ÷ US $2.74 = €9.12.

J. Balance of Trade — Higher Level

Balance of Trade = Visible Exports – Visible Imports.
If visible exports > visible imports, we have a surplus.
If visible exports < visible imports, we have a deficit.

K. Balance of Payments — Higher Level

Balance of payments is the difference between all money coming into a country (total exports) and all money going out of a country (total imports).

Balance of payments = total exports – total imports.
If total exports > total imports — surplus on balance of payments.
If total exports < total imports — deficit on balance of payments.

Example — Higher Level

Visible exports €16,629m. Invisible exports €900m.
Visible imports €13,195m. Invisible imports €970m.

BALANCE OF PAYMENTS:			€
Balance of Trade	Visible exports		16,629m
	Visible imports		13,195m
	Balance of trade surplus		3,434m
Invisible Trade	Invisible imports	970m	
	Invisible exports	900m	
	Deficit on invisible trade		–70m
	Balance of payments surplus		3,364m

N.B. Balance of payments includes visible and invisible trade.

L. Business Terms

Balance of Payments Total exports – total imports.
Balance of Trade Visible exports – visible imports.
CAP Common Agricultural Policy.
Currency Money of a country.
Deficit Imports greater than exports.
Embargo Ban on certain imports.
EMU Economic and Monetary Union.
EU European Union.
Exporting Selling goods and services to other countries.
Free Trade No duties to be paid on imports.
Import Substitution Producing goods in Ireland to replace imported goods.
Importing Buying goods and services from other countries.
Invisible Export Services sold abroad.
Invisible Import Services purchased from abroad.
Invisible Trade Services imported and exported.
Maastricht Treaty Treaty signed by twelve member states setting up the European Union.
Quota Limit on amount of goods imported.
Rate of Exchange Value of one currency in terms of another currency.
SEA — Single European Act Laid down framework for internal market.
Surplus Exports greater than imports.
Visible Export Physical goods sold abroad.
Visible Import Physical goods purchased from abroad.
Visible Trade Physical goods imported and exported.

Examination-Style Question and Solution

Question 1.

This is a Question on Balance of Payments.

1. (a) The following figures refer to SOMBIA international trade.

	€
Export of visible goods	950 million
Export of invisible items	280 million
Import of visible goods	640 million
Import of invisible items	360 million

From the above figures, calculate:

(i) the Balance of Trade, and

(ii) the Balance of Payments on Current Account. (Show your workings.) (12)

1. (b) (i) Which country buys the largest percentage of Ireland's exports? (4)

(ii) Suggest **one** thing which **each** of the following groups could do to help the Irish Balance of Payments?

- Irish Consumers (Shoppers)
- Irish Producers (Manufacturers). (8)

Source: Junior Certificate Higher Level.

Solution to Question 1.

1. (a) *Balance of Trade and Balance of Payments*

	€	€
Export of visible goods	*950m*	
—Import of visible goods	*640m*	
Balance of trade surplus		*310m*
Export of invisible items	*280m*	
— Import of invisible items	*360m*	
Deficit on invisible trade		*—80m*
Surplus on Balance of Payment Current Account		*230m*

1. (b) *(i) The UK.*

(ii) Irish consumers could buy Irish goods and services.

Irish producers could:

- *Use Irish raw materials*
- *Become more competitive and efficient.*

BUSINESS BACKGROUND

Chapter 14 — Forms of Business

In Ireland businesses are owned by one person, two or more people, or by the state.

MAIN FORMS OF BUSINESS UNIT

☛ Sole Trader — owned by one person.
☛ Co-operatives — owned by eight or more people, called members.
☛ State Companies — owned by state.
☛ Private Limited Company — owned by at least two people, called shareholders.

A. Sole Trader

A sole trader is a person who owns and manages his own business.

CHARACTERISTICS	TYPES	ADVANTAGES	DISADVANTAGES
(1) Owned by **one person**. (2) Owner makes **all decisions**. (3) Owner keeps all **profit** — suffers all losses. (4) Owner has **unlimited liability**.	(1) Retailers. (2) Services. (3) Professional Services.	(1) Easy to set up. (2) Personal attention to customers. (3) Owner makes all decisions. (4) Owner can keep all profit. (5) May give credit. (6) May offer a delivery service.	(1) Unlimited liability — if the business fails, the sole trader can also lose his/her own private assets. (2) Lack of capital hinders expansion. (3) Prices may be higher than in supermarkets. (4) Extra work outside trading hours. (5) Owner bears all losses. (6) No continuity of business — on death, the business ceases to exist

B. Co-operatives

A co-operative is a business owned and run by its members.

The first co-operative was in Rochdale in England. The first Irish co-operative was established in Drumcollogher in Limerick in 1889.

CHARACTERISTICS	FORMATION	ADVANTAGES	DISADVANTAGES
(1) To become a member a person must buy one share. (2) Each member has one vote. (3) Profit is distributed among members. (4) Members have limited liability. (5) Managed by a committee.	(1) Eight people are required. (2) Apply to Registrar of Friendly Societies. (3) Certificate of Incorporation is issued. (4) Report annually to Registrar of Friendly Societies.	(1) Shareholders have limited liability. (2) One vote per member. (3) Members own co-operative — a big incentive to do their business with co-operative. (4) Profits are returned to members.	(1) Lack of finance. (2) No incentive to buy more shares. (3) Management committee may not have the business expertise to run a modern business.

TYPES OF CO-OPERATIVE

(1) Producer Co-operatives

Producer co-operatives are mainly agricultural co-operatives. They collect the raw material from the farmers, e.g. milk, process it and sell the finished product, e.g. cheese.

(2) Consumer Co-operatives

These co-operatives buy directly from the manufacturer and sell to members and non-members.

(3) Worker Co-operatives

These are set up where businesses close down and the workers decide to put in money and set up a worker co-operative.

(4) Financial Co-operatives, e.g. credit unions

These are set up by people sharing a common interest, e.g. same town, same job (ASTI Credit Union for teachers). They encourage savings and provide loans at a reasonable rate of interest.

CO-OPERATIVES BECOMING PUBLIC LIMITED COMPANIES — PLCs

One of the major problems co-operatives have had in the past is the **lack of capital for expansion**. To overcome this problem, some of the major co-operatives have converted their status from co-operatives to PLCs (Public Limited Companies). For example, Kerry Group PLC, Glanbia PLC.

ADVANTAGES OF CONVERTING TO PLCs

(a) Finance is available by selling shares to the public.
(b) Shareholders can sell their shares at the Stock Exchange.

C. State Ownership

State companies are owned and controlled by the state.

REASONS FOR STATE INVOLVEMENT	FORMATION	CHARACTERISTICS	ADVANTAGES	DISADVANTAGES
(1) To provide **essential services.** (2) To develop the country's **natural resources.** (3) To rescue firms in **danger of closing down.** (4) To promote **Irish businesses at home and abroad.** (5) To provide **training for unemployed**, e.g. FÁS.	Most state companies were set up by passing an Act of the Oireachtas.	(1) Owned, financed and controlled by the government. (2) Each state company is responsible to a government minister. (3) The minister appoints a board of directors to run the company. (4) Profit is reinvested in the company or given to the government.	(1) Provide essential services. (2) Provide a lot of employment.	(1) Some are in a monopoly situation with no competition, which may lead to inefficiency. (2) No profit motive, which also leads to inefficiency. (3) Some state firms suffer **large losses** borne by taxpayer.

NAMES, INITIALS AND MAIN ACTIVITY OF STATE COMPANIES

NAME	INITIALS	MAIN ACTIVITY
(1) Production		
Electricity Supply Board	ESB	Provision of electricity throughout Ireland.
Bord na Móna		Development of peat resources. Production of turf, briquettes and peat moss.
Bord Gáis Éireann	BGE	Distribution of natural gas.
Coillte		Planting of forests and sale of timber.
(2) Transport		
Coras Iompair Éireann		Provision of transport by roads and rail throughout Ireland.
Three Companies:		
(a) Dublin Bus	CIE	Dublin city bus service.
(b) Bus Éireann		Bus service for rest of Ireland.
(c) Iarnród Éireann (Irish Rail)		Rail service for passengers and goods throughout the country.
(3) Marketing/Export		
Enterprise Ireland		Encourages development of indigenous industry (Irish-owned).
Fáilte Ireland		Promotion of Irish tourist industry.
An Bord Bia		Responsible for promotion of Irish food and drinks products.
Bord Iascaigh Mhara	BIM	Promotion of Irish Sea fishing industry.
(4) Training		
Foras Aiseanna Saothair	FÁS	Training workers and the unemployed.
(5) Research		
Teagasc		Research in agriculture and horticulture.
(6) Communications		
Radio Telefís Éireann	RTE	Radio and television services.
An Post		National postal service.
(7) Promotion and development		
IDA Ireland		Encourages transnational companies to set up in Ireland.
(8) Health Insurance Services		
Voluntary Health Insurance	VHI	Provision of hospital insurance cover.

NATIONALISATION

State takes over a firm previously owned by shareholders.

PRIVATISATION

State sells off a state company to the public. A number of state companies have been privatised, including Irish Life, Irish Sugar Company, now called Greencore, Telecom Éireann, now called Eircom.

REASONS FOR PRIVATISATION

(1) Raises finance for government.
(2) State no longer responsible for these state companies.

HOW STATE COMPANIES ARE FINANCED

(1) Borrowing.
(2) Grants.
(3) Issuing government stock to public.
(4) Charging for services.

D. Private Limited Company (Ltd)

A private limited company is where a group of people numbering between two and fifty come together and form a business. The owners are called shareholders. They invest money in the company. The profit is divided up among the shareholders and distributed in the form of **dividends**.

CHARACTERISTICS	ADVANTAGES	DISADVANTAGES
(1) Between two and fifty shareholders. (2) Shareholders have limited liability. (3) 'Ltd' written after the name. (4) Shares cannot be sold to the public. (5) The annual accounts are sent to the Registrar of Companies. They are not published.	(1) Shareholders have limited liability. (2) Extra capital available. (3) Continuity of existence.	(1) Costly to set up. (2) A lot of legal requirements when forming a company. (3) Shares cannot be transferred to the general public.

FORMATION OF A PRIVATE LIMITED COMPANY

(1) To form a private limited company, you must have at least two shareholders and a maximum of fifty. The company is **owned** by these shareholders.
(2) The people involved in the formation of a company are called the **Promoters**. They employ:
(a) An accountant — to advise on financial affairs.
(b) A solicitor — to prepare the legal documents, which must be sent to the Registrar of Companies:

☛ Memorandum of Association
☛ Articles of Association
☛ Declaration of Compliance with Companies Acts 1963–1990
☛ Statement of Capital of the Company.

DOCUMENTS INVOLVED IN THE FORMATION OF A COMPANY

(1) Memorandum of Association

This sets out the relationship of the company to the general public, i.e. rules and regulations governing company's dealing with public.

CONTENTS		SAMPLE MEMORANDUM OF ASSOCIATION	
(a) Name of company with 'Ltd' after last word.	⇛	(a) Name of company is *Lakeside Fruit Farm Ltd.*	
(b) Objectives of company (i.e. type of business).	⇛	(b) Objects for which company is established are *fruit-growing.*	
(c) Statement of limited liability.	⇛	(c) The liability of the company is limited.	
(d) Share capital of company. How much money can be raised from selling shares.	⇛	(d) The share capital of the company is *€50,000* divided into *50,000 shares @ €1 each.*	
		We the several persons whose names, addresses and descriptions are subscribed wish to be formed into a company in pursuance of the Memorandum of Association and we agree to take the number of shares in the capital of the Company set opposite our respective names.	
(e) Names of those forming the company and number of shares taken.	⇛	(e) Name, address and description of each subscriber.	Number of shares taken by each subscriber.
	⇛	*John O'Mahony* **Director** *Cork*	*15,000*
	⇛	*Claire O'Mahony* **Director** *Cork*	*15,000*
(f) Date and signatures	⇛	(f) Date *01. 1. 15*	Signatures: *John O'Mahony* *Claire O'Mahony*

(2) Articles of Association

This document sets out the internal rules and regulations of the company.

CONTENTS		SAMPLE ARTICLES OF ASSOCIATION	
Name of Company	⇛	Articles of Association of *Lakeside Fruit Farm Ltd*	
(a) Details of share capital.	⇛	(a) Share capital of company is *€50,000 divided into 50,000 shares @ €1 each.*	
(b) Shareholders' voting rights.	⇛	(b) Shareholders' voting rights. *One vote per share.*	
(c) Regulation regarding General Meetings.	⇛	(c) General Meetings *AGM will be held on first Tuesday in January.*	
(d) How directors are to be elected.	⇛	(d) Election of directors *at AGM and will hold office for one year.*	
(e) Powers and duties of directors.	⇛	(e) Powers and duties of directors. *Responsible for day-to-day running of company.*	
(f) Borrowing powers of company.	⇛	(f) Borrowing powers of company. *Up to €1,000,000.*	
(g) Procedure for winding up company.	⇛	(g) How company can be wound up. *Company can be wound up if it becomes insolvent.*	
(h) Directors' names and addresses.	⇛	(h) DIRECTORS' NAMES	AND ADDRESSES
		John O'Mahony	*Cork*
		Claire O'Mahony	*Cork*
(i) Date and signature	⇛	(i) Date *01.1.15*	Signatures *John O'Mahony* *Claire O'Mahony*

(3) Declaration of Compliance with Companies Acts 1963–1990

This document states that the company will comply with the Companies Acts 1963–1990.

(4) Statement of Capital of the Company

This document states the **Authorised Share Capital** of the company, i.e. the maximum amount of capital that the company can raise.

REGISTRAR OF COMPANIES

The documents are sent to the Registrar of Companies. The Registrar will check all the documents carefully to see if they are in order. If everything is in order a **Certificate of Incorporation** is issued.

CERTIFICATE OF INCORPORATION

(1) This is the birth certificate of a company.
(2) It has a separate legal existence from its owners.
(3) The shareholders have limited liability.
(4) Company can sue and be sued in its own name.

BOARD OF DIRECTORS

When the company is incorporated it will hold a meeting of shareholders, who elect a board of directors to run the company on a day-to-day basis. They report to the shareholders annually on the performance of the company at the Annual General Meeting (AGM).

RECORDING SHARE CAPITAL IN THE BOOKS OF A PRIVATE LIMITED COMPANY

From the memorandum and articles we see that on 1 January 2015 John and Claire O'Mahony formed a private limited company called Lakeside Fruit Farm Ltd. They each purchased 15,000 shares @ €1 each in the company. The money received by the company was lodged in a company bank account. On 10 January they purchased equipment for €20,000.

(1) Record the issue of the shares in the ordinary Share Capital A/C and Bank A/C.
(2) Record the purchase of the equipment in the appropriate accounts.
(3) Make out the trial balance of Lakeside Fruit Farm Ltd on 11 January 2015.

EXPLANATION
Basic Rule of Double Entry Book-Keeping
Debit — Receiving Account
Credit — Giving Account

(1) Lakeside Fruit Farm Ltd has received €30,000, which was lodged in the bank. **Debit bank account** (receiving account). Company now owes €30,000 to its shareholders, John and Claire O'Mahony, who purchased the shares. **Credit share capital account** (giving account).

Bank Account

		€			€
01.1.15	Ordinary Share Capital A/C	30,000	10.1.15	Equipment A/C	20,000
			11.1.15	Balance C/d	10,000
		30,000			30,000
11.1.15	Balance C/d	10,000			

Ordinary Share Capital Account

					€
			01.1.15	Bank	30,000

(2) On 10 January 2015 Lakeside Fruit Farm Ltd purchased equipment for €20,000. **Debit equipment account** (receiving account). **Credit bank account** (giving account).

Equipment Account

		€	
10.1.15	Bank	20,000	

(3) Trial Balance of Lakeside Fruit Farm Ltd on 11.1.15
The trial balance brings together the balance from the accounts and lists them in two separate columns, **Debit** and **Credit**.

Bank €10,000 Debit.
Ordinary Share Capital €30,000 Credit.
Equipment €20,000 Debit.

The trial balance must balance.

Trial Balance of Lakeside Fruit Farm Ltd on 11.1.15

		Debit €	Credit €
	Bank	10,000	
	Ordinary Share Capital		30,000
	Equipment	20,000	
		30,000	30,000

E. Business Terms

AGM — Annual General Meeting Annual meeting of shareholders.
Articles of Association Sets out internal rules and regulations of the company.
Auditor Checks accounts of a business.
Authorised Share Capital Maximum amount of capital that can be raised through selling of shares.
Board of Directors Appointed by shareholders to run the company.
Certificate of Incorporation Birth certificate of a company.
Co-operative A business owned and run by members.
Credit Union An institution which encourages savings and provides loans at reasonable interest rates.
Dividend Part of profit that each shareholder receives from a company.
Double Entry Book-Keeping In book-keeping there are two sides to every transaction. The receiving (Debit) and giving (Credit).
Issued Share Capital Actual amount of shares that the company has sold.
Limited Liability Investor can lose only capital invested in a business.
Memorandum of Association Outlines company's dealing with public.
Nationalisation State taking over a private enterprise company.
Private Limited Company A company that is owned by between two and fifty shareholders. It has limited liability.

Privatisation State sells a state company to the public.
Producer Co-operative A co-operative which produces a product.
Promoters People involved in the formation of a company.
Registrar of Companies Office for keeping information on all companies formed in Ireland.
Shareholder A person who buys shares in a company.
Sole Trader A person who owns and runs his own business.
State-Owned Company A business owned and controlled by the state.
Trial Balance A list of balances from all accounts in the ledger.
Unlimited Liability An investor can lose money invested in a business and his own personal assets if business fails.

Examination-Style Question and Solution

Question 1.

Answer all sections. This is an Integrated Company Formation Question.

On 1 January 2013 Ann Smyth of 2 Top St, Carlow, and Patrick Daly of 15 Cork Rd, Carlow, formed a private Limited Company called WOOD FUN LTD. They prepared a Memorandum of Association and sent it and all the other necessary documents to the Registrar of Companies. A Certificate of Incorporation was then issued.

The objects of the company are to manufacture and sell wooden toys.

The authorised share capital of Wood Fun Ltd is 40,000 €1 ordinary shares.

On 11 January 2013 Ann Smyth purchased 15,000 shares and Patrick Daly purchased 16,000 shares. The money received from the issue of these shares was lodged to the company bank account.

On 12 January the company purchased by cheque equipment costing €15,000.

You are required to:

1. (a) Complete the Memorandum of Association on the blank document supplied with this paper. (15)
1. (b) Name one other document which should be sent to the Registrar of Companies when forming a company. (5)
1. (c) Record the issue of the shares on 11 January 2013 in the Ordinary Share Capital Account and the Bank Account of Wood Fun Ltd. (5)
1. (d) Record the transaction that took place on 12 January 2013 in the appropriate accounts. (10)
1. (e) Prepare a Trial Balance for Wood Fun Ltd on 13 January 2013. (5)

MEMORANDUM OF ASSOCIATION

1. **The Name of the Company is** ______________________

2. **The Objects for which the Company is established are:**

____

____

3. **The Liability of the members is limited.**

4. **The Share Capital of the Company is** ______________ **divided into** ______________________

____

WE, the several persons whose names, addresses and descriptions are subscribed wish to be formed into a Company in pursuance of the Memorandum of Association and we agree to take the number of shares in the Capital of the Company set opposite our respective names.

Name, Address and Description of each Subscriber	Number of Shares taken by each Subscriber

Dated ______________

Source: Junior Certificate Higher Level. **(40 marks)**

Solution to Question 1.

For use with Question 1 (a)

MEMORANDUM OF ASSOCIATION

1. **The Name of the Company is** *Wood Fun Ltd*

2. **The Objects for which the Company is established are:**
The manufacture and sale of wooden toys

3. **The Liability of the members is limited.**

4. **The Share Capital of the Company is** *€40,000* **divided into** *40,000 €1 ordinary shares*

WE, the several persons whose names, addresses and descriptions are subscribed, wish to be formed into a Company in pursuance of the Memorandum of Association and we agree to take the number of shares in the Capital of the Company set opposite our respective names.

Name, Address and Description of each Subscriber	Number of Shares taken by each Subscriber
Ann Smyth, 2 Top Street, Carlow	*15,000*
Patrick Daly, 15 Cork Road, Carlow	*16,000*

Dated *1 January 2013*

1. (b) *Any document from the following: Articles of Association, List of Directors, Statement of Capital, Declaration of Compliance with the Companies Act.*

1. (c) & (d)

Ordinary Share Capital Account

			11/1/13	Bank	31,000

Equipment Account

12/1/13	Bank	15,000			

Bank Account

11/1/13	Ordinary Share Capital	31,000	12/1/13	Equipment	15,000
			13/1/13	Balance C/d	16,000
		31,000			31,000
14/1/13	Balance B/d	16,000			

1. (e)

Trial Balance as on 13 January 2013

Date	Details	Debit €	Credit €
	Ordinary Share Capital		31,000
	Equipment	15,000	
	Bank	16,000	
		31,000	31,000

Chapter 15 — Finance for Business

Why companies need finance	Length of time money is needed	Match use with source	Collateral required on loans
(1) Purchase assets (2) Pay expenses	Short-term (0–1 yr) Medium-term (1–5 yrs) Long-term (over 5 yrs)	Purchase premises ⇛ Long-term source Purchase stock ⇛ Short-term source	(1) Title deeds (2) Personal guarantor (3) Life policies (4) Stocks and shares

SOURCES OF FINANCE

Short-Term Sources (0–1 year)		
Purpose	**Sources**	**Explanation**
Purchase of stock Payment of wages	Taxation	VAT, PAYE, PRSI, paid every two months, used as a free loan until collection.
Insurance	Trade credit	Buy goods on credit, usually thirty days = free loan.
Telephone, rent	Bank overdraft	Overdraw current account up to a certain limit.
	Expenses accrued	Delayed payment of bills — use of free money.
	Factoring	Selling debtors for cash.

Medium-Term Sources (1–5 yrs)		
Purpose	**Sources**	**Explanation**
Vehicles Furniture and fittings	Hire purchase	Pay by instalments. The firm will not own goods purchased until last instalment is paid.
Computers	Term loan	Loan for a period up to five years, given for specific reason and repaid by instalments.
	Leasing	Similar to renting, pay rentals but the firm will never own asset.

Long-Term Sources (5 yrs upwards)		
Purpose	**Sources**	**Explanation**
Land Premises Extensions Equipment Machinery	Capital	Invested by owner — sole trader/partnership. Companies sell shares to public — shareholders.
	Retained earnings	Profit made retained in business.
	BES	Business Expansion Scheme. A person who invests in a company in BES scheme can write off amount invested against income tax.
	Sale and leaseback	Sell an asset for cash and arrange to lease it back.
	Mortgage	Long-term loan — title deeds of premises are given as collateral.
	Government grants and EC grants	Government agencies provide grants to business, e.g. Fáilte Ireland, BIM, FÁS, IDA Ireland. Non-repayable.

Examination-Style Question and Solution

Question 1.

Tick the most suitable source of finance for each of the following items required by Ideal Motors Ltd:

Items	**Sources**		
	Short-Term	Medium-Term	Long-Term
Buildings			✓
Computer		✓	
Cars for resale	✓		
Advertising	✓		

Source: Junior Certificate Higher Level. **(4)**

Examination-Style Question and Solution

Question

Answer A and B. This is an Integrated Business Finance and Loan Application Question.

(A) Outline **four** sources of finance, other than loans, which a business can use for the purchase of office equipment (12)

(B) Gear Ltd is a sportswear manufacturer operating from Back Four Street, Drogheda, Co. Louth. It has two directors, Ian Harte and Gary Kelly. It owns premises worth €550,000 and has machinery and delivery vans valued €20,000. Gear Ltd has a weekly income of €20,000 and feels that this can be increased to €30,000 by building an extension to the factory costing €100,000 and purchasing new machinery costing €50,000. Gear Ltd has reserves of €45,000 and is eligible for a €30,000 grant.

On 1 May 2015 it applied for a seven year loan from the Ulster Bank for the remainder. The loan was granted on 10 May 2015.

You are required to:

(i) Calculate the amount of the loan required;

(ii) Complete the Loan Application Form *using the blank loan application form supplied with this paper*;

(iii) Record the receipt of the loan in the *Ulster Bank and Bank Accounts supplied with this paper.* (28)

(40 Marks)

Source: Junior Certificate Higher Level.

For use with question (B)(i)

For use with question (B) (ii)

ULSTER BANK LOAN APPLICATION FORM	
COMPANY DETAILS NAME: ADDRESS:	
NAMES OF DIRECTORS: NATURE OF BUSINESS:	
ANNUAL INCOME: AMOUNT OF LOAN REQUIRED	€ €
PURPOSE OF LOAN: LENGTH REQUIRED FOR: SECURITY AVAILABLE:	
SIGNATURES OF DIRECTORS: DATE:	;

For use with question (B) (iii)

Date	Details	F	Amount	Date	Details	F	Amount
			Ulster Bank A/C				
			Bank A/C				

PLEASE ENCLOSE WITH YOUR ANSWERBOOK

Solution to integrated business finance and loan application question.

A. *Hire purchase: the business buys the office equipment from a retailer, the retailer is paid by the HP company, the business repays the HP company plus interest. The business does not own the goods until after the last repayment is made.*

Leasing: the business rents the equipment thus releasing finance for other uses. The equipment will never be owned by the business.

Deferred payment: the business buys the equipment but is allowed pay for it later. The equipment is owned by the business from the date of purchase.

Retained Earnings: the business can save part of its profit and then use cash to buy the equipment.

Term loan: business buys equipment and the loan is repaid by instalments.

B (i)

	€
Finance needed	*150,000*
Finance available	*75,000*
Loan required	*75,000*

B (ii)

ULSTER BANK LOAN APPLICATION FORM	
COMPANY DETAILS NAME: ADDRESS:	*Gear Ltd* *Back Four St* *Drogheda* *Co. Louth*
NAMES OF DIRECTORS:	*Ian Harte and Gary Kelly*
NATURE OF BUSINESS:	*Sportswear Manufacturer*
ANNUAL INCOME: AMOUNT OF LOAN REQUIRED:	*€1,040,000* *€75,000*
PURPOSE OF LOAN: LENGTH REQUIRED FOR: SECURITY AVAILABLE:	*Extension to factory* *Purchase of new machinery* *7 years* *Premises €550,000, machinery & vans €120,000*
SIGNATURE OF DIRECTORS: DATE:	*Ian Harte* *Gary Kelly* *1/5/15*

Date	Details	F	Amount	Date	Details	F	Amount
			Ulster Bank A/C				
				10.5.15	Bank A/C	GL	75,000
			Bank A/C				
10.5.15	Ulster Bank A/C	GL	75,000				

Chapter 16 — Financial Planning for Business

John and Claire O'Mahony, owners of Lakeside Fruit Farm Ltd, wish to purchase ten acres of land at a cost of €80,000 to extend their soft fruit-growing business. They also wish to purchase a delivery van at a cost of €20,000. They are seeking a bank loan of €100,000 repayable over ten years.

A. Applying for a Loan

Borrower must be clear on:

(1) Purpose of loan.
(2) Size of loan.
(3) Repayment period.
(4) Security available.
(5) Rates of interest.
(6) Monthly payment.

B. What Information Must Be Presented to Bank When Seeking a Loan?

(1) Letter of application.
(2) Loan application form.
(3) Business plan.
(4) Cash flow forecast.
(5) Final accounts over two or three years.
(6) Projected accounts.
(7) Details of collateral.
(8) Proof of ability to repay.

(1) LETTER OF APPLICATION FOR LOAN

See p. 120.

(2) LOAN APPLICATION FORM: ALLIED IRISH BANKS

Name of Business	*Lakeside Fruit Farm Ltd.*
Address of Business	*Long Lane Cork.*
Name(s) of Owners	*John O'Mahony/Claire O'Mahony.*
Address of Owners	*Long Lane Cork.*
History of Business	*Our fruit business has been in existence for two years. It has made a profit every year.*
Qualifications of Management	*John has a degree in horticulture, Claire has a diploma in fruit-growing.*
Bank Accounts	*Deposit and current account in AIB Cork.*
Purpose of Loan	*Purchase land and a delivery van.*
Amount of Loan	*€100,000.*
Repayment Period	*Ten years.*
Ability to Repay	*See accounts and projected profit/loss account.*
Security Available	*Deeds of land.*
Marketing Details	*Wholesale/Retail market in Cork.*
Signed	*John O'Mahony/Claire O'Mahony* **Date** *10 March 2017.*

LAKESIDE FRUIT FARM LTD
Long Lane — Cork

VAT No. 2684168

Tel (021) 892145
Telex (021) 364185
Fax (021) 892146

10 March 2017

To Mr G. Murphy
Manager
AIB
Cork

Dear Mr Murphy

We want to apply for a bank loan of €100,000 to purchase ten acres of land and a delivery van.

We have been involved in growing fruit for two years and throughout this time we have been renting land. We have now decided to purchase land of our own costing €80,000. We also need a delivery van costing €20,000.

We plan to repay this loan over a ten-year period making an annual payment out of profit.

We enclose a completed loan application form, details of our business are contained in our business plan. We also enclose a Cash Flow Forecast and our Projected Trading and Profit and Loss Account indicates that the business will be successful and profitable.

We also enclose a copy of our accounts over the last two years. We have decided that the deeds of the land will be put forward to the bank as security for the loan.

We await a favourable response.

Yours sincerely

John and Claire O'Mahony.

Encl. 5

(3) BUSINESS PLAN

When applying for a loan, it will be necessary to make out a Business Plan which will show how the owners see their business developing in the future. A business that fails to plan, plans to fail. A good business plan should cover the following areas: management, marketing, finance and production.

Contents of a Business Plan

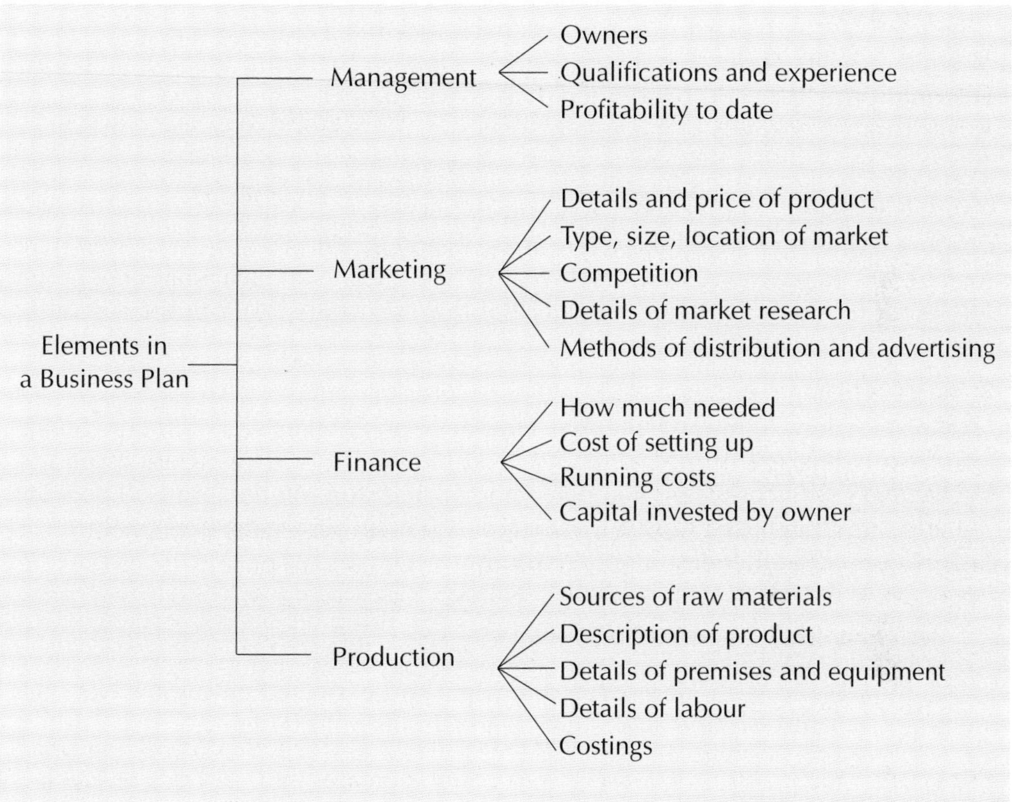

Costings

There are two costs involved in producing a product:

(1) Fixed costs — Must be paid irrespective of how much is produced.

(2) Variable Costs — Increase as production increases.

Fixed costs + variable costs = Total costs.

$$\textbf{Cost per unit} = \frac{\textbf{Total Cost}}{\textbf{Unit Produced}} + \textbf{Mark-Up} = \textbf{Selling Price}$$

Why are business plans necessary?

(1) Required when applying for a loan.

(2) Help management making decisions.

(3) To compare actual with planned performance.

LAKESIDE FRUIT FARM LTD BUSINESS PLAN

1. MANAGEMENT
Lakeside Fruit Farm Ltd is a private limited company set up in January 2015. **Owners:** John and Claire O'Mahony. **Qualifications:** John has a degree in horticulture and Claire has a diploma in fruit-farming.

2. MARKETING
Products: Raspberries, strawberries, loganberries, blackcurrants.
Market: Wholesale/retail market in Cork, shop on the farm, local jam factory.
Distribution: The fruit is distributed daily to the market.
Advertising: Weekends in the local papers.

3. FINANCE
Capital invested: The owners have each invested €15,000 in the business. **Purpose of finance:** To purchase ten acres of land for €80,000 and a delivery van for €20,000. **Repayment:** Over a ten-year period, by annual payment out of profit. **Enclosed:** (i) Financial accounts over the last two years; (ii) a projected set of accounts; (iii) a cash flow forecast.

4. PRODUCTION
Fruit production: April until October. **Employment:** Owners work full-time on the farm and twenty part-time students are employed fruit-picking during season. **Packaging:** Fruit is prepared and packed in a large store on the farm. All packing materials are purchased from a local supplier. **Enclosed:** Production costings.
Signed: John O'Mahony, Claire O'Mahony.

(4) CASH FLOW FORECAST

A Cash Flow Forecast shows **expected receipts** and **expected payments**: Net Cash, Opening Cash and Closing Cash (similar to a household budget).

Receipts of a business

Sales, owners' capital, sale of assets, receipts from debtors, bank interest received, loans received, government grants.

Payments of a business

Purchases of stock, purchase of premises, machinery, equipment, computers, wages, rent, rates, insurance, heat and light, repayment of loans, telephone, advertising.

Reasons for Preparing a Cash Flow Forecast

A business prepares a cash flow forecast for the following reasons:
(1) To find out if the business can live within its means, i.e. receipts greater than payments.
(2) To identify future liquidity problems.
(3) To obtain a bank loan.
(4) To supply information required when drawing up a business plan.
(5) To show whether repayments can be met.

CASH FLOW FORECAST 2017 LAKESIDE FRUIT FARM LTD

	Jan.	Feb.	Mar.	Apr.	May	June	July	Aug.	Sept.	Oct.	Nov.	Dec.	Total
Receipts													
Sales	9,000	7,000	2,000	10,000	17,000	26,000	25,000	20,000	16,000	11,000	6,000	9,000	158,000
Government Grant	—	—	—	—	—	—	—	—	—	—	—	—	
Loan	—	—	—	—	100,000	—	—	—	—	—	—	—	100,000
A Total Receipts	9,000	7,000	2,000	10,000	117,000	26,000	25,000	20,000	16,000	11,000	6,000	9,000	258,000
Payments													
Purchases	2,000	1,800	600	3,000	4,000	6,000	4,000	5,000	2,000	4,000	4,500	4,600	41,500
Wages	—	—	—	2,500	3,800	4,500	4,200	3,500	3,000	5,000	2,000	—	28,500
Rent of Land	300	300	300	300	300	300	300	300	300	300	300	300	3,600
Telephone	80	—	150	—	180	—	160	—	130	—	180	—	880
Advertising	40	30	60	80	100	250	200	160	150	200	250	200	1,720
Purchase of Land	—	—	—	—	80,000	—	—	—	—	—	—	—	80,000
Purchase of Van	—	—	—	—	20,000	—	—	—	—	—	—	—	20,000
B Total Payments	2,420	2,130	1,110	5,880	108,380	11,050	8,860	8,960	5,580	9,500	7.230	5,100	176,200
C Net Cash (A – B)	6,580	4,870	890	4,120	8,620	14,950	16,140	11,040	10,420	1,500	–1,230	3,900	81,800
D Opening Cash	200	6,780	11,650	12,540	16,660	25,280	40,230	56,370	67,410	77,830	79,330	78,100	200
Closing Cash (C + D)	6,780	11,650	12,540	16,660	25,280	40,230	56,370	67,410	77,830	79,330	78,100	82,000	82,000

(5) TRADING AND PROFIT AND LOSS ACCOUNT

Trading and Profit and Loss Account of Lakeside Fruit Farm Ltd for Years Ending 31 December 2015 and 31 December 2016

Trading and Profit and Loss Account for Year Ending 31/12/15			Trading and Profit and Loss Account for Year Ending 31/12/16		
		€			€
Sales		127,000	Sales		136,000
Purchases		48,200	Purchases		47,100
Gross Profit		78,800	Gross Profit		88,900
Less Expenses			**Less Expenses**		
Wages	16,200		Wages	19,100	
Rent	3,600		Rent	3,600	
Telephone	700		Telephone	750	
Advertising	1,200	21,700	Advertising	1,530	24,980
Net Profit		57,100	**Net Profit**		63,920

(6) PROJECTED PROFIT FOR 2017

From the cash flow forecast, we can prepare a projected trading and profit and loss account for 2017.

Lakeside Fruit Farm Ltd Projected Trading and Profit and Loss Account for Year Ending 31 December 2017

	€	€
Sales		158,000
Purchases		41,500
Gross Profit		116,500
Less Expenses		
Wages	28,500	
Rent	3,600	
Telephone	880	
Advertising	1,720	
Total Expenses		34,700
Projected Net Profit		**81,800**

(7) DETAILS OF COLLATERAL/SECURITY

A bank will look for collateral from a business that is borrowing money. Lakeside Fruit Farm Ltd is offering the deeds of the land as collateral. Other types of collateral offered on business loans are:

(a) Deeds of premises.

(b) Personal written guarantee by the owners.

(8) PROOF OF ABILITY TO REPAY

The net profit shown by the accounts for 2015, 2016 and projected for 2017 is as follows:

Accounts	2015	2016	Projected 2017
Net Profit	€57,100	€63,920	€81,800

The trend is towards increasing profit.

C. Recording the Loan in the Books of the Company

When the business receives the loan, it must be recorded in the books as follows:

- ➢ Debit bank account of business.
- ➢ Credit loan account AIB bank (Lender).
- ➢ Assume the loan was received on 20 May 2017.

Bank Account — Lakeside Fruit Farm

		€			
20 May 2017	Loan AIB	100,000			

Loan Account AIB Bank

					€
			20 May 2017	Bank	100,000

Examination-Style Question and Solution

Question 1.

Answer (a), (b) and (c). This is a Cash Flow Statement Question.

1. (a) On a separate sheet supplied with this paper is a partially completed Cash Flow Statement. You are required to complete this form for the months of March, April, May and June, as well as all the Total columns.

The following information should be taken into account.

- ➢ Monthly sales are expected to increase by 30% beginning in April.
- ➢ A European Union (EU) grant of €40,000 for equipment is expected in May.
- ➢ The shareholders are to invest an additional €50,000 in the business in June.
- ➢ Light and heat is expected to decrease by 15% in the months of March and May.
- ➢ Rent and wages are expected to remain the same every month.
- ➢ A new advertising campaign during May will cost €10,000.
- ➢ A second motor vehicle will be purchased in April at a cost of €30,000.
- ➢ New equipment costing €170,000 will be purchased in April.
- ➢ Purchases will increase each month by 12% beginning in March. (28)

1. (b) State **two** important pieces of information which NAMBOOG LTD can obtain from this Cash Flow Statement. (6)

1. (c) NAMBOOG LTD forgot to allow for overtime payments of €5,000 for the period. State how this omission will affect the net cash position at the end of June. (6)

Source: Junior Certificate Higher Level. **(40 marks)**

Cash Flow Statement of Namboog Ltd
for Period Jan.–June

	JAN. €	FEB. €	MARCH €	APRIL €	MAY €	JUNE €	TOTAL FOR JAN.–JUNE €
RECEIPTS							
Sales	40,000	40,000					
EU Grant	—	—					
Share Capital	—	—					
A Total Receipts	40,000	40,000					
Payments							
Light and Heat	1,600	—					
Rent	500	500					
Wages	2,500	2,500					
Advertising	—	—					
Motor Vehicles	—	25,000					
New Equipment	—	—					
Purchases	16,000	16,000					
B Total Payments	20,600	44,000					
C Net Cash (A – B)	19,400	–4,000					
D Opening Cash	3,000	22,400	18,400				
Closing Cash (C + D)	22,400	18,400					

Solution to Question 1.
1. (a) Cash Flow Statement of Namboog Ltd for Period Jan.–June

	JAN. €	FEB. €	MARCH €	APRIL €	MAY €	JUNE €	TOTAL FOR JAN.–JUNE €
RECEIPTS							
Sales	40,000	40,000	40,000	52,000	52,000	52,000	276,000
EU Grant	—	—			40,000		40,000
Share Capital	—	—				50,000	50,000
A Total Receipts	40,000	40,000	40,000	52,000	92,000	102,000	366,000
Payments							
Light and Heat	1,600	—	1,360		1,360		4,320
Rent	500	500	500	500	500	500	3,000
Wages	2,500	2,500	2,500	2,500	2,500	2,500	15,000
Advertising	—	—			10,000		10,000
Motor Vehicles	—	25,000		30,000			55,000
New Equipment	—	—		170,000			170,000
Purchases	16,000	16,000	17,920	20,070	22,478	25,175	117,643
B Total Payments	20,600	44,000	22,280	223,070	36,838	28,175	374,963
C Net Cash (A – B)	19,400	–4,000	17,720	–171,070	55,162	73,825	–8,963
D Opening Cash	3,000	22,400	18,400	36,120	–134,950	–79,788	3,000
Closing Cash (C + D)	22,400	18,400	36,120	–134,950	–79,788	–5,963	–5,963

ALTERNATIVE

The last entry in the question, 'Purchases will increase each month by 12% beginning in March', may have a different interpretation. If it is understood to be an increase of 12% on February figure of €16,000, then the purchases figures for March, April, May and June will be €17,920 each month. The figures for total payment, net cash, opening cash and closing cash will have to reflect these figures.

1. (b) *(i) There will be net cash deficits in the months of February (€4,000) and April (€171,070).*

(ii) There will be an overall net cash deficit of €8,963 for period January to June.

(iii) There will be a closing cash deficit of €5,963 at the end of the period.

1. (c) *The extra overtime payments of €5,000 will increase the net cash deficit at the end of June from €8,963 to €13,963.*

Examination-Style Question and Solution

Question

Answer (A) and (B). This is a Self-Employment and Business Plan Question.

(A) State **two rewards** and **two risks** of being self-employed. (8)

(B) Mary Burke and John Smyth decide to set up a sandwich making and delivery business. The name of their company is SAMBOS Ltd, located at 25 Low Street, Kells, Co. Meath
Mary Burke is managing director.
Their market research has provided the following information:
- there are two thousand potential customers;
- there are four businesses in the area supplying sandwiches but none of them offers a delivery service;
- they estimate that they can sell five hundred sandwiches per day at €1.85 each.

They estimate their costs as follows: Equipment €5,500; Delivery van €12,000; Lease of premises €14,000; Working capital €7,500.

They have savings of €5,500 to invest in the business and can obtain a grant of €10,000 if they produce a Business Plan. They seek your help in preparing this plan.

(i) Calculate the amount of money they would need to borrow in order to set up this business;
(ii) Outline **two** suitable methods of advertising and promoting their sandwiches;
(iii) Complete the blank Business Plan document, supplied with this paper, using today's date.

(32)
(40) marks

Source: Junior Certficate Higher Level.

For use with Question (B) (iii)

BUSINESS PLAN

COMPANY DETAILS	
Name of Company	______________________
Address of Company	______________________
	______________________
Shareholders /Owners	______________________
	______________________
Managing Director	______________________
	______________________
PRODUCT	
Description of Product	______________________
	______________________
MARKET RESEARCH	
Size of Market	______________________
Competitors	______________________
Price per unit sandwich	______________________
SALES PROMOTION	
Methods	______________________
FINANCE	
Total Required	______________________
Amount Available	______________________
Loan Required	______________________
SIGNED	______________________
	______________________
DATE	______________________

PLEASE ENCLOSE WITH YOUR ANSWERBOOK

Solution to Self-Employment and Business Plan Question.

Self-employment and business plan

(A) Two rewards of being self-employed:

(i) Keep all the profit;

(ii) Make all the decisions;

(iii) Be one's own boss.

Two risks of being self-employed:

(i) Lose one's investment if the business fails;

(ii) Has unlimited liability, could lose one's personal wealth (house, etc.) if the business fails.

(iii) Final decisions up to the owner, may not make the correct decision.

(iv) Stress — Family problems.

(B) (i) **Amount of money required:**

	€	€
Equipment	*5,500*	
Delivery Van	*12,000*	
Lease of premises	*14,000*	
Working Capital	*7,500*	*39,000*
Less amount of money available	€	€
Own savings	*5,500*	
Grant	*10,000*	*15,500*
Amount of money required		***23,500***

(B) (ii) Two suitable methods of advertising and promoting sandwiches.
Leaflets drop, Local paper, Local radio, Personal callers, Free samples, Street signs, Billboards, Local TV, Cinema.

(B) (iii) **Business Plan**

COMPANY DETAILS	
Name of Company	*Sambos Ltd*
Address of Company	*25 Low Street*
	Kells
	Co. Meath
Shareholders/Owners	*Mary Burke, John Smyth*
Managing Director	*Mary Burke*
PRODUCT	
Description of product	*Sandwich making and delivery*
MARKET RESEARCH	
Size of market	*Two thousand customers*
Competitors	*Four businesses but no delivery services*
Price per unit sandwich	*€1.85*
SALES PROMOTION	
Methods	*Leaflets, free samples*
FINANCE	
Totalrequired	*€39,000*
amount available	*€15,500*
loan required	*€23,500*
Signed	*Mary Burke*
	John Smyth
Date	*16/6/15*

Chapter 17 — Commercial Banks and Business

Begin by rereading chapter 8 — Money and Banking.

A. Summary of Services Provided by Commercial Banks for Business

(1) SAVING

Deposit account.

(2) MONEY TRANSFER FACILITIES

(a) Cheque payments.
(b) Bank draft — a cheque drawn by a bank on its own bank account.
(c) Standing order — to make certain fixed payments, e.g. rent, insurance, interest payments.
(d) Direct debit — to make variable payments from an account at regular intervals, e.g. ESB, telephone.
(e) Credit transfer (bank giro) — to pay ESB or telephone bills, make VAT returns.
(f) Paypath — wages transferred directly into employee's bank account.

(3) CARD PAYMENTS

(a) ATM (Automated Teller Machines) — a business can lodge, withdraw, request a statement, order a cheque book or pay a bill.
(b) Company credit cards — used in business to pay for lunches, hotel accommodation, petrol/diesel.

(4) TRANSFERRING MONEY ABROAD

(a) Foreign draft — to pay a creditor abroad.
(b) Traveller's cheques — used by salespeople travelling abroad.

(5) LENDING

(a) Bank overdraft.
(b) Term loan — given for a **stated reason** for a **specified period of time**, it has an **agreed repayment schedule**.
(c) Commercial mortgage — for purchasing property.

(6) SAFE KEEPING

(a) Strongroom facilities — a business can store important documents and other valuables in the bank's strongroom.
(b) Night safe facilities — money can be lodged in the bank late at night through a chute located in the bank wall. A leather wallet and key are provided.

(7) FOREIGN EXCHANGE

(8) FINANCIAL SERVICES

(a) Financial advice.
(b) Income tax advice.

(c) Facility for **purchase and sale of shares**.
(d) Advice on **insurance** or **assurance**.
(e) Help with **financial planning**, e.g. cash flow statements.

(9) HELP WITH EXPORTING
(a) Foreign currency **exchange**.
(b) Checking **creditworthiness** of foreign customers.
(c) **Information** on foreign markets.
(d) Arranging **collection of payment** from abroad.
(e) **Export credit insurance** covers risk of non-payment.
(f) **Loans**, while firms are waiting for payment from foreign customers.

(10) BANK STATEMENTS AND BANK RECONCILIATION STATEMENTS ARE DEALT WITH FULLY IN CHAPTER 8.

B. Operating a Business Bank Account

(1) Usually two signatures required on all cheques and withdrawal forms.
(2) Record all lodgments and payments in the business bank account.
(3) Request a weekly bank statement.
(4) Prepare bank reconciliation statement regularly.

SOME INFORMATION THAT A PRIVATE LIMITED COMPANY CAN PROVIDE WHEN OPENING A CURRENT ACCOUNT IN A BANK
(1) Memorandum of association/articles of association.
(2) Signatures of people who can write company cheques.
(3) Name and address of company, names of directors.
(4) Certificate of incorporation.
(5) Objectives of the company.
(6) Details of company accounts.

FACTORS THAT BANKS CONSIDER WHEN GRANTING A LOAN
(1) Amount of money requuired.
(2) Purpose of the loan.
(3) Period of time the loan is required for.
(4) Ability to repay loan.
(5) Security available.
(6) Business history.
(7) Market research details.
(8) Creditworthiness of busiess seeking the loan.

Higher Level

Chapter 18 — Insurance for Business

There are many risks in business and every business should be adequately insured.

A. Reasons for Business Insurance

(1) **Protection of assets** against fire, theft, etc.
(2) Protection against **legal action** as a result of accidents to the public or staff.
(3) **Legal reasons** — motor insurance.

B. Main Types of Business Insurance

(1) **Motor insurance** — compulsory on all company vehicles.
(2) **Employer's liability** — covers claims by employees arising out of accidents at work.
(3) **Fire insurance** — covers damage to property and contents.
(4) **Burglary/Theft insurance** — covers damage arising from a break-in and theft of contents or property.
(5) **Cash in transit insurance** — covers theft of cash while in transit between the business and the bank.
(6) **Goods in transit insurance** — covers theft or damage to goods while being transported.
(7) **Fidelity guarantee insurance** — compensates an employer for loss of cash arising from the dishonesty of employees.
(8) **Plate glass insurance** — covers the breakages or damage to expensive shop window glass.
(9) **Sprinkler leakage insurance** — covers loss or damage caused to stock by water as a result of accidental switching on of the sprinkler system used for fire-fighting.
(10) **Consequential loss insurance** — covers the firm for loss of profits while a business is closed as a result of a fire or flood.
(11) **Public liability insurance** — covers claims made by members of the public who are injured while on the firm's property.
(12) **Bad debts insurance** — covers a loss arising because a debtor does not pay what he owes.
(13) **Product liability insurance** — provides cover against a claim made by a person that he was harmed or suffered a loss or damage through using the firm's products.
(14) **PRSI (Pay-Related Social Insurance)** — PRSI is a payment to the government. The employee pays a percentage of gross wages, but the employer must also make a contribution for each employee on the payroll.
(15) **Key person insurance** — provides compensation for the loss of valuable employees through death, for example, the managing director or a highly talented employee.

C. Non-Insurable Risks

(1) Bankruptcy.
(2) Stock becoming obsolete (out of date).
(3) Bad management decisions.

D. Recording the Payment of Insurance in the Books of the Business

When insurance is paid, money goes out of the business.

— Debit insurance account (expense).

— Credit bank account (asset).

Example

A payment of €600 was made by cheque for insurance on 1 September 2016.

Bank Account (Asset)

			1/9/16	Insurance	600

Insurance Account (Expense)

1/9/16	Bank	600	1/9/16	Profit & Loss A/C	600

The figure of €600 insurance will appear under expenses in the profit and loss account.

Profit and Loss Account

	<u>Expenses</u>		
	Insurance		600

Examination-Style Questions and Solutions

Question 1.

Teckno Office Supplies Ltd is not satisfied with its present insurers and has asked HIBO Insurance Co. Ltd to give it a quotation for insuring the following:

Buildings valued €180,000; machinery valued €60,000; five delivery vans valued €15,000 each; stock of office supplies valued €280,000; cash held in office €1,500.

Hibo Insurance Co. Ltd supplied the following quote for one year's insurance:

Insurance for buildings and machinery €3 per €1,000 value; motor van insurance third party fire and theft €600 per van; stock insurance €10 per €1,000 value; cash insurance €10 per €500. New business introductory offer: 10% discount off total premium.

Teckno accepted the quotation and took out insurance on everything at replacement value except buildings, which it insured for €120,000.

1. (a) Give two reasons why Teckno should take out insurance. (6)

1. (b) Calculate the total cost of the insurance premium. (8)

1. (c) In the event of fire damage to buildings of €60,000, how much compensation would Teckno receive from the insurance company? Show calculations. (9)

1. (d) Teckno paid this premium on 1.7.14 by cheque. Complete this cheque on the blank provided below. (5)

Date ________ 20

To ________

For ________

Balance € 30,000

Amount Lodged

046 Total € 30,000

Amount this Cheque ________

Bal. forwd ________

500046

Allied Irish Banks 93–34–81

107/108 MAIN STREET BRAY CO WICKLOW 20

Pay ________ or order

________ €

TECKNO LTD

____

S. MURRAY

"500046" "93"3481" 05001052 "02"

1. (e) The insurance account in Teckno's ledger has an opening debit balance of €3,500. Record the payment to Hibo Insurance Co. in this account in Teckno's ledger. (6)

1. (f) Teckno's trading year ends on 28.2.15. Show the relevant extracts of the profit and loss account and balance sheet of Teckno, in respect of the insurance account. (6)

Source: Junior Certificate Higher Level. **(40 marks)**

Solution to Question 1.

1. (a) *Two reasons for taking out insurance:*

(i) Insurance helps reduce the risks the business might have.

(ii) The law requires Teckno Office Supplies Ltd to have motor insurance.

(iii) In case of loss due to fire, theft, claims by employees, or claims by members of the public.

1. (b) *Calculate the total cost of the insurance premium.*

PREMIUM CALCULATION:

Buildings	*€120,000*	@	*€3 per €1,000*	*120 × €3 =*	*€360*
Machinery	*€60,000*	@	*€3 per €1,000*	*60 × €3 =*	*€180*
Five delivery vans	*€15,000*	@	*€600 per van*	*5 × €600 =*	*€3,000*
Stock	*€280,000*	@	*€10 per €1,000*	*280 × €10 =*	*€2,800*
Cash	*€1,500*	@	*€10 per €500*	*3 × €10 =*	*€30*
					€6,370
Less 10% New Business Introductory Offer					*€637*
Total cost of premiums to Teckno Office Supplies Ltd					*€5,733*

1. (c) *Compensation for fire damage to buildings of €60,000*

Calculation:

Buildings valued @ €180,000 insured for €120,000, i.e. buildings insured for 2/3 of value. The principle of average clause applies here. The insurance company will pay 2/3 of €60,000 = €40,000.

Teckno Office Supplies Ltd will receive €40,000.

1. (d) *Complete cheque on blank document supplied.*

Counterfoil	
Date	*1 July 2014*
To	*Hibo Insurance Ltd*
For	*Insurance 1/7/14–30/6/15*
Balance	€ 30,000
Amount Lodged	
046 Total	€ 30,000
Amount this Cheque	*€5,733*
Bal. forwd	*€24,267*
500046	

Allied Irish Banks 93–34–81

107/108 MAIN STREET BRAY CO WICKLOW *1/7/2014*

Pay *Hibo Insurance Co Ltd* or order

Five thousand seven hundred and thirty-three Euro € *5,733—*

TECKNO LTD

S. Murray

S. MURRAY

"500046" "93"3481" 05001052 "02"

1. (e) *Record balance and payment to Hibo Insurance Company in Teckno's ledger.*

Insurance Account

Date	Details	Total €	
1/7/14	*Balance*	*3,500*	
1/7/14	*Bank*	*5,733*	

1. (f) *Extracts from profit and loss account and balance sheet in respect of insurance.*

Profit and Loss Account (Extract) for Year Ending 28 February 2015

Less Expenses	€	€
Insurance	*9,233*	
Less Insurance Prepaid (1/3)	*1,911*	*7,322*

Balance Sheet (Extract) as at 28 February 2015

Current Assets		€
Insurance Prepaid		*1,911*

Question 2.

Answer all sections. This is an Insurance Premium Calculation and Recording Question.

Shopfitters Ltd has decided to change its insurers and has asked Sword Insurers Ltd to give it a quotation for insuring the following:

Buildings €135,000; machinery €70,000; three delivery vans valued at €18,000 each; stock of shopfittings €85,000; cash held in the office €1,250.

Sword Insurers Ltd supplied the following quotation for one year's insurance:

Insurance for buildings and machinery €3.50 per €1,000 value; motor van insurance third party fire and theft €710 per van; stock insurance €11.50 per €1,000 value; cash insurance €12 per €500.

New business introductory offer: 20% discount off total premium.

Shopfitters Ltd accepted the quotation and took out insurance on everything at replacement cost (as stated above) except the machinery, which it insured for €50,000.

Shopfitters Ltd paid the premium by cheque on 1 July 2015.

Answer the following:

2. (a) Calculate the amount of the premium paid by Shopfitters Ltd on 1 July 2015. (Show your workings clearly.) (16)

2. (b) The Insurance Account in Shopfitters Ltd ledger has an opening debit balance of €1,700. Record the payment to Sword Insurers Ltd on 1 July 2015.

Balance the **Insurance Account** on 31 December 2015 (the end of its trading year), showing clearly the amount to be transferred to the Profit and Loss Account. (12)

2. (c) In the event of fire damage to machinery of €35,000, how much compensation would Shopfitters Ltd receive? (Show your workings.) (8)

2. (d) Name two other types of insurance you think Shopfitters Ltd should have. (4)

Source: Junior Certificate Higher Level. **(40 marks)**

Solution to Question 2.

2. (a) *Calculate premium paid by Shopfitters Ltd.*

Buildings	*€135,000@*	*€3.50 per €1,000*	*135 × €3.50 =*	*€472.50*
Machinery	*€50,000@*	*€3.50 per €1,000*	*50 × €3.50 =*	*€175.00*
Three delivery vans	*€18,000@*	*€710 per van*	*3 × €710 =*	*€2,130.00*
Stock	*€85,000@*	*€11.50 per €1,000*	*85 × €11.50 =*	*€977.50*
Cash	*€1,250@*	*€12 per €500*	*2.5 × €12 =*	*€30.00*
				€3,785.00
	Less 20% new business introductory offer			*€757.00*
	Total amount of premium paid by Shopfitters Ltd			*€3,028.00*

2. (b) *Insurance Account*

Debit — Insurance Account — Credit

Date	Details	Fo	Total €	Date	Details	Fo	Total €
1/7/15	*Balance*	*B/d*	*1,700*	*31/12/15*	*P & L A/C*		*3,214*
1/7/15	*Bank*	*CB*	*3,028*	*31/12/15*	*Balance*	*C/d*	*1,514*
			4,728				*4,728*
1/1/16	*Balance*	*B/d*	*1,514*				

2. (c) *Compensation for fire damage to machinery €35,000.*

Calculations:

Machinery valued €70,000 is insured for €50,000, i.e. it is insured for 5/7 of its value. The average clause principle applies in this partial loss of €35,000. The insurance company will pay €35,000 x 5/7 = €25,000.

2. (d) *Public liability, employer's liability, fidelity guarantee, cash in transit, plate glass, goods in transit, etc.*

Higher Level

Chapter 19 — Communications

Communication is the exchanging of information. The message should be **brief**, **clear** and **simple**.

A. Factors to Be Considered When Choosing a Form of Communication

(1) Cost — How expensive is the method of communication: telephone call v. letter?
(2) Speed — How fast can the information be transferred?
(3) Safety — Will the item reach its destination safely?
(4) Written record — It is important to keep a written record for future reference.
(5) Secrecy — If information is confidential, choose a secret form of communication.
(6) Destination — Over what distance is the communication, national or international?
(7) Accuracy — Will method chosen transfer the information exactly?

B. Who Does a Business Communicate With?

(1) Directors, managers, employees, supervisors — **internal communication**.
(2) Customers, public, shareholders, insurance companies, bank, suppliers, tax office — **external communication**.

C. Internal and External Communication

Internal Communication	External Communication
1. Person to person	1. Meeting
2. Notice-board	2. Radio and TV
3. Meeting	3. Trade fairs and exhibitions
4. Intercom	4. Newspapers
5. Paging	5. Publications
6. Walkie-talkie (portable radio)	6. Letters and business documents
7. Memorandum (memo)	7. Computers
8. Internal report	8. Films, slideshows and videos
9. Closed-circuit TV	9. RTE Aertel and BBC Ceefax
10. Computers	10. Eircom
11. Internal newspapers, magazines	11. An Post
12. Graphs, bar charts, pictograms, pie charts	12. Internet • Electronic mail (e-mail) • World Wide Web (www)
13. Internal telephone.	13. Video conferencing

Agencies Involved in Communication

EIRCOM SERVICES

(1) **Telephone** — Popular form of communication for local, national and international calls.
(2) **Call Answering** — Takes messages if person is not available to answer phone.
(3) **Call Waiting** — Informs person on the phone that another call is coming in and allows the person to take the two calls at same time.
(4) **Call Forwarding** — Allows subscriber to divert calls to another phone.
(5) **Freephone** — 1800 plus the Freephone number: allows person to call a business and business pays for the call.
(6) **Telemessages** — Phone a message to Eircom and it will be delivered the next day.
(7) **Tele-conferencing** — A meeting or conference can be held over the telephone.
(8) **Video Conferencing** — A way of conducting meetings without travelling to the meeting. Video cameras are used to transmit the picture and sound of the meeting over the telephone.
(9) **Fax (facsimile)** — Exact copy of a document can be transmitted over the telephone to another fax machine
(10) **Internet** — This gives access to the World Wide Web and email.

AN POST

An Post offers a wide range of services in communications.

(1) **Postal services**

All services have been designed according to what is important to the customer.

- **Standard post**: If cost is the main concern, standard post should be used. It offers a cost-effective worldwide delivery.
- **Registered post**: If security is the main concern, registered post should be used. It offers the securest delivery method available.
- **Express post**: If speed and next-day delivery are required, express post should be chosen. It offers a guaranteed next-working-day delivery within the Republic of Ireland, with optional signature and insurance available for a small fee.
- **Courier post**: If the item is especially urgent, courier post is the service to use. It provides a next-day delivery before 12.00 p.m. in major urban areas within the Republic of Ireland. International delivery times vary according to destination.

(2) **Publicity Post** — Delivery of unaddressed leaflets to every household in a specific area for a fee.
(3) **Post Aim** — Allows a business to send letters to all its customers for about half the normal price.
(4) **Freepost** — Allows customers to write to a business free. Customers must write FREEPOST on the envelope
(5) **Business Reply Service** — Business provides special business reply envelope.

D. Methods of Communication

ORAL	WRITTEN	VISUAL	ELECTRONIC
Person to person Meeting Telephone Intercom Paging Walkie-talkie Tele-conferencing	Notice-board Memo Report Letter and business documents Newspapers Fax An Post	Films, slides and videos Aertel Ceefax Graphs Bar chart Pictogram Pie charts	Electronic Data Interchange (EDI) Internet • Electronic mail (e-mail) • World wide web (www) Video conferencing
Advantage Fast **Disadvantage** No written record	**Advantage** Written record	**Advantages** 1. Easy to understand 2. Very effective	**Advantage** Fast

E. Visual Communication/Charts and Graphs

There are four main ways of showing information visually.
Line graph, bar chart, pie chart, pictogram.

(1) LINE GRAPH

A line graph shows a trend, i.e. how things change over time.

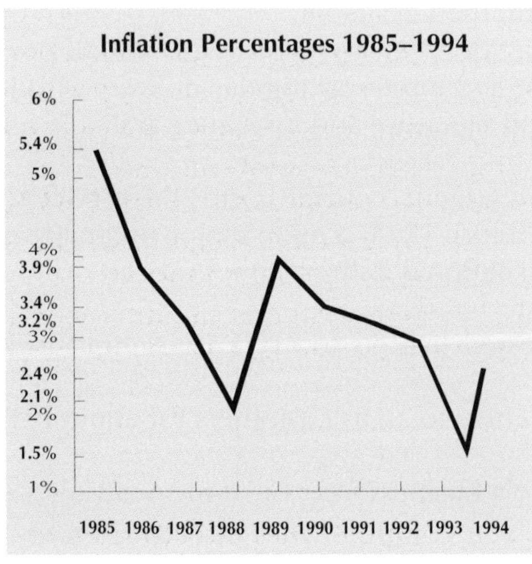

Source: Central Statistics Office.

(2) BAR CHART

A bar chart is very useful when making comparisons. Information is displayed in a series of bars.

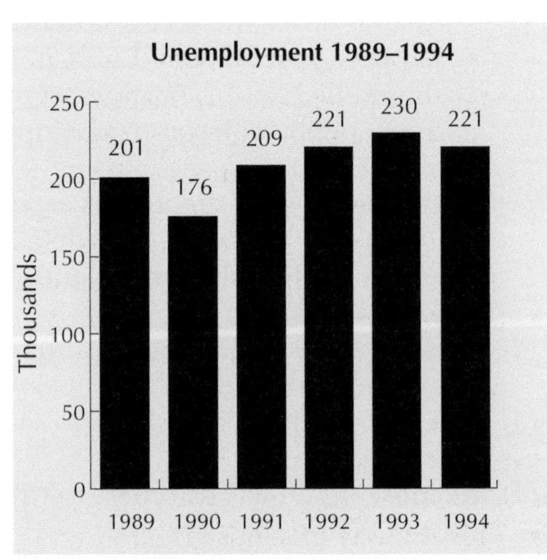

Source: Central Statistics Office.

(3) PIE CHART

A pie chart is a circle divided into sections, each section showing figures as a percentage of the total.

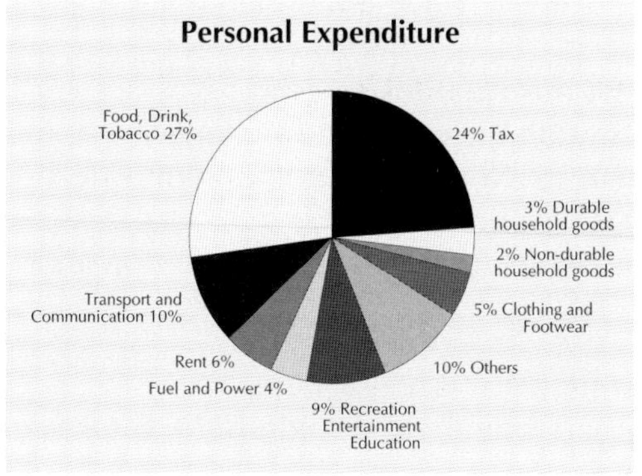

Source: Central Statistics Office.

(4) PICTOGRAM

Here pictures or symbols are used to represent figures.

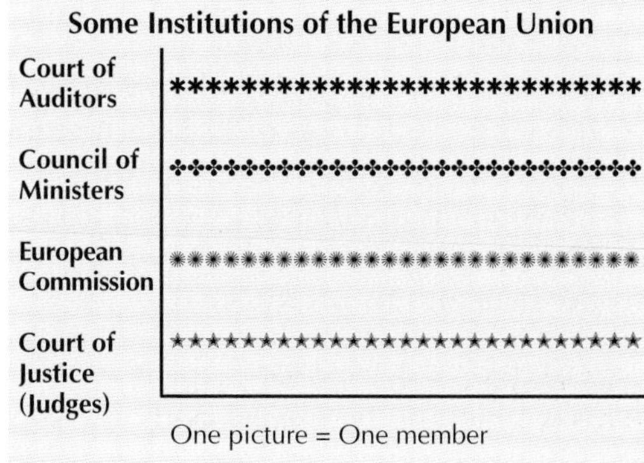

Modern Communication Technology

ELECTRONIC DATA INTERCHANGE (EDI)

- EDI allows the information in a standard document, for example an invoice or purchases order, to be transferred directly from one computer to another without recourse to a printed copy.
- EDI is dependent on users having compatible technology. It is a faster, cheaper and more reliable means of exchanging information than traditional paper-based exchanges.

THE INTERNET

- The Internet is an international network linking computers across telephone lines. Millions of computers in different countries are connected to each other through the telephone system. Once connected, any computer can exchange information with any other computer on the network for the price of a local call.
- Firms connect to the Internet through an Internet service provider (ISP). They need a computer and a modem connected to a telephone line. A modem is a device that connects a computer to the telephone line and the Internet.
- Companies throughout the world are rapidly discovering that the Internet is a valuable tool for business, giving them a chance to see and be seen on the world stage.

Internet Services

ELECTRONIC MAIL (E-MAIL)

- This is a way of sending typed messages and computer files directly from one computer to another over the Internet. It is the most popular use of the Internet.
- It is a fast, efficient, convenient and cheap way of sending messages.
- Each user has a unique e-mail address.
- You can send a copy of your messages to any number of people at the same time.

- Files containing text, spreadsheets, and graphics can be attached to your e-mail messages.
- Messages are held in a 'mailbox', access to which can be controlled by your own password.

WORLD WIDE WEB (WWW)

- The World Wide Web is the world's biggest information gateway.
- It is a vast collection of linked documents available over the Internet.
- A special program called a Browser (such as Netscape Navigator or Internet Explorer) is needed to give you access to the web.
- Many businesses have their own websites on which they display information about the firm and its products.

E-COMMERCE/E-BUSINESS

This is a method by which goods and services are bought and sold on the Internet.

VIDEO CONFERENCING

This is a meeting held between people who are in different places. Visual and sound signals are transmitted over a telephone line, and all participants can see and hear each other. It eliminates the cost of travelling to meetings. A telephone line, camera and monitor are needed.

Chapter 20 — Chain of Production and Channels of Distribution

A. Types of Production

(1) **Primary production** (extractive industries), e.g. agriculture, forestry, fishing, mining.
(2) **Secondary production** (manufacturing industries), e.g. brewing, food processing.
(3) **Tertiary production** (service industries), e.g. banking, insurance, transport.

B. Public Sector and Private Sector

Public sector — working for government, e.g. teachers.
Private sector — all other workers not employed by government, e.g. bank officials.

C. Channels of Distribution

Channels of distribution are the ways that goods go from the manufacturer to the consumer.

The most common channels of distribution are:

1.

Suitable for fitted furniture, buying a computer direct from the manufacturer, e.g. Dell.

2.
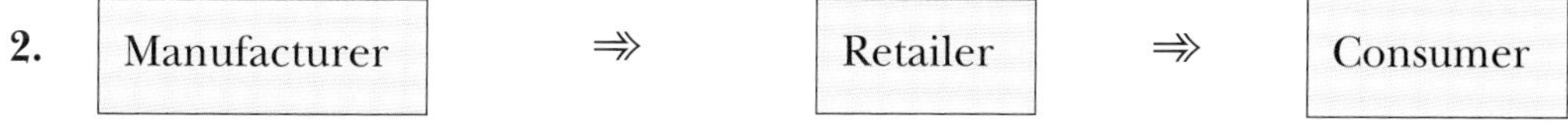

Used where retailer buys direct from manufacturer, e.g. Tesco, Dunnes Stores. Newspapers and magazines are distributed in this way.

3.
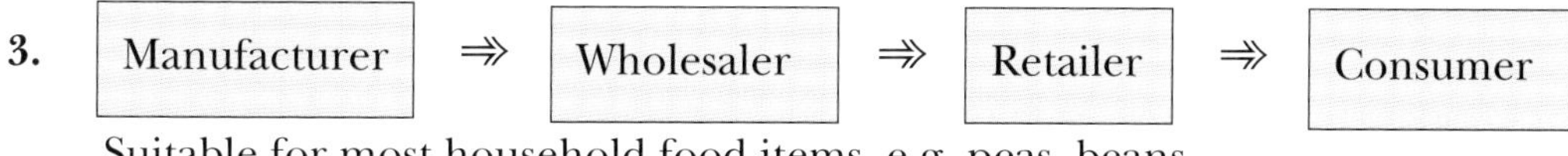

Suitable for most household food items, e.g. peas, beans.

D. Manufacturer

The manufacturer turns raw materials into finished goods.

E. Wholesaler

The wholesaler buys in bulk from manufacturer and sells in smaller quantities to the retailer.

SERVICES TO MANUFACTURER	SERVICES TO RETAILER
(1) Buys in bulk. (2) Blends, grades, packs goods. (3) Advertises manufacturer's goods. (4) Gives information.	(1) Gives credit to retailer. (2) Delivers goods to retailer. (3) Provides wide choice of goods. (4) Informs retailers about new products.

TYPES OF WHOLESALER

(1) Traditional wholesaler
Retailer sends in order. Goods are delivered to retailer's premises. Credit is given.

(2) Specialist wholesaler
Specialises in a certain range of goods.

(3) Cash and carry wholesaler
Sells a wide variety of goods. Retailer goes to the wholesaler's premises, selects and pays for goods and transports them to his premises.

WHY WOULD THE WHOLESALER BE OMITTED FROM A CHANNEL OF DISTRIBUTION?

(1) Storage may not be required.
(2) If it is important to get product to consumer quickly.
(3) If product has short shelf life.
(4) Retailer wishes to buy in bulk from manufacturer.

F. Retailer

The retailer buys goods from the wholesaler and sells to the consumer.

FUNCTIONS OF RETAILER

(1) Sells goods or services at a convenient location.
(2) Offers a wide range of goods to the consumer.
(3) May give **credit.**
(4) May **deliver** goods.
(5) May offer personal service and advice.
(6) Brings new products to the attention of the consumer.

TYPES OF RETAILER

(1) Independent shops/Sole traders
☛ Small shops owned and managed by one person.
☛ **Examples:** butcher, newsagent.

(2) Multiple shops/Chain stores
☛ A number of shops/branches owned by same firm.
☛ Multiple shops **specialise** in a particular type of product, e.g. Eason's.
☛ Chain stores **sell a wide range** of goods, e.g. Tesco, Dunnes.

(3) Department stores
☛ Sell a wide range of goods in many different departments.
☛ **Examples:** Roches Stores, Marks & Spencer, Brown Thomas.

(4) Supermarkets
☛ Large self-service stores selling a variety of goods, e.g. Dunnes Stores, Superquinn.

(5) Shopping centres
☛ A number of shops under one roof usually located on the outskirts of large towns or cities.

(6) Franchising
☛ Retailer has permission to use name and logo.
☛ **Examples:** McDonald's, Burgerland.

(7) Voluntary groups
☛ A number of small retailers link with a wholesaler to form a group.
☛ **Examples:** Super Valu, Spar, Gala.

(8) Mail order
☛ Customer chooses goods from catalogue.
☛ **Example:** Family Album, Argos.

(9) Vending machines
☛ Machines that sell cigarettes, drinks, sweets.

(10) Petrol stations
☛ Sell a wide range of goods and services.

(11) Street or roadside traders
☛ People who sell from a stall on the street or on the roadside.

(12) Mobile shops
Traders who move around and sell from a van.

(13) Door-to-door sales
People who go from door to door selling, e.g. encyclopaedias, insurance.

DEVELOPMENTS IN RETAILING

(1) Late-night shopping and Sunday trading.
(2) In-store banking — Customers can pay directly from their bank accounts e.g. Laser.
(3) Bar codes — Bar code scanner — stores prices, acts as cash register, produces receipt and updates stock levels.
(4) Increase in the use of environmentally friendly products.
(5) More foreign competition e.g. ALDI, LIDL.
(6) Greater use of credit cards.
(7) Many retailers providing a delivery service.
(8) Growth of franchising, e.g. McDonald's.
(9) Increase in the sale of fast foods.
(10) Growth in the number of shopping centres.
(11) E-Commerce — Sale of goods and services over the Internet.

Examination-Style Question and Solution

Question 1.

Write in each box whether the following forms of Industry are:

Primary, Secondary or Services

(a) MINING	Primary
(b) BANKING	Services
(c) PEN FACTORIES	Secondary

Source: Junior Certificate Ordinary Level. (4)

Chapter 21 — People at Work

A. Work

Performing a task **without payment**, such as club members doing voluntary work, e.g. GAA.

B. Employment

☛ Working **for payment**, i.e. employees of firms.

C. Nature and Extent of Employment

☛ People who are employed work in three main areas: agriculture, industry, services.
☛ People who cannot find employment are said to be unemployed.
☛ The labour force = those who are employed and those available for work.
☛ Employment in agriculture is falling.
☛ Employment in services is increasing.
☛ Employment in industry is static.
☛ Unemployment is falling.

D. Unemployment

People are unemployed when they are willing to work for payment but cannot find a job.

REASONS FOR UNEMPLOYMENT

(1) Fall in the number employed in agriculture.
(2) New technology replacing workers.
(3) Firms have reduced staff numbers because of competition.
(4) Business closing down and relocating to other country to avail of lower wage rates.

HOW TO REDUCE UNEMPLOYMENT

(1) Put more money into job creation.
(2) Encourage more enterprise and self-employment.
(3) Become more competitive abroad and increase sales, thus creating more jobs.
(4) Introduce early retirement and job-sharing schemes.
(5) Buy more Irish-produced goods and create more jobs.

E. Emigration

Leaving the country in search of employment.

F. Self-Employment

WHY PEOPLE BECOME SELF-EMPLOYED

(1) Cannot find employment.
(2) Made redundant.
(3) See an opportunity to start own business.

REWARDS OF SELF-EMPLOYMENT

(1) Own boss, make your own decisions.
(2) Receive all the profit.
(3) Decide what hours to work.
(4) Decide what to sell.
(5) Greater job satisfaction.
(6) Potential to make a great deal of money.
(7) Greater motivation.

RISKS OF SELF-EMPLOYMENT

(1) Business may fail. Loss of investment.
(2) Work long hours.
(3) Provide all the money (capital).
(4) Overworked/Stress/Family problems.
(5) Unlimited liability. Could lose personal assets, house, etc.
(6) All responsibility rests on employer.

G. Organisation of the Workplace

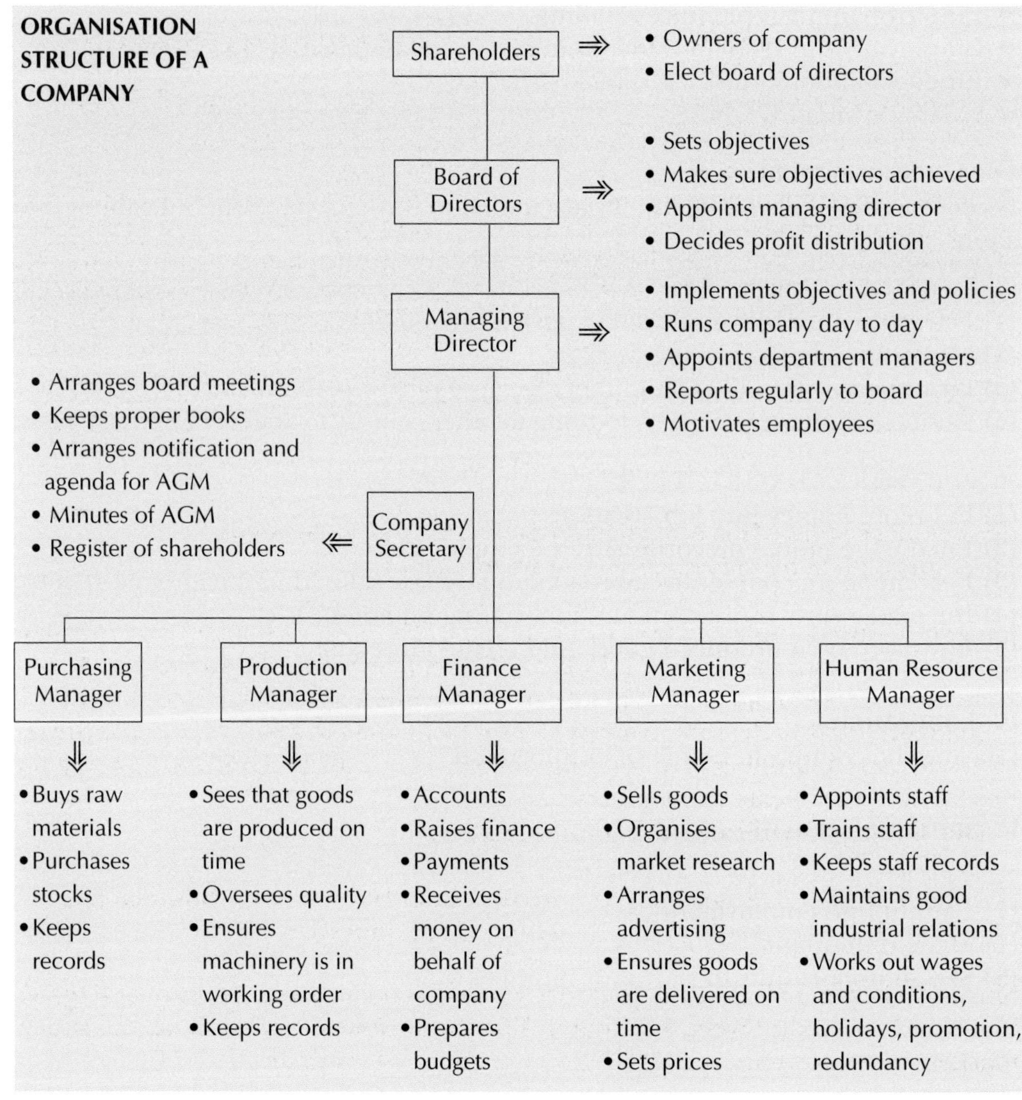

H. Types of Job

(1) **Services** — providing a service to individuals or to business, e.g. teacher.
(2) **Administration** — in either a management or a supervisory role.
(3) **Artistic/Creative** — using one's imagination or creative abilities, e.g. artist.
(4) **Technical** — understanding how things work, e.g. computer programmer.
(5) **Manual** — physical work, e.g. builder.
(6) **Clerical** — office work.

TYPES OF SKILL

(1) **Unskilled** — no qualifications and no training, e.g. builder's labourer.
(2) **Semi-skilled** — trained to do a particular task, e.g. machine operator.
(3) **Skilled** — trained in a trade, usually having served an apprenticeship, e.g. electrician.
(4) **Professional** — professional qualification, such as a university degree, e.g. teacher.

I.

RIGHTS OF EMPLOYEES	RESPONSIBILITIES OF EMPLOYEES
All employees have the right to: 1. Safe, clean and healthy working conditions. 2. Fair wages for work done. 3. To be allowed statutory annual holidays. 4. Equal pay, equal promotion opportunities. 5. Membership of a trade union if they wish. 6. Their legal entitlements as laid down in employment legislation.	All employees are obliged to: 1. Do an honest day's work. 2. Be punctual. 3. Obey all rules, regulations and instructions. 4. Protect employer's property and stock. 5. Co-operate with other employees. 6. Work for the best interest of the firm. 7. To maintain confidentiality re business matters.

Examination-Style Question and Solution

Answer all sections. This is a question on Work and Employment.
(To be completed in the application for employment form.)

Joan Hills, who is single and lives 37 High Street, Mullingar is hoping to get employment as a sales assistant at Winton Ltd., Mullingar. Joan will be 20 years old on 14 July 2009. She loves reading, walking and horse-riding. Her telphone no. is 0506-98755.

Joan attended Ballymore primary school from 1994 to 2002. Her post-primary education was at Mullingar community college from 2002 to 2007, when she sat for her Leaving Certificate examination.

Her Leaving Certificate subjects and grades were:

Irish D	English C	Mathematics D	Business B
French D	Biology E	Home Economics C	

Since her Leaving Certificate, Joan has worked as a check-out assistant at Regan's Supermarket, Main Street, Mullingar. But she is now out of work, as the supermarket closed down in April 2009 because the owner retired.

Joan is a very healthy person whose only injury was a broken wrist in 2008 when she had a fall from her horse. Joan has never been outside Ireland.

On 31 May 2009, Joan completed the application form for employment as a sales assistant at Winton Ltd.

(A) Using the above information, complete the application form for Joan. Use the blank application form with this question. (30)

(B) Explain the difference between work and employment, giving one example of each. Write your answer in your answer book. (10)

(C) Self-employment (running your own business) has its rewards and also its risks. In your answer book state **two** rewards and **two** risks of self-employment. (20)

(60 marks)

Source: Junior Certificate Ordinary Level.

For use with question on work and employment.

Winton Ltd	**Application for Employment as sales assistant**				
	PERSONAL DETAILS				
Name					
Address					
Date of Birth			Telephone No.		
Marital Status			Nationality		
	EDUCATION				
Primary School		From		To	
Postprimary School		From		To	
Leaving Certificate Year		*Enter Subjects and Grades below*			
	EMPLOYMENT *Please give details of your most recent employment*				
Name of Firm					
Address					
Position Held		From		To	
Reason for Leaving					
	GENERAL INFORMATION				
Please state your interests and hobbies					
Give dates and details of any injury or illness in the last three years					
I certify that, to the best of my knowledge, the above particulars are correct.					
Signed			Date		

Solution to question on work and employment.

Winton Ltd	**Application for Employment as sales assistant**					
	PERSONAL DETAILS					
Name	*Joan Hills*					
Address	*37 High Street, Mullingar*					
Date of Birth	*14/7/89*	Telephone No.	*0506–98755*			
Marital Status	*Single*	Nationality	*Irish*			
	EDUCATION					
Primary School	*Ballymore Primary School*	From	*1994*	To	*2002*	
Postprimary School	*Mullingar Community College*	From	*2002*	To	*2007*	
Leaving Certificate Year	*2007*	*Enter Subjects and Grades below*				
Irish D *Biology E*	*Business B*	*English C*				
French D	*Home Economics C*	*Mathematics D*				
	EMPLOYMENT					
	Please give details of your most recent employment					
Name of Firm	*Regan's Supermarket*					
Address	*Main St, Mullingar*					
Position Held	*Check-out Assistant*	From	*2007*	To	*04/2009*	
Reason for Leaving	*Supermarket closed down*					
	GENERAL INFORMATION *Please state your interests and hobbies*					
Reading, walking and horseriding.						
Give dates and details of any injury or illness in the last three years						
2008 – Broken wrist, horseriding accident						
I certify that, to the best of my knowledge, the above particulars are correct.						
Signed	*Joan Hills*	Date	*31/5/09*			

(B) *Difference between Work and Employment*

Work includes any job you do whether you are paid or not.

Employment is work you are paid for.

Example of Work: Working in the garden at home.

Example of Employment: Working in a supermarket

(C) *Self-Employment*

Rewards
- *You are your own boss*
- *Keep all the profits*

Risks
- *Suffer unlimited liability*
- *May suffer from stress due to long working hours*

Chapter 22 — Being an Employer

A.

RIGHTS OF EMPLOYER	RESPONSIBILITIES OF EMPLOYER
1. To decide on the **objectives** and **policies** of the business. 2. To hire suitable staff. 3. To dismiss dishonest or unsuitable staff. 4. To expect loyalty from staff.	1. To make sure workplace is safe and healthy. 2. To give employees contract of employment in writing. 3. To give statutory holiday entitlements. 4. To pay agreed wages. 5. Not to discriminate when advertising, recruiting or promoting staff. 6. To give female employees maternity leave. 7. To give equal pay to men and women. 8. To deduct PAYE and PRSI from employees and remit it to Collector General of Taxes.

B. Procedure for Employing Staff

(1) Draw up job description.
(2) Advertise the job.
(3) Short-list candidates.
(4) Interview candidates.
(5) Select the most suitable candidate.
(6) Inform the successful candidate.
(7) Prepare a written **contract of employment.**
(8) New employee is **introduced to the firm**. A **period of training** is organised.
(9) New employee supplies a tax credit certificate. New employee is then registered for PAYE and PRSI.

C. Calculating Wages

Employees are paid by time rate, piece rate or on a commission basis.

(1) TIME RATE

Employees are paid a certain rate per hour or per day.

(2) PIECE RATE

Employees' gross pay would depend on output/the number of units produced.

(3) COMMISSION

Calculated as a percentage of the value of sales. This is usually used for paying sales personnel.

Gross Pay = Basic Pay + Overtime + Commission

Net Pay = Gross Pay – Deductions

D. Income Tax Forms

(1) P60

At the end of the tax year each employee receives a P60, which shows amount of pay, tax and PRSI deducted during the tax year.

(2) P45 CESSATION CERTIFICATE

Given to an employee leaving the firm. This shows amount earned and how much tax and PRSI has been paid to date.

(3) P12

This is the taxpayer's income tax return for the year. It also acts as an application form for a tax credit.

E. Wages Slip

When employees are paid they receive their pay plus a payslip. This shows gross pay, deductions and net pay.

Example

Michael Ryan earns a basic wage of €250. He earned €50 overtime. His Tax Credit is €27 per week. His deductions are PAYE 27%, PRSI 10% of gross, union €10 and VHI €15.

Calculate his net wage and complete the payslip.

Solution

Workings:

(i) Calculation of PAYE

Gross wage (€250 + €50) = €300 × 27% = €81
– Tax Credit €27
PAYE = **€54**

(ii) Calculation of PRSI (**N.B.** PRSI is calculated on gross wages)
PRSI = 10% of gross wages = 10% €300 = **€30**

(iii) Total Deductions
PAYE €54 + **PRSI** €30 + **Union** €10 + **VHI** €15 = €109
Total deductions: €109.

(iv) Find Net Pay

Net Pay = Gross Wages – Deductions
€300 – €109 = €191 = Net pay

PAYSLIP

Name	Basic	Pay O/T	Gross	Tax Credit	PAYE	PRSI	Union	VHI	Total Deductions	Net Pay
MICHAEL RYAN	€250	€50	€300	€100	€54	€30	€10	€15	€109	€191

F. Wages Book

The employer will keep a record of all wages/salaries paid in a wages book. From the wages book the employer can calculate the total cost of wages and employer's PRSI. The wages slip is an extract from the wages book.

Example

Wages book of Premier Ltd which employs three people, including Michael Ryan, whose payslip is shown above. Assume employer's rate of PRSI is 12%, employee PRSI 10%, employee PAYE 27%.

WAGES BOOK OF PREMIER LTD

Date	Employee	Basic	O/T	Gross	Tax Credit	PAYE	PRSI	Union	VHI	Total Deductions	Net Pay	Employer PRSI	Total PRSI
20/1/16	Michael Ryan	250	50	300	27	54	30	10	15	109	191	36	66
20/1/16	Mary Lucey	370	30	400	27	81	40	10	20	151	249	48	88
20/1/16	John Murphy	190	10	200	27	27	20	10	12	69	131	24	44
	TOTALS	810	90	900	81	162	90	30	47	329	571	108	198

G. Payment of Wages and Salaries

Wages and salaries may be paid in any one of the following ways:

(1) By cash.

(2) By cheque — safe method of payment.

(3) By credit transfer directly into the bank account of employee (PayPath).

BY CASH

If wages are paid by cash the employer will have to do a cash analysis to show the breakdown of the wages into the various denominations of money required for paying each employee. The following cash analysis will show the exact cash required to pay the three employees of Premier Ltd.

NOTE/COIN ANALYSIS OF PREMIER LTD

NAME	Net Pay	€500	€200	€100	€50	€20	€10	€5	€2	€1	50c	20c	10c	5c	2c	1c
Michael Ryan	191	0	0	1	1	2	0	0	0	1	0	0	0	0	0	0
Mary Lucey	249	0	1	0	0	2	0	1	2	0	0	0	0	0	0	0
John Murphy	131	0	0	1	0	1	1	0	0	1	0	0	0	0	0	0
Total	571	0	1	2	1	5	1	1	2	2	0	0	0	0	0	0

H. Recording the Total Cost of Wages in Books of Premier Ltd

- ➢ Debit wages account. €1,008 | Gross Wages + Employer's PRSI
- ➢ Credit bank account. €1,008 | €900 + €108

Wages Account

		€			€
20.1.16	Bank	1,008	20.1.16	Profit and Loss Account	1,008

Bank Account

					€
			20.1.16	Wages	1,008

Wages account is closed off to the profit and loss account. Figure will appear under expenses.

Profit and Loss Account for week ending 20.1.16

	Expenses		
	Wages	1,008	

I. Employee Records

Employers keep records on all employees.
(1) Personal details.
(2) Job application form.
(3) Curriculum vitae.
(4) Job performance.
(5) Behaviour — absence, lateness, personal days taken.
(6) Copy of contract of employment.
(7) PAYE and PRSI records.

WHY ARE EMPLOYEE RECORDS KEPT?
(1) A reference if an employee leaves.
(2) Promotion decisions.
(3) PAYE and PRSI records are compulsory.

INFORMATION GIVEN ON A CV
(1) Personal details
(2) Educational details
(3) Work experience details
(4) Interests/Hobbies
(5) Referees.

Examination-Style Question and Solution

Question 1.
Answer (a) and (b) and (c). This is a Person at Work Question.

1. (a) Teresa Clancy recently applied for a job advertised as follows in the Sunday newspapers.

MORGAN INSURANCE BROKERS LTD
General Insurance Clerk required

Typing and computer knowledge an advantage.

Basic Pay €312 gross for 39-hour week,
Overtime also a possibility.
Subsidised canteen and travel.
Flexitime

Applications, in writing, should be sent to:

The Human Resources Manager,
Morgan Insurance Brokers Ltd,
Cork Road, Waterford.

Morgan Insurance is an equal opportunities employer.

Explain **any four** of the terms **underlined** in the above advertisement. (16)

1. (b) Teresa Clancy got the job. Last week she worked a total of 48 hours.

➢ Overtime is paid at €12 per hour. Her tax credit is €84 per week. Her rate of tax is 40%, PRSI 10% of gross and her other weekly deductions are union fee €3, VHI €6.

➢ Calculate her net wage and complete the pay slip, using supplied blank at the end of the question (show your workings). (18)

1. (c) State two methods, other than on a time basis, by which an employee can be paid. (6)

Name	Basic	Pay O/T	Gross	Tax Credit	PAYE	PRSI	Union	VHI	Total Deductions	Net Pay
T. Clancy										

Source: Junior Certificate Higher Level. **(40 marks)**

Solution to Question 1.

1. (a) *Basic Pay: Gross pay excluding overtime. Pay for working normal/standard week (usually 39 hours).*
Overtime: Pay for working more than normal hours or for working more than 39 hours a week. Such hours are paid at a rate per hour above the standard rate.
Subsidised: Canteen prices are lower than commercial prices, as the firm is willing to pay part of the cost.
Flexitime: Employees can complete their agreed hours of work at times that suit them.
Human Resources Manager: Person in charge of staff, appointing staff, training staff, staff records.
Equal Opportunities: Job open to both men and women.

1. (b) Document for use with part B.

PAYSLIP

Name	Basic	Pay O/T	Gross	Tax Credit	PAYE	PRSI	Union	VHI	Total Deductions	Net Pay
T. Clancy	*€312*	*€108*	*€420*	*€84*	*€84*	*€42*	*€3*	*€6*	*€135*	*€285*

WORKINGS

Basic pay *€312 for 39 hours*

Overtime *9 hours × €12 per hour = €108*

Gross pay = *Basic pay €312 + O/T €108 = €420*

Tax Credit *€84 per week given in question*

PAYE *is:* *Gross Pay = €420 × 40% = €168*
– Tax Credit = €84
PAYE = €84

PRSI = *10% of gross = €42, union €3, VHI €6 (see question)*

Total deduction = *PAYE + PRSI + union + VHI*
€84 + €42 + €3 + €6 = €135

Net pay = *Gross pay €420 – Deductions €135 = €285.*

1. (c) *Piece rate, commission.*

Chapter 23 — Industrial Relations

A. Introduction

Industrial relations is the term used to describe the relationship between management and employees. If relationships are good, workers will be well motivated, morale and productivity will be high. There will be industrial peace, no strikes and good co-operation between employers and employees. If industrial relations are poor, employees are discontented resulting in poor motivation, absenteeism, high labour turnover and low productivity.

B. What Is a Trade Union?

A trade union is a group of workers who join together to protect their interests and rights and who try to improve their wages and conditions of work.

C. Functions of a Trade Union

(1) To protect the rights of its members.
(2) To negotiate wages and salaries for members.
(3) To negotiate conditions of work.
(4) To negotiate with employers if a dispute occurs.
(5) To protect members from unfair dismissal.
(6) To negotiate in a redundancy situation.

BENEFITS OF JOINING A TRADE UNION

(1) Higher standard of living for members — improved wage rates, improved conditions.
(2) Greater job security if union is powerful.
(3) Increased bargaining power, one voice for all workers.
(4) The benefit of having skilled negotiators on behalf of employees.
(5) Protection against discrimination or unfair treatment.
(6) Support members if in dispute with employer.

D. Types of Trade Union

(1) **Industrial unions** — represent all workers in an industry, e.g. Irish Bank Officials' Association (IBOA).
(2) **Craft unions** — members have a trade or craft, e.g. Brick and Stonelayers' Trade Union.
(3) **White-collar unions** — members are usually professional, e.g. teachers' unions: ASTI, TUI, INTO.
(4) **General unions** — members come from a variety of occupations, e.g. SIPTU (Services, Industrial, Professional and Technical Union).

E. How to Join a Trade Union

(1) Contact shop steward (union representative).

(2) Fill up application form.
(3) Pay annual subscription.

F. Functions of a Shop Steward

(1) Acts as intermediary between union members and union head office.
(2) Represents members.
(3) Recruits new members.
(4) Attends union meetings.
(5) Collects subscriptions.
(6) Communicates information to members from head office.
(7) Communicates workers' problems to union head office.
(8) Discusses and resolves problems with the Human Resource Manager or Supervisor.

G. Irish Congress of Trade Unions (ICTU)

ICTU represents all trade unions. It is the governing body of trade unions. It represents trade unions in negotiations with employers and the government with regard to pay and working conditions.

H. Irish Business Employers' Confederation (IBEC)

IBEC represents all employers in negotiations with trade unions and the government. It gives a voice to members on all aspects of industrial relations.

I. Management Role

This is very important for good industrial relations. The Human Resources manager will deal with the shop steward if a dispute arises.

J. What Is a Dispute?

A dispute is a disagreement between employees and management.

K. Main Causes of Disputes/Strikes

(1) Poor wages and working conditions.
(2) Dismissal of employees.
(3) Employees being made redundant — redundancy payments.
(4) Demarcation disputes — 'who does what?'
(5) Promotion, procedures.
(6) Unfair treatment by management.
(7) Poor relationships between workers and management.

L. Types of Industrial Action (Strikes)

(1) STRIKE

Workers withdraw labour, i.e. refuse to work. There are two types of strike:

(a) Unofficial strike — not approved by trade union.
(b) Official strike — approved by trade union.

(2) ALL-OUT STRIKE

All unions in the firm stop work in support of the union on strike.

(3) WORK TO RULE (i.e. GO SLOW)

Workers go to work but do only the bare essentials.

(4) A 'SIT-IN'

Employees sit in in the premises where they work.

PICKETING

Workers on strike usually **picket** the employer's premises.

M. How to Resolve an Industrial Dispute

The following steps are involved in the resolution of an industrial dispute:

(1) The worker and the supervisor discuss the problem. If there is no solution:

(2) The shop steward and manager discuss the problem. If there is no solution:

(3) A trade union official and manager discuss the problem. If there is no solution:

(4) An acceptable third party, e.g. Labour Relations Commission, attempts to bring both parties together. This is called **conciliation**. If there is no solution:

(5) An acceptable third party such as the Labour Court is asked to make a decision, which the disputing parties usually accept. This is called **arbitration**.

N. Functions of Labour Relations Commission (LRC)

(1) **Conciliation service.** Parties are brought together, and are encouraged to come up with a settlement themselves.

(2) **Advisory service**. LRC offers advice to employers and employees on industrial relations matters.

(3) It appoints **Rights Commissioners**. Investigates disputes concerning individual workers or small groups of workers.

(4) It appoints **Equality Officers**. Investigates disputes on issues of equality and discrimination in the workplace.

O. Labour Court

The Labour Court is a court of last resort to help to settle industrial disputes.
Function of labour court:

- Investigates disputes
- Court of Appeal
- Investigates breaches of codes of practice
- Registers employment agreements.

P. Difference Between Conciliation and Arbitration

Conciliation

- A third party/Labour Relations Commission or mediator brings both sides of a dispute together and helps them find a resolution.
- The proposal of the conciliator is not binding in industrial relations.

Arbitration

- Both parties in a dispute present their case to an independent body/Labour Court, which then recommends a resolution.
- The parties may agree to the recommendation of the arbitrator.
- It is normal for the disputing parties to accept the finding of the arbitrator.

Q. Equality in Employment

(1) It is illegal to discriminate on the grounds of marital status, gender, family status, religious belief, age, disability, race, membership of traveller community, sexual orientation.

(2) There must be equal pay for men and women.

R. National Wage Agreement

This is a pay agreement between the social partners, i.e. ICTU (workers), IBEC (employers) and the government. It is binding on all employers and employees nationally.

S. Business Terms

Arbitrator A person who investigates the dispute and makes a recommendation. It is normal for both parties to accept the finding of the arbitrator.
ASTI Association of Secondary Teachers of Ireland.
Conciliation A service to try to get both parties to solve the dispute themselves.
Craft Union Members have trade or craft.
Demarcation Dispute 'Who Does What' job dispute.
General Union Represents workers from all occupations.
IBEC Irish Business Employers' Confederation — represents employers.
IBOA Irish Bank Officials' Association.
ICTU Irish Congress of Trade Unions — represents all unions in Ireland.
Industrial Relations Relationship between management and employees.
Industrial Union Represents all workers in a particular industry.
INTO Irish National Teachers' Organisation.
Labour Court Court of last resort for solving disputes. Decisions not binding.
Labour Relations Commission Set up to try to settle disputes.
Lightning Strike Sudden stoppage — no warning given.
Lock-Out Employer locks workers out of premises.
Official Strike A strike that union approves.
Overtime Ban Workers refuse to work extra hours.
Picket Workers on strike walking outside business carrying placards.
Promotion Movement to a position of more authority and more responsibility.
Redundancy Workers being 'laid off' — no work.
Token Stoppage Short work stoppage.
Trade Dispute A disagreement between employees and management.
Trade Union Employees join together to protect interests and rights.
TUI Teachers' Union of Ireland.

Union Dues Union subscriptions, i.e. fee paid for union membership.
Unofficial Strike A strike that union does not approve.
White-Collar Unions Professional people who provide services.
Work to Rule Go slow — workers do basic duties only.

SECTION THREE — ENTERPRISE

MARKETING AND DISTRIBUTION

Chapter 24 — Marketing

A. Market

A market is a place where goods are bought and sold.

B. Types of Market

(1) Retail Market — where goods and services are sold to the public.
(2) Wholesale Market — where goods and services are sold to retailers.
(3) Street Market — fruit, vegetables, clothes.
(4) Stock Exchange — where stocks and shares are bought and sold.
(5) Export Market — exporting to other countries.

C. Target Market

The target market is the total number of potential customers for a product or a service, e.g. the target market for Junior Certificate Business Studies Revision Notes is Junior Certificate students studying Business Studies.

D. Market Segmentation

Producing many different models of the same product to satisfy customers.

E. Marketing

Marketing is concerned with all the stages involved in getting the product or service to the final customer.

F. Four 'P's of Marketing/Marketing Mix

(1) Product — Product/service that company offers to the target market. It includes quality and packaging.
(2) Place — This is where the product is available to the target consumers.
(3) Price — Amount of money customer has to pay to obtain the product.
(4) Promotion — This consists of the activities that communicate the merits of the product and persuade the target customer to buy.

To be successful a business must have the **right product** on sale in the **right place** at the **right price** using the **right promotion**.

G. Market Research

Market research involves researching, gathering, recording and analysing information about a market. The main objective is to find out information.

H. Reasons for Market Research

To find out:
(1) Who will buy the product.
(2) What price should be charged.
(3) What methods of advertising should be used.
(4) Best packaging to use.
(5) What competition is in the market.

I. Methods of Collecting Information for Market Research

(1) DESK RESEARCH

This involves researching existing material, e.g. examining business records, looking up suitable internet sites, examining census of population, Central Statistics Office.

(2) FIELD RESEARCH

This involves getting information directly from the customer.
(a) Observation — Researcher watches and records behaviour rather than asking questions.
(b) Questionnaire — Document containing a series of structured questions designed to generate information.
(c) Telephone interview — Researcher telephones the people being surveyed.
(d) Personal interview — Researcher asks questions and records responses.
(e) Panels — Consumer panels provide information about some activity on an ongoing basis.

J. Test Marketing

A new product is tested on a small number of people to find their reaction.

K. Product Development

It is important to **improve existing products** and **develop new products.** If a new product is to be successful, it must be
- ➢ of better quality
- ➢ better value
- ➢ better presented.

FACTORS THAT A BUSINESS SHOULD CONSIDER BEFORE DECIDING TO PRODUCE A NEW PRODUCT

(1) Is there a demand for the product?
(2) Will it be profitable?
(3) What kind of product should it be?
(4) What price should be charged?
(5) How should it be promoted?

(6) In what place should it be sold?
(7) What type of packaging should be used?
(8) What is the target market?
(9) How is it different from/better than competitors' products?

L. Advertising

Advertising is informing consumers about products or services.

M. Aims of Advertising

(1) To give information to consumers.
(2) To persuade consumers to buy.
(3) To launch new products.
(4) To project a good image of the firm.

N. Types of Advertising

(1) **Informative advertising** — giving information to the consumer.
(2) **Persuasive advertising** — trying to convince the consumer.
(3) **Competitive advertising** — comparing with competitors.
(4) **Generic advertising** — industry promotes the product.

O. Advertising Media, i.e. Where to Advertise

(1) Newspapers (Press)
(2) Television
(3) Radio
(4) Posters and Hoardings
(5) Magazines
(6) Cinemas
(7) Trade Fairs and Exhibitions
(8) Leaflets
(9) Window Displays
(10) Vehicle Displays
(11) Shopping Bags
(12) Journals
(13) Internet.

P. Steps Involved in an Advertising Campaign

(1) Identify target market, i.e. potential customers.
(2) Choose medium, e.g. radio, TV.
(3) Decide on the message, e.g. song, slogan, cartoon.
(4) Decide on personnel, e.g. pop star, soccer star.

A good advertisement will:

- ➢ Attract our attention.
- ➢ Provide information.

- ➢ Stay in our memories, e.g. 'Magic Moments' for Quality Street.
- ➢ Create desire.
- ➢ Stimulate action.

Q. Sales Promotion

This is used to back up advertising and the aim is the same — to increase sales. Techniques include:

(1) Free samples
(2) Special offers
(3) Coupons/Tokens
(4) 'Money-Off Vouchers'
(5) In-store promotions
(6) Competitions and draws

R. Selling Techniques

(1) BRANDING

A brand is a name/sign/symbol/design used by a firm to identify its products and distinguish them from other similar products. Examples include Levi's, Reebok, Primark, Cadbury, Tayto and St Bernard.

(2) LOSS LEADERS

Selling products below cost.

(3) TRADE MARKS AND LOGOS

A trade mark is the name given to the product or firm, while a logo is the symbol, which is usually written in a very distinctive style, e.g.

(4) MERCHANDISING

Arranging products on shelves or in display cabinets for maximum impact on the consumer.

S. Public Relations (PR)

Presenting a good image of the company to the public.

DUTIES OF PUBLIC RELATIONS OFFICER

(1) Issuing press releases.
(2) Arranging trade fairs and exhibitions.
(3) Arranging sponsorship.
(4) Arranging radio and TV coverage of events.
(5) Organising company literature for employees and the public.

T. Sponsorship

Many firms sponsor major events or sports teams. For example, Eircom sponsors the Irish international soccer team, Vodaphone — Manchester United FC.

U. Export Markets

Exports are essential if Irish firms are to survive and expand.
Difficulties in Exporting
(1) Language.
(2) Currency.
(3) Documentation.
(4) Transport costs.
(5) Risk of non-payment is very great.

Recording the payment of advertising in the books of the Business

Example: A payment of €10,000 was made by cheque for advertising on 31/12/16

Bank A/C

					€
			31/12/16	Advertising	10,000

Advertising A/C

		€			€
31/12/16	Bank	10,000	31/12/16	Profit & loss a/c	10,000

The figure for €10,000 advertising will appear under Expenses in the Profit and Loss Account.

Profit and Loss Account for year ending 31/12/16

			€
	Expenses Advertising		10,000

V. Business Terms

Branded Goods Well-known goods easily identifiable by customers.
Consumer Panel Group of consumers who give reaction to a product.
Desk Research Looking up materials already in files.
Field Research Obtaining information directly from consumers.
Import Substitution Replacing imported product with Irish-made product.
In-Store Promotion Customers taste a product in large stores.
Logo Distinctive style of writing a firm's name.
Loss Leader Selling a product at a loss to attract customers.
Market A place where goods are bought and sold.
Market Research Gathering and recording information about a market.
Market Segmentation Dividing market into different segments.

Marketing All stages in getting product to the consumer.
Marketing Mix Four Ps of marketing: product, place, price, promotion.
PRO Public Relations Officer.
Product Development Updating and improving existing products and developing new products.
Product Life Cycle Different stages that sales of a product go through.
Sales Promotion Methods other than advertising used to promote products.
Sampling Researching a number of people representative of the whole market.
Sponsorship Where a firm finances an event or team.
TAM Ratings Television Audience Measurement.
Target Market Total number of potential customers for a product.
Test Marketing Testing a product on a few customers.
Trade Mark A name that a firm uses on its products.

Examination-Style Question and Solution

Question 1.

Fitzwear Ltd is a wholesale firm selling fashion clothes for the teenage and early twenties market to shops throughout Ireland. Fitzwear Ltd divides the country into the five regions shown in the table below:

	Total	Dublin	Rest of Leinster	Munster	Connaught	Ulster
2013	€200,000	€70,000	€30,000	€40,000	€20,000	€40,000
2014	€230,000	€50,000	€40,000	€60,000	€30,000	€50,000

The Managing Director, Ms S. Fitzgerald, has stated that she is disappointed with the Dublin sales figures for 2014 and that she has not enough information on this market.

1. (a) Identify the target market for Fitzwear's products from the information above. (3)
1. (b) Give two reasons why the company divides the country into regions. (6)
1. (c) On graph paper prepare a bar chart illustrating the table above for the two years. (13)
1. (d) Give two reasons why you think the Managing Director is disappointed with the Dublin sales figures for 2014. (4)
1. (e) Assume you are T. Delany, sales manager of the company. Write a report to the Managing Director on 3/1/2015 about the Dublin market, indicating:
(i) How more information could be obtained about this market, and
(ii) Three suitable methods for promoting the products. (14)

Source: Junior Certificate Higher Level. **(40 marks)**

Solution to Question 1.

1. (a) *Target market — teenagers and people in their early twenties.*

1. (b) Why Divide Country into Regions?

(i) *Sales representatives can be assigned to a region and they will get to know the area and its needs well.*

(ii) *Problem areas can be easily identified and catered for.*

(iii) *You can set up warehouses in each region, thus making distribution easier.*

1. (c) Bar Chart

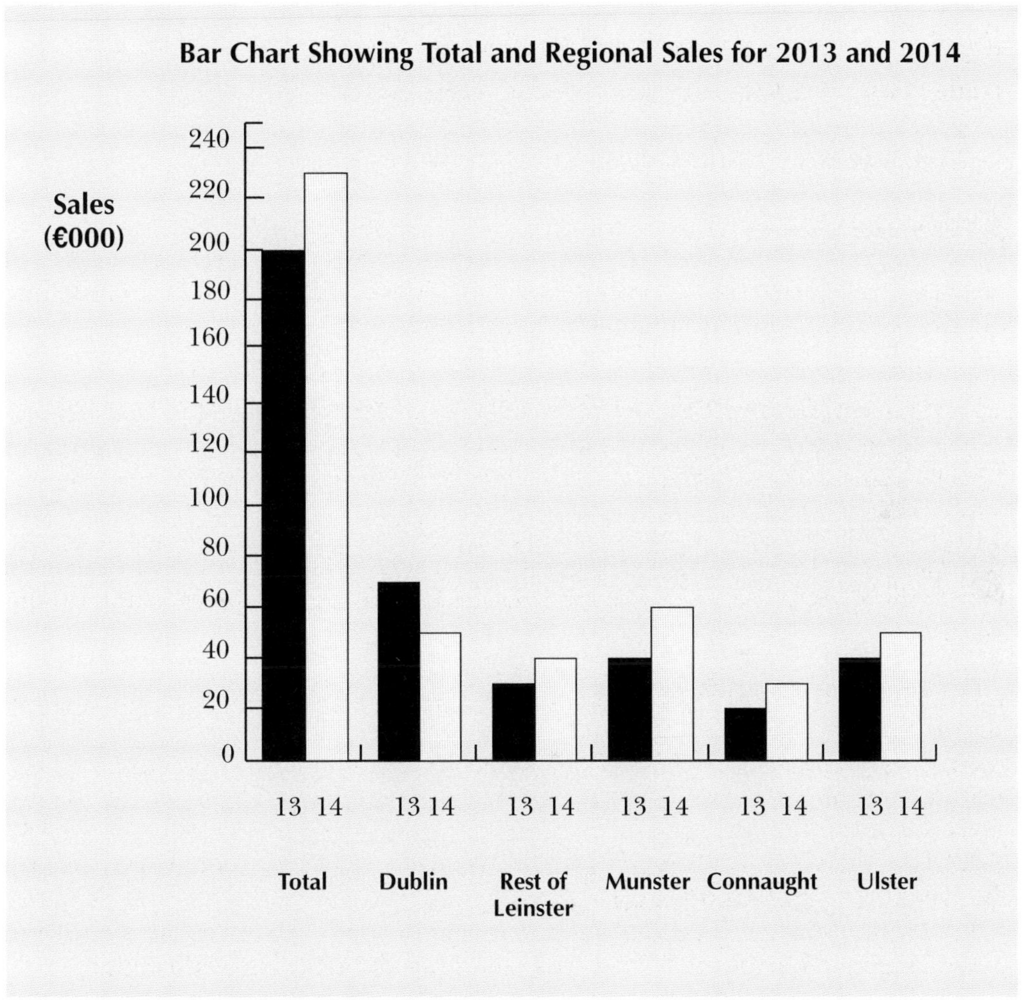

1. (d) Reasons Why Managing Director is Disappointed with Dublin Sales Figures

(i) *Sales in Dublin have fallen in 2014.*

(ii) *This has taken place in the context of an overall increase in sales and an increase in all other regions in 2014.*

1. (e) Report from Sales Manager to Managing Director on the Dublin Market

To: *Managing Director, Ms S. Fitzgerald*

Introduction

I was asked by the Managing Director to prepare a report on the Dublin region indicating

(i) How more information could be obtained about this market, and

(ii) Three suitable methods for promoting the products.

Body of Report

I have spent a number of weeks researching this market and I enclose my findings below.

(a) *Fitzwear can get more information about the market using the following methods:*

(i) Questionnaires
(ii) Observation
(iii) Telephone interviews
(iv) Personal interviews
(v) Panels
(vi) Desk research

This market research should provide the company with the following information:

(i) The target market.
(ii) The price to charge.
(iii) The competition in the market.
(iv) The best method of advertising to use.

(b) *The following methods should be used to promote the products:*

(i) Local radio advertising.
(ii) Organising a fashion show.
(iii) Advertising in a fashion magazine.

I am available to discuss any of these points when required.

Signed

T. Delany
Sales Manager
3 January 2015

Chapter 25 — Delivery Systems

A. Importance of Delivery in the Chain of Distribution

A good efficient delivery system is important to business.

(1) To deliver raw materials to the manufacturer.
(2) To deliver finished goods.
(3) To transport workers to their jobs.
(4) To transport goods abroad.

B. Factors to Be Considered When Choosing a Delivery System

(1) Cost — Cost of different transport systems adds to the price of the goods.
(2) Reliability — System chosen must be reliable and punctual.
(3) Speed — Speed of delivery is an important factor especially for perishables or something urgently required.
(4) Safety — Important for valuable goods and people.
(5) Distance — Distance between buyer and seller will be an important factor in choosing a delivery system.
(6) Type of goods — will influence the delivery system chosen. Is the product perishable, bulky or fragile?

C. Types of Delivery System

The following are the main types of delivery system used in Ireland.

TYPES	ADVANTAGES	DISADVANTAGES
ROAD	1. Fast over short distances 2. Door-to-door deliveries 3. Minimum handling 4. Flexible, convenient and cheap	1. Congestion/Poor roads — delays 2. Bad weather — delays 3. Not suitable for bulky goods 4. Slow over long distances
RAIL	1. Fast over long distances 2. Suitable for bulky goods 3. Reliable 4. Cheap for bulky goods	1. Not flexible — fixed timetable 2. Lot of handling 3. Fixed routes 4. Expensive over short distances
SEA	1. Suitable for bulky goods 2. Cheaper than air 3. Suitable for containers 4. Good facilities at ports 5. Modern ships — large loads	1. Slow over long distances 2. Weather conditions — delays 3. Not flexible — fixed timetable 4. Must link with other forms of transport 5. High insurance costs
AIR	1. Fast 2. Suitable for expensive goods 3. Good safety record 4. Less packing — reduced cost 5. Modern aircraft — large loads	1. Expensive 2. Bad weather — delays 3. Must link with other forms of transport 4. Not flexible — fixed timetable 5. Not suitable for bulky goods
PIPELINE	1. Safe 2. Cheap to maintain	1. Expensive to install 2. Suitable only for liquids or gases

D. Modern Developments in Delivery Systems

A. ROAD TRANSPORT DEVELOPMENTS

(1) Motorways/Dual Carriageways/Ring Roads

These have been constructed around our major towns and cities, mainly with EU funding.

(2) Toll Roads/Toll Bridges

Built by private firms that charge a fee.

(3) Quality bus corridors and cycle lanes

Special lanes that buses and cyclists can use have been provided in major cities.

(4) Dublin Port Tunnel

This tunnel allows heavy transport to bypass Dublin city on their journey to Dublin Port.

(5) Metric speed limits

In January 2005, speed limits changed from Mph to Kph (metric), improving safety.

B. RAIL TRANSPORT DEVELOPMENTS

An Luas – The Light Rail system in Dublin.

C. SEA TRANSPORT DEVELOPMENTS

The introduction of high speed ferries.

D. AIR TRANSPORT DEVELOPMENTS

1. New terminal at Cork airport.
2. Plans to build a second terminal at Dublin airport.

E. Calculating Delivery Time

When calculating delivery time we must:

(1) Work out distance involved (use a distance table).
(2) Calculate average speed of vehicle (km per hour).
(3) Allow for stopovers, traffic delays and time for loading and unloading.

Formula for Calculating Time

$$\frac{\text{Distance}}{\text{Average Speed per Hour (km)}}$$

Examination-Style Question and Solution

Question 1.

Look at the distance table and answer the following questions:

1. (a) How many kilometres from Tralee to Limerick?

Distance Table (km)

Dundalk									
256	Ennis								
238	70	Galway							
240	37	105	Limerick						
92	16	144	148	Mullingar					
246	246	274	210	204	Rosslare				
168	195	138	232	135	326	Sligo			
346	94	162	105	254	290	288	Tralee		
242	164	220	130	170	82	292	210	Waterford	
118	228	254	190	185	19	306	275	62	Wexford

1. (b) How long would it take for a lorry to travel from Galway to Waterford at an average speed of 44 kilometres per hour? **(5)**

Source: Junior Certificate Ordinary Level.

Solution to Question 1.

1. (a) *105 km.*

1. (b) $\text{Time} = \frac{\text{Distance}}{\text{Av. speed}} = \frac{220 \text{ km}}{44} = 5 \text{ hrs}$

F. Calculating Delivery Costs

As delivery expenses increase the cost of the goods, it is important to choose the cheapest method of transport. It is also important to be able to calculate the cost of delivery accurately. Cost of delivery will depend on whether:

(1) Firm uses its own vehicles

OR

(2) Firm uses a courier.

(1) FIRM USES OWN VEHICLES

When using own vehicles there are two costs involved.

Fixed costs must be paid no matter how much the vehicle is used and must be divided out over each day the vehicle is used in the year, e.g. maintenance, road tax, vehicle insurance.

Variable costs vary with the usage of the vehicle and are associated with a particular delivery, e.g. petrol/diesel, wages.

REASONS WHY A BUSINESS MIGHT USE ITS OWN FLEET OF DELIVERY VANS

(1) Transport is available when required — flexibility.
(2) Vehicles can be used for advertising.
(3) Business not affected by a strike of transport hauliers or of Iarnrod Éireann.
(4) Return load can be collected.
(5) It is not confined to a fixed timetable.
(6) It can be cheaper in the long term than hiring outside transport.
(7) It is more secure and requires less handling of the goods.

Sample Question and Solution on Cost of Delivery

Question

Calculate the total cost of a journey from Cork to Dublin and back to Cork from the following data:

- Distance from Cork to Dublin 260 km.
- Diesel van will do 10 km per litre of diesel.
- Cost of diesel is €1 per litre.
- Van driver's wages are €100 a day.
- Annual van tax is €250.
- Annual van insurance is €750.
- Annual repairs €500.
- The company operates 250 days in the year.

Solution — Cost of Delivery Calculation.

	Total distance		*260 km × 2 (return journey)*	=	*520 km*
	Number of litres used		$\frac{520}{10}$	=	*52 litres*
Variable Costs	*Cost of diesel*	=	*52 litres × €1*	=	*€52*
	Driver's wages			=	*€100*
Fixed Costs	*Motor tax per day*	=	$\frac{€250}{250 \text{ days}}$	=	*€1*
	Insurance per day	=	$\frac{€750}{250 \text{ days}}$	=	*€3*
	Repairs per day	=	$\frac{€500}{250 \text{ days}}$	=	*€2*
	Total cost of delivery			=	*€158*

Recording the total cost of delivery in the books of the business.

Assume cost is €158 × 250 days = €39,500

Bank Account

					€
			31/12/16	Delivery/carriage out	39,500

Delivery /carriage out A/C

		€			€
31/12/16	Bank	39,500	31/12/16	Profit & Loss account	39,500

The figure of €39,500 delivery expenses will appear under Expenses in the Profit and Loss A/C.

Profit and Loss account for year ending 31/12/16

			€
	Expenses Delivery Expenses		39,500

(2) FIRM USES A COURIER

A pharmacy needs to send a small parcel of 10 kgs urgently from Dublin to New Ross. It wishes to use a courier. DHL International quotes the following collection fee and fee per kilogram (kg):

	Dublin	Rest of Leinster
Collection Fee	€50	€60
Fee per Kg	€1	€1.10

Courier Cost	Collection fee	= €50
	Fee per kg €1 × 10 kgs	= €10
	Cost of courier delivery	= €60

G. Business Terms

C & F — Carriage and Freight Price quoted includes all costs to the port of destination — except insurance.

Chartering Renting/Hiring a ship for a specific journey or a specific time.

CIF — Carriage Insurance Freight Price quoted includes all costs to the port of destination.

Coastal Shipping Transports goods around coast from one port to another.

Containers A container is a large metal box into which goods are packed. The container is sealed and loaded onto the mode of transport being used.

Couriers Will deliver fast for a fee, e.g. An Post — SDS; Irish Rail — Fastrack; DHL International.

DART — Dublin Area Rapid Transport.

Euro-tunnel Links England and France underground. High speed trains operate regularly, linking England with mainland Europe.

Ex-Works Price quoted assumes buyer must collect the goods from seller's premises. All costs of transport must be paid for by the buyer.

FAS — Free Alongside Ship Price quoted includes delivery as far as ship.

Ferries Carry passengers and vehicles.

FOB — Free On Board Price quoted includes delivery as far as ship plus loading.

Juggernaut Articulated truck.

Liner Carries passengers and cargo — travels on a fixed route.

Lo-Lo — Lift-On Lift-Off Containers on ships or trucks.

LUAS — The light-rail system in Dublin.

Pallets Pallets are wooden platforms for moving heavy goods.

Pipeline Used to transport water, gas, oil, sewage.

Refrigerated Truck A truck with cold-storage facilities.

Rent-a-Van A business can rent a van or truck for a period of time for a fee.

Road Tax Money paid by vehicle owners to government for upkeep of roads.

Ro-Ro — Roll-On Roll-Off Ferry service.

Ryanair Privately owned Irish airline.

Specialised ships Built to carry specific cargo, e.g. oil tanker.

Tramp Ship No fixed timetable or route.

Tachograph A small device attached to commercial vehicles, it records (a) Distance; (b) Speed; (c) Time. A driver cannot drive more than four hours continuously or more than eight hours per day.

Examination-Style Question and Solution

Question 1.

Answer all sections. This is a Distribution of Goods/Cost of Transport Question.

1. (a) The wholesaler plays an important role in the distribution of goods.
State three services the wholesaler provides to the manufacturer and three services the wholesaler provides to the retailer. (12)

1. (b) Transport is very important in the distribution of goods.
List four factors a business should take into account when deciding on what type of transport to use. (8)

1. (c) (i) Murphy Electric Ltd asks you to calculate the total cost of a journey from Galway to Dublin and back again to Galway from the following data:

- ➢ The distance from Galway to Dublin is 216 km.
- ➢ Their diesel van can do 8 km per litre of diesel.
- ➢ The cost of diesel is 45c per litre.
- ➢ The van driver's wages are €60 per day.
- ➢ The Annual Motor Tax is €450.
- ➢ The Annual Motor Insurance is €925.
- ➢ The Annual Repairs are €625.
- ➢ The company operates 250 working days in the year. (14)

(ii) The invoice value of the goods delivered to Dublin is €18,460. Express the total cost of the return journey as a percentage of this figure. (3)
(iii) Give one reason why it is important to know this percentage. (3)

Source: Junior Certificate Higher Level. **(40 marks)**

Solution to Question 1.

1. (a) Services Wholesaler Provides to Manufacturer

(i) Buys in bulk from manufacturer.
(ii) Stores the goods until they are sold.
(iii) Advises manufacturer of the opinions of retailers about the products.

Services Wholesaler Provides to Retailer

(i) Sells goods in small quantities to retailer.
(ii) Gives credit to retailer.
(iii) Provides a delivery service to retailer.
(iv) Provides retailer with a wide variety of goods.

1. (b) Four Factors in Deciding on Type of Transport

(i) Cost
(ii) Reliability
(iii) Speed
(iv) Safety
(v) Distance
(vi) Type of goods

1. (c) (i) Cost of Delivery Calculation

	° *Total distance (216 km × 2)*		=	*432 km*
	° *Number of litres of diesel used*	$\frac{432}{8}$	=	*54 litres*
Variable Costs	° *Cost of diesel*	*54 litres × 45c*	=	*€24.30*
	° *Wages*		=	*€60*
Fixed Costs	° *Motor tax per day*	$\frac{€450}{250\ days}$	=	*€1.80*
	° *Insurance per day*	$\frac{€925}{250\ days}$	=	*€3.70*
	° *Repairs per day*	$\frac{€625}{250\ days}$	=	*€2.50*
	Total cost of delivery		=	*€92.30*

(ii) Cost of Delivery as a Percentage of Value of Goods Delivered

Formula = $\frac{\text{Cost of Delivery} \times 100}{\text{Value of Goods Delivered}} = \frac{€92.30 \times 100}{€18,460} = 0.5\%$

(iii) Reason Why It Is Important to Know This Percentage

It costs 0.5% of the value of the goods to deliver the goods. Other methods of transporting the goods should be looked at to find out whether they could be delivered more cheaply.

BUSINESS TRANSACTIONS AND BUSINESS DOCUMENTS

Chapter 26 — Purchases and Sales

1. PURCHASES

A. Effective Purchasing

Purchasing the **right goods** in the **right quantity** at the **right price** at the **correct time**.

B. Enquiring About Goods and Services

When suitable suppliers are identified, contact can be made by letter, telephone, fax or personal call. A number of suppliers may be contacted with **an enquiry** about prices, quality, delivery terms, discount terms and payment terms. Most suppliers will reply by means of **a quotation** and on comparing these a decision can be made from which company to **order** the goods.

C. Prices

(1) Price list — a list of all goods and their price.
(2) Catalogue — a book containing details and descriptions of all goods for sale.
(3) Quotation — contains details about the price at which the seller is prepared to supply his goods.

D. Delivery Terms

(1) Carriage paid — price quoted includes all transport costs (paid by seller).
(2) Ex-works/Ex-factory — buyer pays for delivery.
(3) Free on rail — price quoted includes delivery of goods by the seller to the nearest railway station.

E. Discount Terms

(1) TRADE DISCOUNT

Discount given by the seller to the buyer off the list price of the goods to enable the buyer to make a profit when he resells the goods. Trade discount is deducted on the invoice.

(2) CASH DISCOUNT

Discount given to the buyer to encourage him to pay promptly.

F. Payment Terms

(1) CWO (Cash With Order) — customer must pay when ordering.
(2) COD (Cash On Delivery) — customer must pay on delivery.

G. VAT — Value Added Tax

VAT is a tax on goods and services sold. Businesses with a certain turnover must register for VAT. They will pay VAT on their purchases and must charge VAT on their sales.

2. SALES

A. Selling on Credit

A credit sale is where goods are sold and the customer pays for them at a later date.

WAYS OF CHECKING THE CREDIT RATING OF A NEW CUSTOMER BEFORE SELLING ON CREDIT

(1) Get credit reference from customer's bank.
(2) Get credit reference from previous suppliers.
(3) Get our bank to check with customer's bank.
(4) Get sales personnel to check customer.
(5) Get credit agency to check customer.
(6) Look up *Stubbs Gazette.*

B. Stock Control (Higher Level)

It is very important for a business to have the correct level of stock at all times. This is the optimum stock level.

OVERSTOCKING COSTS	UNDERSTOCKING COSTS
1. Cash tied up. 2. More storage space required. 3. Higher insurance costs. 4. More security staff required. 5. Risk of pilferage. 6. Risk of stock becoming obsolete.	1. Loss of orders. 2. Loss of sales. 3. Loss of customers. 4. Loss of profit.

To ensure that a firm has always the correct amount of stock, it is important to have a proper stock control system.

SETTING UP A STOCK CONTROL SYSTEM

(1) Code every item in stock.
(2) Decide the correct level of stock for each item.
(3) Develop a method of recording stock.
(4) Carry out regular stocktaking.

C. Computerised Stock Control

When a business is computerised, the computer will give an automatic update on stock position. Each time a product is sold the bar code on the product is passed over a scanner and the stock count of the product is reduced by one.

D. Mark-Up and Margin (Higher Level)

The aim of being in business is to make a profit. A business will buy goods at cost and add on its profit to give the selling price.

COST + PROFIT = SELLING PRICE

Mark-up and margin are expressed as percentages.

Example Cost price €100 Selling price €120 ∴ Profit = €20

Mark-up — Profit expressed as a percentage of cost.

$$\text{Mark-Up} = \frac{\text{Profit x 100\%}}{\text{Cost Price}} = \frac{\text{€20 x 100\%}}{\text{€100}} = 20\%$$

Margin — Profit expressed as a percentage of selling price.

$$\text{Margin} = \frac{\text{Profit x 100\%}}{\text{Selling Price}} = \frac{\text{€20 x 100\%}}{\text{€120}} = 16.66\%$$

E. Filing

Filing is the storing of documents so that they can be easily and quickly found when required. There are many methods of filing. The most common are alphabetical and numerical.

(1) ALPHABETICAL

This is where the customer files are arranged in the filing cabinet in alphabetical order. Steel cabinets are used. A folder is used for each customer and the name of the customer is written on a tab.

(2) NUMERICAL

Each customer file is given a number rather than the customer name. Files are arranged in the filing cabinet in numerical sequence. A card index system showing each customer's name and address and file number is used in conjunction with numerical filing.

It is very important to file all business documents carefully, so that they can be found when needed.

Examination-Style Questions and Solutions

Question 1.
Given a cost price of €40 and a selling price of €45.60, calculate the percentage mark-up. (4)

Solution to Question 1.

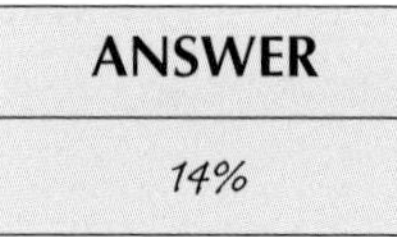

ANSWER
14%

Workings

$$\text{Mark-Up} = \frac{\text{Profit} \times 100}{\text{Cost Price}} = \frac{€5.60 \times 100}{€40.00} = 14\%$$

Source: Junior Certificate Higher Level.

Question 2.
Given a buying price of €50 and a selling price of €60, calculate the percentage profit 'margin'. (4)

Solution to Question 2.

ANSWER
16.66%

Workings

$$\text{Profit Margin} = \frac{\text{Profit} \times 100}{\text{Selling Price}} = \frac{€10 \times 100}{€60.00} = 16.66\%$$

Source: Junior Certificate Higher Level.

Chapter 27 — Business Letters / Report Writing

Business letters are an important form of communication. A letter will reveal what a business is like. A good business letter should be accurate, brief and clear.

Examination-Style Question and Solution

Question 1.
This question is about writing a Letter.
(To be completed in your Answer Book.)

Sarah McKenna is Treasurer of Fairways Golf Club, Links Road, Cork. The annual subscription for members is €1,000. On 20 April 2014 she received a cheque for €300 from Jack Palmer, one of the members, who lives at 29 Salt Road, Mallow. Mr Palmer stated that he would pay the rest of the annual subscription in September.

Sarah immediately wrote a letter to Mr Palmer, thanking him for the €300 and enclosing a Receipt. In the letter, she pointed out that the Golf Club was not in a position to wait until September for the rest of his annual subscription, as this would not be fair to all the other members who had already paid in full. She also stated that, according to the rules, anyone whose full annual subscription was not paid by 1 May would no longer be a member of the club. She hoped that Mr Palmer would forward the balance due before that date.

1. (a) Assume you are Sarah McKenna. Write the letter that Sarah sent to Mr Jack Palmer.

Source: Junior Certificate Ordinary Level. **(45)**

Solution to Question 1. **LETTER**

[1] Fairways Golf Club
Links Road
Cork

Tel (021) 926311

[2] 20 April 2014

[3] Mr Jack Palmer
29 Salt Road
Mallow

[4] Re: Annual Subscription

[5] Dear Mr Palmer

[7] **[6]** I wish to **thank you for your cheque** of €300, for which a receipt is enclosed. Unfortunately, the Golf Club **is not in a position to wait until September for the rest of your annual subscription**, as this would not be fair to all the other members who have paid in full.

According to the rules, **anyone whose full subscription is not paid before the first of May will cease to be a member** of this club.

[8] I hope you can **forward the balance due of €700** before that date.

[9] Yours sincerely

[10] Sarah McKenna
Treasurer.

[11] ENC 1

LAYOUT OF A BUSINESS LETTER

[1] Address of sender — This is printed information on the top of company or club notepaper as follows:

Full name and address of company or club, telephone number, fax number and VAT number.

[2] Date — The most acceptable order for the date in a business letter is day, month, year.

[3] Inside address — This is the person to whom the letter is addressed.

[4] Re — Regarding — This outlines what the letter is about.

[5] Salutation — This is the greeting with which every letter begins, i.e. Dear Sir, Dear Madam.

[6] Introduction — If the letter is a reply to a letter received thank the writer and briefly mention the subject-matter (state what the letter is about).

[7] Body of the Letter — The body of the letter should be written in clear concise English. It should be divided into paragraphs.

[8] Follow-up — Stating what should happen next.

[9] Complimentary Close — This is the ending of a business letter and must match the salutation. The most used are Yours faithfully/Yours truly, Yours sincerely.

[10] Signature and position/Title of letter writer

[11] Enc — Enclosures 1 — This shows that something else has been enclosed with the letter, e.g. receipt, and the number of items.

WHAT MARKS ARE AWARDED FOR IN BUSINESS LETTERS

(1) Format/Layout — Address of sender, date, inside address, salutation, Yours sincerely, signature, regarding, enclosures.
(2) Content/Body of Letter — Generally four points of information are required as bold underlined in the solution.
(3) English — Marks are awarded for paragraphs, punctuation, grammar, spelling.
(4) Presentation/Neatness — Marks will be awarded for a well-presented and neat letter.

LAYOUT OF A REPORT

1. Title of report
2. Address of report writer
3. Date
4. Who the report is for
5. Introduction — reasons for report and how the information was collected
6. Main body of report — conclusions and recommendations
7. Follow-up — report writer available to discuss report
8. Signature of report writer
9. Position/Title of report writer
   (see reports on pages 170, 257, 291, 303 and 309)

Chapter 28 — Business Transactions and Business Documents

A. Cash Transaction

A cash transaction is where goods are purchased and payment is made at the time of purchase either by cash or by cheque.

B. Credit Transaction

A credit transaction is where goods are purchased and payment is made at a later date.

C. Business Documents

Business documents are a very efficient way of putting business transactions on paper. They give both the buyer and the seller a written record of the transaction.

(1) LETTER OF ENQUIRY

A letter of enquiry is sent to a supplier enquiring about the prices, terms and conditions under which he is prepared to supply his goods.

SAMPLE TRANSACTION

Murphy TV, Hi-Fi & Video Ltd wish to enquire about electrical equipment from Panasonic Ireland Ltd.

LETTER OF ENQUIRY

Murphy TV, Hi-Fi & Video Ltd
10 Princess Street — Cork

Tel (021) 639425
Fax (021) 639426

VAT Reg. No.: 258364X

Panasonic Ireland Ltd
Sandyford Industrial Est.
Dublin 18

10 May 2016

Dear Sir or Madam

Please send me a quotation for the following goods:

50 Panasonic 21″ Nicam Stereo TVs
50 Panasonic HD Nicam Videos
50 Panasonic Mini Hi-Fi Systems

Yours sincerely

John Murphy

Purchasing Director

N.B. Murphy TV, Hi-Fi & Video Ltd may send letters of enquiry to a few different suppliers.

(2) QUOTATION

A quotation is a document from a supplier stating the prices and the details of discounts, delivery and VAT. The following is the quotation sent by Panasonic Ireland Ltd.

QUOTATION No. 205

PANASONIC IRELAND LTD
Sandyford Industrial Est.
Dublin 18

Tel (01) 9986241 Vat. Reg. No. 924651N
Fax (01) 9986242

Murphy TV, Hi-Fi & Video Ltd
10 Princess Street
Cork

13 May 2016

Dear Sir

Thank you for your enquiry. Our quotation is as follows:

Quantity	Description	Unit Price	Delivery
50	Panasonic 21″ Nicam Stereo TVs	€499	Ready
50	Panasonic HD Nicam Videos	€459	Ready
50	Panasonic Mini Hi-Fi Systems	€279	Ready

Yours sincerely

Gary Richards

Sales Director

TERMS OF SALE:
VAT 20% on all models. Trade Discount 10%. Carriage Paid.

This quotation will be compared with other quotations before a supplier is decided on.

(3) ORDER

An order is a document sent by the buyer ordering the goods required.

ORDER No. 648

Murphy TV, Hi-Fi & Video Ltd
10 Princess Street
Cork

Tel (021) 639425 **Vat Reg. No.: 258364X**
Fax (021) 639426

Panasonic Ireland Ltd
Sandyford Industrial Est.
Dublin 18

17 May 2016

Please supply the following goods:

Quantity	Description	Unit Price
50	Panasonic 21″ Nicam Stereo TVs	€499
50	Panasonic HD Nicam Videos	€449
50	Panasonic Mini Hi-Fi Systems	€279

Signed *John Murphy*

Purchasing Director

Treatment of incoming orders

(a) Date-stamp order.
(b) Get goods ready for delivery.
(c) Send order to office for preparation of invoice and delivery docket.
(d) File order.

(4) DELIVERY NOTE

When the goods are delivered, the buyer will sign the delivery docket. It gives a list of the goods delivered. If any goods are missing or damaged, it should be noted on the delivery docket. It is made out in duplicate, one copy given to the buyer and the second copy kept by seller as proof of delivery.

The goods were delivered to Murphy TV, Hi-Fi & Video Ltd on 20 May 2016.

DELIVERY NOTE **No. 74**

PANASONIC IRELAND LTD
Sandyford Industrial Est.
Dublin 18

Tel (01) 9986241 **VAT Reg. No.** 924651N
Fax (01) 9986242

Murphy TV, Hi-Fi & Video Ltd
10 Princess Street
Cork

20 May 2016

Quantity	Description
50	Panasonic 21″ Nicam Stereo TVs
50	Panasonic HD Nicam Videos
50	Panasonic Mini Hi-Fi Systems

Received the above goods in perfect condition.

Signed: *John Murphy*

Purchasing Director

Treatment of incoming delivery dockets

(a) The delivery note should be checked against the order to ensure that the goods received were ordered.

(b) The delivery note should be carefully filed so that it can be checked against the invoice when it arrives.

Treatment of outgoing delivery dockets

(a) Check that the name and address of the buyer are correct.
(b) Check details as per order or invoice.
(c) File copy of delivery docket, or record on computer.
(d) Ensure that the delivery docket is signed by the recipient of the goods.

(5) INVOICE

An invoice is sent from the seller to the buyer. It is the bill for the goods. It shows the quantity, description and price of the goods, details of trade discount and VAT and the total due to the seller.

The invoice is the source document for recording credit sales and credit purchases.

(a) The **seller** writes up his **Sales Day Book** from **invoices sent**.
(b) The buyer writes up his **Purchases Day Book** from **invoices received**.

The invoice received will be checked against the delivery docket to make sure that the buyer received what he is being charged for.

What Seller Should Do Before Sending Invoices/Treatment of Outgoing Invoices
1. Compare prices with the quotation given. 2. Check calculations for accuracy. 3. Check address of customer. 4. Write up sales day book. 5. File a copy of invoice.
What Buyer Should Do on Receiving Invoices/Treatment of Incoming Invoices 1. Compare with order and delivery docket. 2. Check accuracy of prices and calculations. 3. Write up purchases day book. 4. Post to the creditors ledger. 5. File invoice.

The following invoice was sent by Panasonic Ireland Ltd to Murphy TV, Hi-Fi & Video Ltd on 21 May 2016. (See p. 191.)

INVOICE **No. 61**

PANASONIC IRELAND LTD
Sandyford Industrial Est.
Dublin 18

Tel (01) 9986241
Fax (01) 9986242 **VAT Reg. No.** 924651N

21 May 2016

Murphy TV, Hi-Fi & Video Ltd
10 Princess Street
Cork

Quantity	Description	Unit Price	Total (Ex. VAT)
50	Panasonic 21″ Nicam Stereo TVs	€499	€24,950
50	Panasonic HD Nicam Videos	€449	€22,450
50	Panasonic Mini Hi-Fi Systems	€279	€13,950
	Total (ex. VAT)		€61,350
	Less Trade Discount 10%		€6,135
			€55,215
	Add VAT 21%		€11,043
	Total Due		€66,258

Terms of Sale:
Carriage paid.

E & O E

NOTES

(i) The design and layout of invoices may vary.

(ii) E & O E means Errors and Omissions Excepted. This gives the seller the right to correct any errors discovered later.

(iii) On the invoice always deduct the trade discount before adding VAT.

RECORDING INVOICES SENT IN THE SALES DAY BOOK OF SELLER

Books of Panasonic Ireland Ltd (Seller)

SALES DAY BOOK

Date	Details	Inv. No.	Fo	Net	VAT	Total
21/5/16	Murphy TV, Hi-Fi & Video Ltd	61		€55,215	€11,043	€66,258

RECORDING INVOICES RECEIVED IN PURCHASES DAY BOOK OF BUYER

Books of Murphy TV, Hi-Fi & Video Ltd (Buyer)

PURCHASES DAY BOOK

Date	Details	Inv. No.	Fo	Net	VAT	Total
21/5/16	Panasonic Ireland Ltd	61		€55,215	€11,043	€66,258

(6) DEBIT NOTE

A debit note is sent from seller to buyer if

(a) The seller **undercharged** the buyer on the invoice.
(b) The seller **omitted some items** from the invoice.

NB The debit note increases the amount of money buyer owes seller.

If we compare the quotation and the invoice we will see that Panasonic Ireland Ltd **undercharged** Murphy TV, Hi-Fi and Video Ltd by €10 each on the 50 Panasonic HD Nicam Videos (quoted price €459, invoice price €449).

A debit note is issued by Panasonic Ireland Ltd to the buyer as follows.

DEBIT NOTE **No. 104**

PANASONIC IRELAND LTD
Sandyford Industrial Est.
Dublin 18

Tel (01) 9986241
Fax (01) 9986242

VAT Reg. No. 924651N

22 May 2016

Murphy TV, Hi-Fi & Video Ltd
10 Princess Street
Cork

Quantity	Description	Unit Price	Total (Ex. VAT)
50	Panasonic HD Nicam Videos Less Trade Discount 10%	€10	€500 €50
			€450
	Add VAT 20%		€90
	Total Additional Amount Due:		€540

Undercharge on Invoice No. 61

Recording debit notes in sales day book of seller

The seller will record debit notes sent out in his sales day book.

SALES DAY BOOK (SELLER)

Date	Details	Inv. No.	Fo	Net	VAT	Total
22/5/16	Murphy TV, Hi-Fi & Video Ltd	DN 104		€450	€90	€540

(7) CREDIT NOTE

A credit note is sent from seller to buyer if:

(a) The buyer has been **overcharged** on the invoice.

(b) The **buyer returns goods** to the seller and the seller issues a credit note to the buyer.

REASONS FOR RETURNING GOODS

- ➢ Damaged in transit.
- ➢ Not ordered.
- ➢ Faulty.
- ➢ Out of date.

NB The credit note reduces the amount of money buyer owes seller.

Let us assume that Murphy TV, Hi-Fi & Video Ltd returned two Panasonic Mini Hi-Fi Systems because they were faulty.

A credit note is issued by Panasonic Ireland Ltd to the buyer as follows:

CREDIT NOTE **No. 140**

PANASONIC IRELAND LTD
Sandyford Industrial Est.
Dublin 18

Tel (01) 9986241
Fax (01) 9986242

VAT Reg. No. 924651N

24 May 2016

Murphy TV, Hi-Fi & Video Ltd
10 Princess Street
Cork

Quantity	Description	Unit Price	Total (Ex. VAT)
2	Panasonic Mini Hi-Fi Systems	€279	€558
	Total (Ex. VAT)		€558
	Less Trade Discount 10%		€55.80
			€502.20
	Add VAT 20%		€100.44
	Total		€602.64

Faulty Goods Ref. Inv. No. 61
E & O E

NOTES

(i) If trade discount was deducted on the original invoice, it must be deducted on the credit note and debit note.

(ii) If VAT was paid on the original invoice, it must be added in the credit note and debit note.

The credit note is the source document for recording Sales Returns and Purchases Returns.

(a) The seller writes up his **Sales Returns Day Book** from credit notes sent.

(b) The buyer writes up his **Purchases Returns Day Book** from credit notes received.

RECORDING CREDIT NOTES SENT IN SALES RETURNS DAY BOOK OF SELLER

SALES RETURNS DAY BOOK — OF PANASONIC IRL. LTD (SELLER)

Date	Details	Credit Note No.	Fo	Net	VAT	Total
24/5/16	Murphy TV Hi-Fi & Video Ltd	140		€502.20	€100.44	€602.64

RECORDING CREDIT NOTES RECEIVED IN PURCHASES RETURNS DAY BOOK OF BUYER

PURCHASES RETURNS DAY BOOK — OF MURPHY TV, HI-FI & VIDEO LTD (BUYER)

Date	Details	Credit Note No.	Fo	Net	VAT	Total
24/5/16	Panasonic Ireland Ltd	140		€502.20	€100.44	€602.64

TREATMENT OF CREDIT NOTES ISSUED

(1) Check figure and dates for accuracy.

(2) Check that the name and address is correct.

(3) Record the credit note in sales returns book.

(4) File a copy of the credit note.

(8) STATEMENT OF ACCOUNT

STATEMENT OF ACCOUNT **No. 210**

PANASONIC IRELAND LTD
Sandyford Industrial Est.
Dublin 18

Tel (01) 9986241
Fax (01) 9986242

VAT Reg. No. 924651N

31 May 2016

Murphy TV, Hi-Fi & Video Ltd
10 Princess Street
Cork

Date	Details	Debit	Credit	Balance
21/5/16	Invoice No. 61	€66,258		€66,258
22/5/16	Debit Note No. 104	€540		€66,798
24/5/16	Credit Note No. 140		€602.64	€66,195.36

AMOUNT DUE

A statement of account is a document sent from the seller to the buyer at the end of a period of time (usually one month).

It outlines the transactions that took place between the seller and the buyer and shows how much the buyer owes at the end of the period.

Let us assume that Panasonic Ireland Ltd sent a statement of account to Murphy TV, Hi-Fi & Video Ltd on 31 May 2016 as above.

Notes

(i) The statement of accounts is presented on the continuous balance format — thus you get a new balance after each transaction.

(ii) Invoices and debit notes are put into the debit column and are added to the balance figure, increasing the amount owed by the buyer.

(iii) Credit notes and payments (cash or cheque) are put into the credit column and are subtracted from the balance figure, reducing the amount owed by the buyer.

What Seller Should Do Before Sending Statements/Treatment of Outgoing Statements	What Buyer Should Do on Receiving Statements/Treatment of Incoming Statements
1. Check that all transactions are included and correct — compare with copies of relevant documents. 2. Check that all calculations are accurate. 3. Check that name and address of buyer are correct. 4. File copy of statement.	1. Compare statement transactions with relevant documents. 2. Compare statement with account of seller in creditors ledger. 3. Check all calculations. 4. Pay seller amount due. 5. File statement.

(9) PAYMENT

The buyer will usually pay the statement of account promptly by cheque.

Assume Murphy TV, Hi-Fi & Video Ltd pays Panasonic Ireland Ltd by cheque on 5 June 2016.

CHEQUE

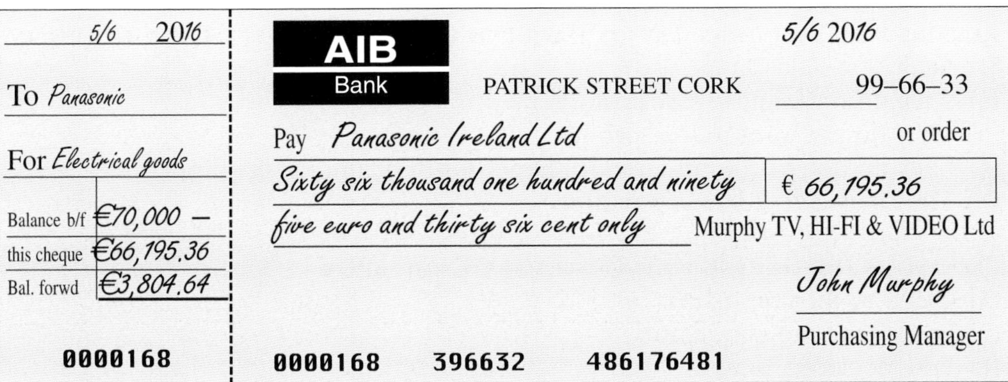

N.B. Balance B/f €70,000 — Assume Murphy TV, Hi-Fi & Video Ltd had €70,000 in its account before writing this cheque.

Treatment of Cheques Issued

(1) Check accuracy, i.e. that it is made out to correct person for correct amount.
(2) Complete stub.
(3) Record in Cash Book (credit side).
(4) Record in debit side of creditor's account in Creditors Ledger.

(10) RECEIPT

When the seller receives the payment, it is usual to issue a receipt to the buyer. This acknowledges payment and when it is received by the buyer it should be filed as proof of payment.

Assume Panasonic Irl Ltd issued a receipt on 10 June 2016.

RECEIPT **No. 802**

PANASONIC IRELAND LTD
Sandyford Industrial Est.
Dublin 18

Received with thanks, Date *10 June 2016*

The sum of *Sixty six thousand one hundred and ninety five Euro and thirty six cent.* IR£ *66,195.36*

FROM *Murphy TV, Hi-Fi & Video Ltd*
10 Princess Street – Cork.

Signed *Jim Kelly*
Accounts Dept

Treatment of Receipts Issued

(1) Check figures and dates for accuracy.
(2) Check that the name and address are correct.
(3) Record receipts issued on the debit side of the Cash Book.
(4) Complete the counterfoil/stub.
(5) Keep copy of counterfoil.

(11) DEALING WITH CUSTOMERS' COMPLAINTS

Reasons Why Businesses Try to Have Few Complaints About Their Goods and Services

(a) They do not want to lose customers.
(b) They do not want to lose profit.
(c) They do not want to incur extra expenses in dealing with complaints.
(d) They may gain a bad reputation.

Procedure for Dealing with Customers' Complaints

(a) Listen to the complaint.
(b) Investigate the complaint.
(c) Take necessary action.
(d) Reply to the complaint.
(e) File and record the complaint for future reference.

Examination-Style Questions and Solutions

Question 1.

Answer all sections. This is a Business Document Question.

William Lyons is the Manager of the Purchasing Department in Office Supplies Ltd. On 21 April 2013 he received the following quotation:

QUOTATION **No. 759**

DESKMAKERS LTD
Industrial Estate, Castlebar, Co. Mayo.

To: Office Supplies Ltd
Canal Road
Roscommon

Date: 20 April 2013
Tel: 094–79555
Fax: 094–89755
Vat No.: IE644311

Model	Description	€ Price Each	Delivery
D42	Office Desks	240.00	Ready
CS6	Swivel Chairs	75.00	Ready
T21	Typewriters	145.00	Ready
F44	Filing Cabinets	280.00	Ready
	VAT 20% extra on all goods. Carriage Paid. For acceptance within 30 days.		

William decides that the typewriters are too costly, but he sends an Order (No. 94) to Deskmakers Ltd for five office desks, ten swivel chairs and six filing cabinets. These goods are delivered in a truck to Office Supplies Ltd on 6 May 2013. William checks the goods when they arrive and finds everything correct. After he signs the Delivery Note, he is handed an Invoice (No. 732) for the goods by the driver of the truck.

1. (a) From the above details, complete Invoice Number 732, using the blank invoice supplied at the end of the question. (30)

1. (b) In the space provided (at the end of the question), give one reason why William should check the invoice against the quotation before paying for the goods. (10)

On behalf of Office Supplies Ltd, William then writes out a cheque in full payment and hands the cheque to the driver to bring back to Deskmakers Ltd.

1. (c) Complete the cheque and counterfoil using the blank supplied at the end of the question. (20)

Documents for Question 1.

1. (a) Invoice

INVOICE **No. 732**

DESKMAKERS Ltd
Industrial Estate, Castlebar, Co. Mayo

To:

Date
Tel: 094–79555
Fax: 094–89755
Vat No.: IE644311
ORDER NO.:

Quantity	Description	Model No.	Price Each (€)	Total
			Total (Excluding VAT)	
			VAT	
			Total (Including VAT)	

E & O E

1. (b) Reason

Quotation

1. (c) Cheque

20	
To	
For	
Balance	€6,315 00
Am't Lodged	
Total	
Am't this chq.	
Bal. forwd	
2355217	

AIB Bank — 20

MAIN STREET, ROSCOMMON 93–77–99

Pay or order

€

OFFICE SUPPLIES LTD

Purchasing Manager

2355217 937799 65477822

Source: Junior Certificate Ordinary Level. **(60 marks)**

Solution to Question 1.

Documents for Question 1.
1. (a) Invoice

INVOICE **No. 732**

DESKMAKERS Ltd
Industrial Estate, Castlebar, Co. Mayo

Date 6 May 2013
Tel: 094–79555
Fax: 094–89755
Vat No.: IE644311
ORDER NO.: 94

To: Office Supplies Ltd
Canal Road
Roscommon

Quantity	Description	Model No.	Price Each(€)	Total
5	Office Desks	D42	€240.00	€1,200.00
10	Swivel Chairs	CS6	€75.00	€750.00
6	Filing Cabinets	F44	€280.00	€1,680.00
		Total (Excluding VAT)		€3,630.00
		VAT		€726.00
		Total (Including VAT)		€4,356.00

E & O E

1. (b) Reason

Quotation To see if he was charged the correct prices as on the quotation.

1. (c) Cheque

6 May 2013
To Deskmakers
For Goods

Balance	€6,315.00
Am't Lodged	
Total	
Am't this chq.	€4,356.00
Bal. forwd	€1,959.00

2355217

AIB Bank

MAIN STREET, ROSCOMMON

6 May 2013

93–77–99

Pay DESKMAKERS LTD or order

Four thousand, three hundred and fifty six Euro only

€ 4,356.00

OFFICE SUPPLIES LTD

William Lyons
Purchasing Manager

2355217 937799 65477822

Question 2.

Answer all sections. This is an Integrated Invoice/Document Question.

On 10 April A. & P. Lawlor Ltd, Furniture Suppliers, Galway, received an order No. 3 from J. Donnelly Ltd, 2 Dublin Road, Sligo, for the following goods:

10 pine tables	@	€350	each excluding VAT
15 TV cabinets	@	€90	each excluding VAT
30 kitchen chairs	@	€8	each excluding VAT
60 bedroom lockers	@	€6	each excluding VAT

A. & P. Lawlor Ltd sent an invoice No. 91 on 13/4/15 to J. Donnelly Ltd. The invoice stated that the trade discount would be 30% of the retail price, and the goods would be delivered by A. & P. Lawlor Ltd on 16/4/15. Furniture is subject to VAT at 20%.

On delivery J. Donnelly Ltd examined the furniture and found that one of the TV cabinets was damaged, and ten of the bedroom lockers had faulty doors. These were returned in the supplier's lorry, and A. & P. Lawlor Ltd issued a credit note No. 65 on 18/4/15. At the end of April A. & P. Lawlor Ltd sent an appropriate document to J. Donnelly Ltd.

2. (a) Complete the invoice of 13/4/15 and the credit note of 18/4/15 on the blank document sheet supplied with this paper. (22)

2. (b) Record the invoice and credit note issued in the books of first entry of A. & P. Lawlor Ltd. (10)

2. (c) Name the document sent by A. & P. Lawlor Ltd to J. Donnelly Ltd at the end of April. (2)

2. (d) Outline how J. Donnelly Ltd should treat incoming invoices. (6)

2. (a) **INVOICE CASH/CREDIT**

A. & P. LAWLOR LTD
Furniture Suppliers
Galway

No.: 91
Telephone: (091) 21354
VAT Reg.: 3174L
Date:

Order No.:
Terms:

Quantity	Description	Unit Price €	Total (Ex. VAT) €
		Total (Ex. VAT)	
		Less: Trade Discount	
		Add: VAT	
		Total Due	

E & O E

2. (a) **CREDIT NOTE**

A. & P. LAWLOR LTD
Furniture Suppliers
Galway

No.: 65
Telephone: (091) 21354
VAT Reg.: 3174L
Date:

Order No.:
Terms:

Quantity	Description	Unit Price €	Total (Ex. VAT) €
		Total (Ex. VAT)	
		Less: Trade Discount	
		Add: VAT	
		Total Due	

E & O E

Source: Junior Certificate Higher Level. **(40 marks)**

Solution to Question 2.

2. (a) **INVOICE CASH/CREDIT**

J. Donnelly Ltd
2 Dublin Road Sligo
Order No.: 3
Terms: Delivery Free

A. & P. LAWLOR LTD
Furniture Suppliers
Galway

No.: 91
Telephone: (091) 21354
VAT Reg.: 3174L
Date: 13/4/15

Quantity	Description	Unit Price €	Total (Ex. VAT) €
10 15 30 60	Pine Tables TV Cabinets Kitchen Chairs Bedroom Lockers	350.00 90.00 8.00 6.00	3,500.00 1,350.00 240.00 360.00
		Total (Ex. VAT)	5,450.00
		Less: Trade Discount	1,635.00
			3,815.00
		Add: VAT	763.00
		Total Due	4,578.00

E & O E

2. (a) **CREDIT NOTE**

J. Donnelly Ltd
2 Dublin Road Sligo
Order No.: 3
Terms: Delivery Free

A. & P. LAWLOR LTD
Furniture Suppliers
Galway

No.: 65
Telephone: (091) 21354
VAT Reg.: 3174L
Date: 18/4/15

Quantity	Description	Unit Price €	Total (Ex. VAT) €
1 10	TV Cabinet Bedroom Lockers (Damaged Goods)	90.00 6.00	90.00 60.00
		Total (Ex. VAT)	150.00
		Less: Trade Discount	45.00
			105.00
		Add: VAT	21.00
		Total Due	126.00

E & O E

2. (b) **SALES DAY BOOK**

Date	Details	Invoices	Fo	€ Net	€ VAT	€ Total
13/4/15	J. Donnelly	91	CL/1	3,815	763	4,578
30/4/15	Credit Sales and VAT A/C			3,815	763	4,578

SALES RETURNS DAY BOOK

Date	Details	Credit Note No.	Fo	Net €	VAT €	Total €
18/4/15	J. Donnelly	65	CL/1	105	21	126
30/4/15	Debit Sales Returns and VAT A/C			105	21	126

2. (c) Document sent by A. & P. Lawlor at end of April

Statement of account.

2. (d) Treatment of Incoming Invoices

(1) Compare with order and delivery docket.
(2) Check accuracy of prices and calculations.
(3) Write up purchases day book.
(4) File invoice.

Question 3.

Answer all sections. This is an Integrated Business Documents Question.

The following details refer to the sale of goods on credit by FAHY LTD to DELFWARE LTD, 10 HIGH ST, CAVAN for the month of May 2016.

On 1 May 2016 there was a balance due of €350 in Delfware's account in Fahy Ltd books.

2016

4 May Fahy sent Invoice No. 6 to Delfware for €10,000
7 May Fahy sent Invoice No. 19 to Delfware for €25,000
11 May Fahy received Cheque from Delfware for €29,000
13 May Fahy sent Credit Note No. 68 to Delfware for goods returned €700 + 15% VAT
17 May Fahy sent Invoice No. 34 to Delfware for €23,000
23 May Fahy sent Credit Note No. 72 to Delfware for goods returned . €1,900 + 15%VAT
27 May Fahy sent Invoice No. 41 to Delfware for €20,000

- On 31 May 2016 Fahy Ltd sent a Statement of Account to Delfware Ltd.
- Delfware paid the amount due on the Statement by cheque.
- Fahy Ltd issued a Receipt on 19 June 2016, signed by Henry Fahy.

You are required to:

3. (a) Record the two credit notes sent on 13 and 23 May 2016 in the appropriate book of first entry of Fahy Ltd. (7)

3. (b) Complete the Statement sent by Fahy Ltd on 31st May 2016 on the blank statement document supplied. (17)

3. (c) Complete the receipt issued by Fahy Ltd on 19 June 2016 on the blank receipt document supplied. (10)

3. (d) In the case of Delfware Ltd, suggest two checks that their book-keeper should carry out before paying the amount due on the Statement. (6)

For Use with Question 3. (Part B)

STATEMENT

FAHY LTD
TUAM RD., GALWAY

To:

Tel: (091) 46377
VAT No. IE43156
Account No. 39

Date:

Date	Details	Debit	Credit	Balance

↑ AMOUNT DUE

For use with Question 3 (Part C).

RECEIPT **No. 658**

FAHY LTD, TUAM ROAD, GALWAY.

Received with thanks, Date ____________

The sum of ____________________ €

FROM

Signed ____________
Accounts Dept

Source: Junior Certificate Higher Level. **(40 marks)**

Solution to Question 3.

SALES RETURNS BOOK

Date	Details	Credit Note No.	Fo	Net €	VAT €	Total €
13/5/16	Delfware	68	DL/1	700	105	805
23/5/16	Delfware	72	DL/1	1,900	285	2,185
31/5/16	Debit Sales Returns and VAT A/C			2,600	390	2,990

For Use with Question 3 (Part B).

STATEMENT

FAHY LTD
TUAM RD, GALWAY

Tel: (091) 46377
VAT No. IE43156
Account No. 39

To: Delfware Ltd
10 High Street
Cavan

Date: 31 May 2016

Date	Details	€ Debit	€ Credit	€ Balance
1 May	Balance			350
4 May	Invoice No. 6	10,000		10,350
7 May	Invoice No. 19	25,000		35,350
11 May	Cheque		29,000	6,350
13 May	Credit Note No. 68		805	5,545
17 May	Invoice No. 34	23,000		28,545
23 May	Credit Note No. 72		2,185	26,360
27 May	Invoice No. 41	20,000		46,360

↑ AMOUNT DUE

For use with Question 3 (Part C).

RECEIPT **No. 658**

FAHY LTD, TUAM ROAD, GALWAY.

Received with thanks,

Date 19 June 2016

The sum of Forty six thousand three hundred and sixty Euro

€ 46,360

FROM Delfware Ltd
10 High Street
Cavan

Signed Henry Fahy
Accounts Dept

3. (d) (i) Check arithmetical accuracy.
(ii) Compare Statement with creditors ledger.
(iii) Check that terms agreed were given.

Chapter 29 — Introduction to Double Entry Book-Keeping, Day Books and Ledger

A. Book-Keeping

Book-keeping is the art of recording business transactions in a systematic manner so that the business will have a permanent record.

B. Double Entry Book-Keeping

Double Entry Principle: Every business transaction has a twofold aspect: **giving** and **receiving**.

C. Fundamental Rule of Double Entry Book-Keeping

Debit	Receiver
Credit	Giver

D. An Account in the Ledger

An account is a space in the ledger set aside for a particular purpose, e.g. cash account, computer account.

Example I

On 1 May a firm spends €2,000 cash on the purchase of a computer.

- ➢ Money goes out of the business — cash account is giving — **Credit Giving Account.**
- ➢ Computer comes into the business — computer account is receiving — **Debit Receiving Account.**

Our two entries are:

(1) Debit computer account.

(2) Credit cash account.

Debit — **Computer A/C** — **Credit**

Date	Details	Total	Date	Details	Total
1 May	Cash	€2,000			

Cash A/C

Date	Details	Total	Date	Details	Total
			1 May	Computer	€2,000

Example II

10 Jan. Purchased machinery on credit from John Keane €10,000.

➢ Two accounts are machinery and John Keane.

(1) Debit machinery account (machinery account — receiving).

(2) Credit John Keane account (John Keane account — giving).

LEDGER

Debit **Machinery A/C** **Credit**

Date	Details	Total	Date	Details	Total
10 Jan.	John Keane	€10,000			

John Keane A/C

Date	Details	Total	Date	Details	Total
			10 Jan.	Machinery	€10,000

E. Day Books

(1) Purchases Day Book — for recording goods purchased on credit for resale.

(2) Purchases Returns Day Book — for recording goods returned by the purchaser.

(3) Sales Day Book — for recording goods sold on credit.

(4) Sales Returns Day Book — for recording goods returned to the seller.

(5) Cash Book — Cash receipts and bank lodgments are entered on the debit side. Cash payments and cheque payments are entered on the credit side.

(6) General Journal — used to record transactions which are not recorded in other books of first entry.

F. Source Documents for Day Books

(1) Seller writes up his sales day book from invoices sent. Purchaser writes up his purchases day book from invoices received.

(2) Seller writes up his sales returns day book from details on credit notes sent. Purchaser writes up his purchases returns day book from credit notes received.

SOURCE DOCUMENTS FOR CASH BOOK

Cash receipts — from cash register, tally roll, or copy of receipts given to cash customers.

Bank lodgments — written up from bank lodgments, counterfoils, bank statements showing receipts paid directly into bank.

Cash payments — written up from cash vouchers showing what the payment was for.

Cheque payments — written up from cheque counterfoils or from bank statements.

G. Layout of Books of First Entry

Layout of the Sales Day Book and Purchases Day Book

Date	Details	Inv. No.	Fo	Net	VAT	Total

N.B. Exactly same layout for returns day books, except credit note number replaces invoice number.

Layout of Cash Book
Layout Number 1: Use analysed cash receipts and lodgments book and analysed cash and cheque payments book, combined with a cash account and a bank account in the ledger.

Layout Number 2: This layout combines the above two books into what is known as The Analysed Cash Book.

H. The Ledger

Every debit entry will have a corresponding credit entry. The ledger is divided into three sections:
(1) **Debtors Ledger** — accounts of people and firms that owe us money.
(2) **Creditors Ledger** — accounts of people and firms to whom we owe money.
(3) **General Ledger** — accounts of a non-personal nature such as expenses, gains, assets and liabilities.

I. Trial Balance

A Trial Balance is a list of all balances standing on the ledger accounts and cash books of a business at the end of the period. Debit balances go to the debit column, credit balances go to the credit column. When totalled, the debit total should correspond to the credit total, thus the entries on the accounts are **arithmetically** correct.

J. Business Terms

Account A page in the ledger in which all transactions relating to a particular person or firm are recorded.
Assets Items that a business **owns**.
Balance The difference between two sides of an account.
Credit An entry on the right-hand side of an account.
Creditor A person or firm to whom money is owed.
Debit An entry on the left-hand side of an account.
Debtor A person or firm who owes money.
Liabilities Items that a business **owes.**
Trial Balance A list of balances from the ledger.

Examination-Style Questions and Solutions

Question 1.

Your total takings in cash in your grocery business on 22 May are €500. Show how you would enter the €500 in both of the following accounts of your business:

Debit **Cash Account** **Credit**

Date	Details	Total	Date	Details	Total
22 May	Sales	500			

Sales Account

Date	Details	Total	Date	Details	Total
			22 May	Cash	500

Source: Junior Certificate Ordinary Level. (5)

Question 2.

Larkin & Co. Ltd paid for repairs to its computer on 4 June with a cheque for €850. Show how you would enter the payment of €850 in both of the following accounts of Larkin & Co. Ltd:

Debit **Bank Account** **Credit**

Date	Details	Total	Date	Details	Total
			4 June	Repairs to computer	850

Repairs Account

Date	Details	Total	Date	Details	Total
4 June	Bank	850			

Source: Junior Certificate Ordinary Level. (5)

Question 3.

In the spaces provided, name the two accounts (in A.N.G. Ltd's books) affected by the following transaction:

A.N.G. Ltd (Engineering Works) purchased a delivery truck from Roches Garage Ltd by cheque on 1 May 2014.

Debit the Delivery Van Account. Credit the Bank Account.

Source: Junior Certificate Higher Level. (4)

Question 4.

Answer either **(a)** or **(b)**:

4. (a) Balance the following Bank Account and bring down the balance:

Debit		Bank Account					Credit
Date	**Details**	**F**	**€**	**Date**	**Details**	**F**	**€**
1 May	Balance	B/d	850	9 May	Wages	GL8	639
4 May	Sales	GL4	755	17 May	Purchases	GL3	247
				31 May	*Balance*	*C/d*	*719*
			1,605				*1,605*
31 May	*Balance*	*B/d*	*719*				

OR

4. (b) Complete the last 3 lines of the 'Balance' column in the following Bank Account:

Bank Account					
Date	**Details**	**F**	**€ Dr**	**€ Cr**	**€ Balance**
1 May	Balance	B/d			850
4 May	Sales	GL4	755		*1,605*
9 May	Wages	GL8		639	*966*
17 May	Purchases	GL3		247	*719*

Source: Junior Certificate Ordinary Level. (5)

Question 5.

Show how the following transaction would be recorded in the ledger of Cablelines Ltd, a TV company.

Cablelines Ltd sold a delivery van on credit to O'Brien Transport Ltd for €4,700.

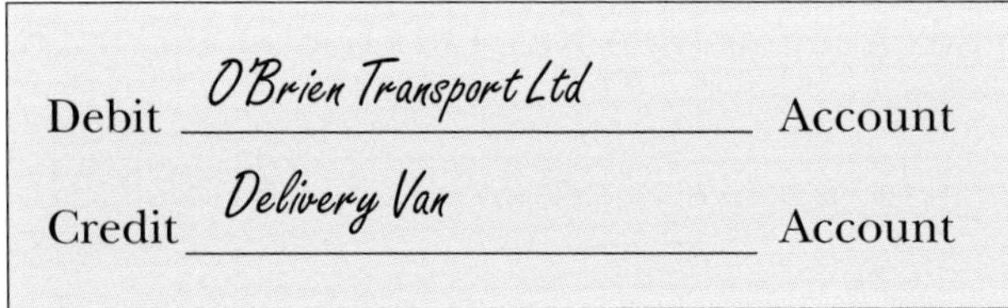
Debit *O'Brien Transport Ltd* Account

Credit *Delivery Van* Account

Source: Junior Certificate Higher Level. (4)

Question 6.
In the space provided, name the two accounts affected by the following transaction in the ledger of Kilcara Hardware Ltd.

Kilcara Hardware Ltd purchased goods for resale on credit from Smith Ltd.

Debit Purchases Account
Credit Smith Ltd Account

Source: Junior Certificate Higher Level. (4)

Chapter 30 — Purchases Day Book and Purchases Returns Day Book

A. Purchases Day Book (PDB)

The purchases day book is used to record goods bought on credit. When you purchase goods, you receive an invoice. The purchases day book is written up from invoices received.

B. Purchases Returns Day Book (PRDB)

The purchases returns day book is used to record the return of goods purchased on credit by a business. When goods are returned, the buyer receives a credit note. The purchases returns day book is written up from the credit notes received.

C. Source Documents for Recording Purchases Day Book and Purchases Returns Day Book

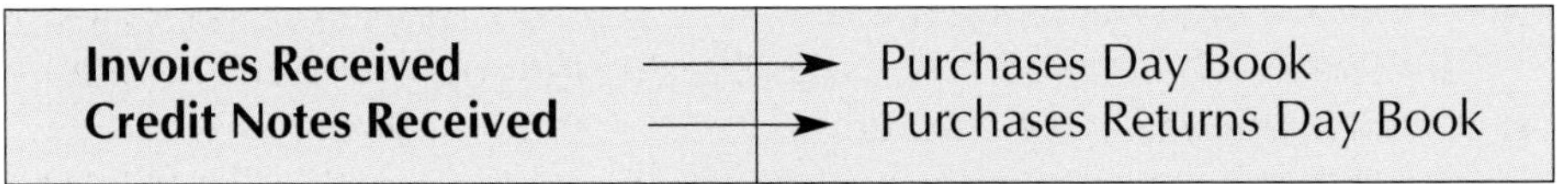

Sample Question and Solution

Question

Write up the purchases day book, purchases returns day book, post to the ledger, balance the accounts, and extract a trial balance.

- 1 Feb. Purchased goods on credit from Motorola Ltd. Invoice No. 186 €2,000 + VAT @ 20%.
- 8 Feb. Returned goods to Motorola Ltd. Received credit note No. 41 €400 + VAT @ 20%.
- 15 Feb. Received invoice No. 149 from Kestrel Ltd €6,000 + VAT @ 20%.
- 24 Feb. Received credit note No. 201 from Kestrel Ltd €200 + VAT @ 20%.

Solution

(1) Day Books

Purchases Day Book — **Page 1**

Date	Details	Invoice No.	Fo	Net €	VAT €	Total €
2015						
1 Feb.	Motorola Ltd	186	CL/1	2,000	400	2,400
15 Feb.	Kestrel Ltd	149	CL/2	6,000	1,200	7,200
28 Feb.	Debit Purchases and VAT A/Cs			8,000	1,600	9,600
				GL/1	GL/2	

Purchases Returns Day Book **Page 2**

Date 2015	Details	Credit Note No.	Fo	Net €	VAT €	Total €
8 Feb.	Motorola Ltd	41	CL/1	400	80	480
24 Feb.	Kestrel Ltd	201	CL/2	200	40	240
28 Feb.	Credit Purchases Returns and VAT A/Cs			600	120	720
				GL/3	GL/2	

CL = Creditors Ledger **GL** = General Ledger

(2) Rules for Posting to Ledger

Posting Purchases Day Book	Posting Purchases Returns Day Book
Debit Purchases account with net amount. **Debit** VAT account with VAT amount. **Credit** Personal accounts with total amount, **i.e.** Credit Motorola Ltd with €2,400. Credit Kestrel Ltd with €7,200.	**Debit** Personal accounts with total amount, **i.e.** Debit Motorola Ltd with €480. Debit Kestrel Ltd with €240. **Credit** Purchases returns account with net amount. **Credit** VAT account with VAT amount.

GENERAL LEDGER

Debit **Purchases A/C No. 1** **Credit**

Date	Details	Fo	Total €	Date	Details	Fo	Total
2015							
28 Feb.	Total PDB	PDB1	8,000				

Debit **VAT A/C No. 2** **Credit**

Date	Details	Fo	Total €	Date	Details	Fo	Total €
2015				2015			
28 Feb.	Total PDB	PDB1	1,600	28 Feb.	Total PRDB	PRDB2	120
				28 Feb.	Balance	C/d	1,480
			1,600				1,600
28 Feb.	Balance	B/d	1,480				

Debit		Purchases Returns A/C No. 3					Credit
Date	Details	Fo	Total	Date 2015	Details	Fo	Total €
				28 Feb.	Total PRDB	PRDB2	600

CREDITORS LEDGER

Debit		Motorola Ltd A/C No. 1					Credit
Date	Details	Fo	Total €	Date	Details	Fo	Total €
2015				2015			
8 Feb.	Purchases Returns	PRDB2	480	1 Feb.	Purchases	PDB1	2,400
28 Feb.	Balance	C/d	1,920				
			2,400				2,400
				28 Feb.	Balance	B/d	1,920

Debit		Kestrel Ltd A/C No. 2					Credit
Date	Details	Fo	Total €	Date	Details	Fo	Total €
2015				2015			
24 Feb.	Purchases Returns	PRDB2	240	15 Feb.	Purchase	PDB1	7,200
28 Feb.	Balance	B/d	6,960				
			7,200				7,200
				28 Feb.	Balance	B/d	6,960

Balancing the accounts

All accounts with more than one entry must be balanced off. Balance in VAT account is €1,480. Balance in Motorola Ltd account is €1,920 and balance in Kestrel Ltd account is €6,960. If an account has only one entry, there is no need to balance it off.

The trial balance

- ➢ The trial balance is a list of balances from the ledger.
- ➢ Debit balances go into the Debit column.
- ➢ Credit balances go into the Credit column.

Trial Balance as on 28 February 2015

Date	Details	Fo	Debit €	Credit €
	Purchases	GL1	8,000	
	VAT	GL2	1,480	
	Purchases Returns	GL3		600
	Motorola Ltd	CL1		1,920
	Kestrel Ltd	CL2		6,960
			9,480	9,480

PRACTICE QUESTION

Write up the purchases day book and purchases returns day book, post to the ledger, balance the accounts and extract a trial balance.

1 Mar. Purchased goods on credit from Nelson Ltd. Invoice No. 214 €7,600 + VAT @ 20%.

10 Mar. Returned goods to Nelson Ltd. Received credit note No. 388 €200 + VAT @ 20%.

16 Mar. Received invoice No. 260 from Experto Ltd €10,000 + VAT @ 20%.

24 Mar. Received credit note No. 181 from Experto Ltd €600 + VAT @ 20%.

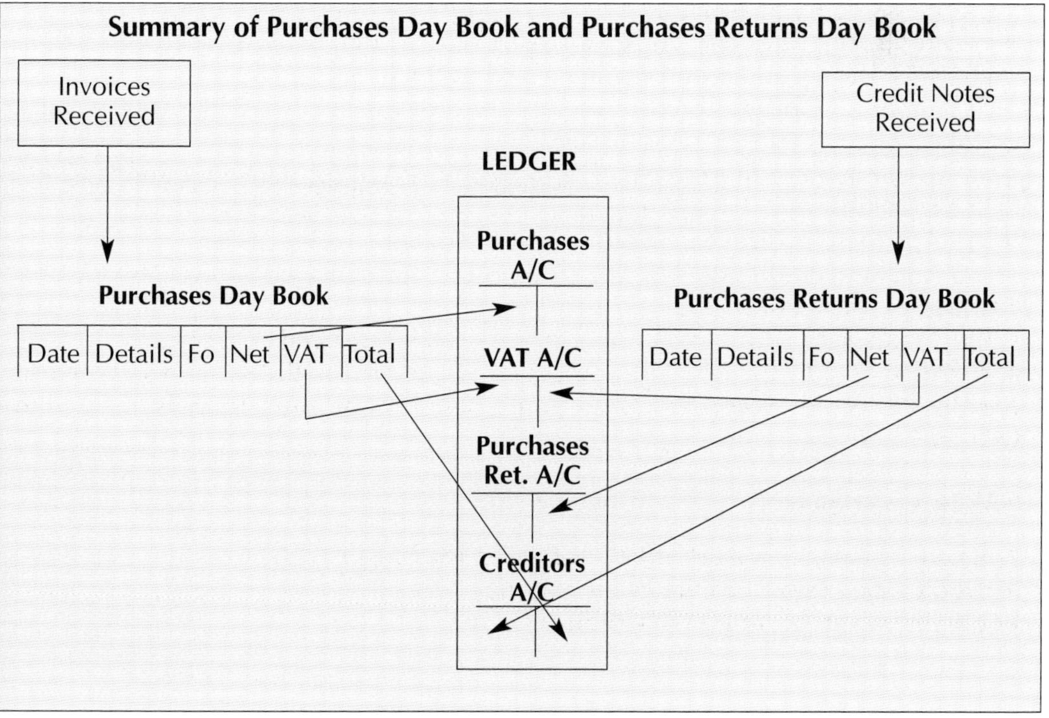

Higher Level

Chapter 31 — Sales Day Book and Sales Returns Day Book

A. Sales Day Book (SDB)

The sales day book is used to record goods sold on credit. When a firm sells goods on credit, it sends an invoice to the buyer. The sales day book is written up from invoices sent.

B. Sales Returns Day Book (SRDB)

The sales returns day book is used to record goods returned to the business previously sold on credit. When goods are returned, the seller issues a credit note. The sales returns day book is written up from credit notes issued.

C. Source Documents for Recording Sales Day Book and Sales Returns Day Book

Invoices Sent ——→	Sales Day Book
Credit Notes Sent ——→	Sales Returns Day Book

Sample Question and Solution

Question

- ➢ Write up the sales day book and sales returns day book, post to the ledger, balance the accounts, and extract a trial balance.
- ➢ 1 Apr. Sold goods on credit to Sapphire Ltd. Invoice No. 238 €9,000 + Vat @ 20%.
- ➢ 6 Apr. Sent a credit note No. 412 to Sapphire Ltd for damaged goods €200 + VAT @ 20%.
- ➢ 15 Apr. Sent invoice No. 324 to Scott Ltd €6,000 + VAT @ 20%.
- ➢ 22 Apr. Sent credit note No. 202 to Scott Ltd for damaged goods €500 + VAT @ 20%.

Solution

(1) Day Books

Sales Day Book **Page 1**

Date 2016	Particulars	Invoice No.	Fo	Net €	VAT €	Total €
1 Apr.	Sapphire Ltd	238	DL/1	9,000	1,800	10,800
15 Apr.	Scott Ltd	324	DL/2	6,000	1,200	7,200
30 Apr.	Credit Sales and VAT A/Cs			15,000	3,000	18,000
				GL/1	GL2	

Sales Returns Day Book **Page 2**

Date	Details	Credit Note No.	Fo	Net €	VAT €	Total €
2016						
6 Apr.	Sapphire Ltd	412	DL/1	200	40	240
22 Apr.	Scott Ltd	202	DL/2	500	100	600
30 Apr.	Debit Sales Returns and VAT A/Cs			700	140	840
				GL/3	GL/2	

DL = Debtors Ledger **GL** = General Ledger

(2) Rules for Posting to Ledger

Posting Sales Day Book	Posting Sales Returns Day Book
Debit Personal accounts with total amount, **i.e.** Debit Sapphire Ltd with €10,890. Debit Scott Ltd with €7,260. **Credit** Sales account with net amount. **Credit** VAT account with VAT amount.	**Debit** Sales Returns account with net amount. **Debit** VAT account with VAT amount. **Credit** Personal accounts with total amount, **i.e.** Credit Sapphire Ltd with €240. Credit Scott Ltd with €600.

GENERAL LEDGER

Debit **Sales A/C No. 1** **Credit**

Date	Details	Fo	Total	Date	Details	Fo	Total €
				2016			
				30 Apr.	Total as per SDB	SDB1	15,000

Debit **VAT A/C No. 2** **Credit**

Date	Details	Fo	Total €	Date	Details	Fo	Total €
2016				2016			
30 Apr.	Total as per SRDB	SRDB2	140	30 Apr.	Total as per SDB	SDB1	3,000
30 Apr.	Balance	C/d	2,860				
			3,000				3,000
				30 Apr.	Balance	B/d	2,860

Debit		Sales Returns A/C No. 3					Credit
Date	Details	Fo	Total €	Date	Details	Fo	Total
2016							
30 Apr.	Total as per SRDB	SRDB2	700				

DEBTORS LEDGER

Debit		Sapphire Ltd A/C No. 1					Credit
Date	Details	Fo	Total €	Date	Details	Fo	Total €
2016				2016			
1 Apr.	Sales	SDB1	10,800	6 Apr.	Sales Returns	SRDB2	240
				30 Apr.	Balance	C/d	10,560
			10,800				10,800
30 Apr.	Balance	B/d	10,560				

Debit		Scott Ltd A/C No. 2					Credit
Date	Details	Fo	Total €	Date	Details	Fo	Total €
2016				2016			
15 Apr.	Sales	SDB1	7,200	22 Apr.	Sales Returns	SRDB2	600
				30 Apr.	Balance	B/d	6,600
			7,200				7,200
30 Apr.	Balance	B/d	6,600				

Balancing the accounts

All accounts with more than one entry must be balanced off. Balance in VAT account is €2,860. Balance in Sapphire Ltd account is €10,560 and balance in Scott Ltd account is €6,600. If an account has only one entry, there is no need to balance it off.

The trial balance

- The trial balance is a list of balances from the ledger.
- Debit balances go into the Debit column.
- Credit balances go into the Credit column.

Trial Balance as on 30 April 2016

Date	Details	Fo	€ Debit	€ Credit
	Sales	GL1		15,000
	VAT	GL2		2,860
	Sales Returns	GL3	700	
	Sapphire Ltd	DL1	10,560	
	Scott Ltd	DL2	6,600	
			17,860	17,860

PRACTICE QUESTION

Write up the sales day book and sales returns day book, post to the ledger, balance the accounts, and extract a trial balance.

1 May Sold goods on credit to Rainbow Ltd. Invoice No. 425 €8,000 + VAT @ 20%.

7 May Sent a credit note No. 553 to Rainbow Ltd for damaged goods €800 + VAT @ 20%.

21 May Sent invoice No. 411 to Goldstar Ltd. €7,000 + VAT @ 20%.

23 May Sent credit note No. 901 to Goldstar Ltd for damaged goods €200 + VAT @ 20%.

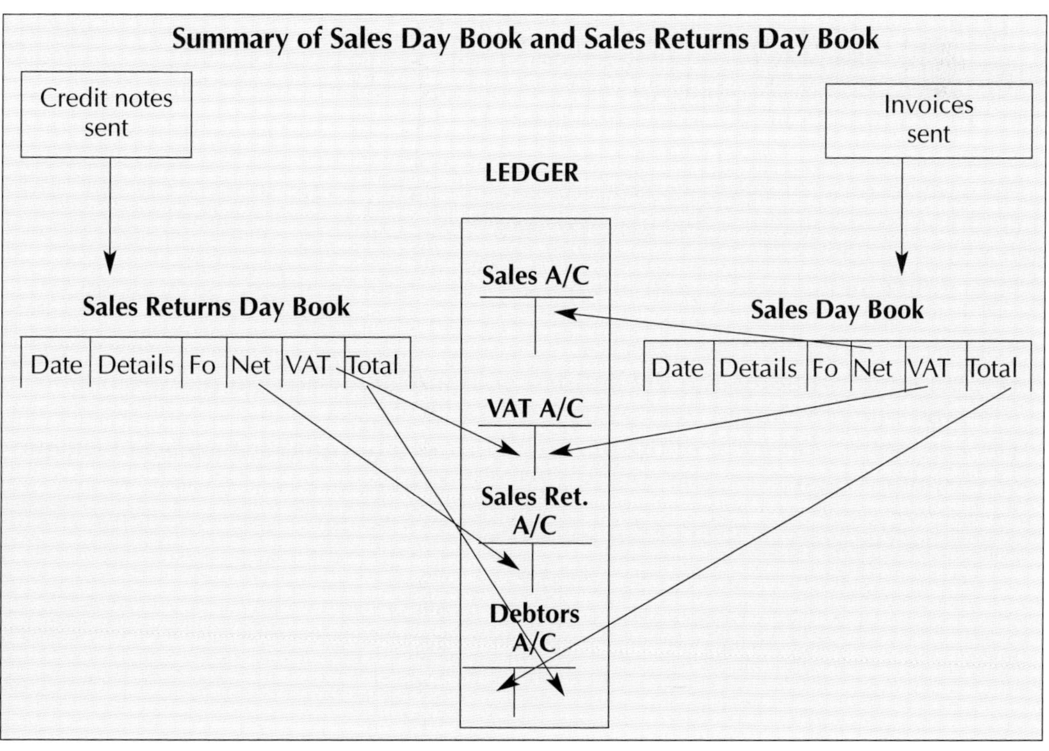

Chapter 32 — Cash Book (Including VAT)

A. Cash Book

The cash book is used to record money received by the business and money paid out by the business. Cash transactions are entered in the cash column, and transactions by cheque are entered in the bank column.

B. Format of Cash Book

The layout of the cash book may vary from one business to another.

METHOD I — TWO SEPARATE CASH BOOKS

Use (1) analysed cash receipts and lodgments book and (2) analysed cash and cheque payments book, plus a cash account and bank account in the ledger.

OR

METHOD II — ANALYSED CASH BOOK

This combines the above two books.

(1) Information in the analysed cash receipts and lodgments book would appear on the debit side of the analysed cash book.

(2) Information in the analysed cash and cheque payment book would appear on the credit side of the analysed cash book.

No cash account or bank account are needed in the ledger, as the cash and bank columns are balanced in the analysed cash book.

N.B. Either method will answer any question at Junior Certificate Business Studies.

RULES FOR WRITING UP CASH BOOKS

(1) Any money coming into the business goes into analysed cash receipts book, or debit side of analysed cash book.

(2) Any money going out of the business goes into the analysed cash and cheque payments book, or credit side of analysed cash book.

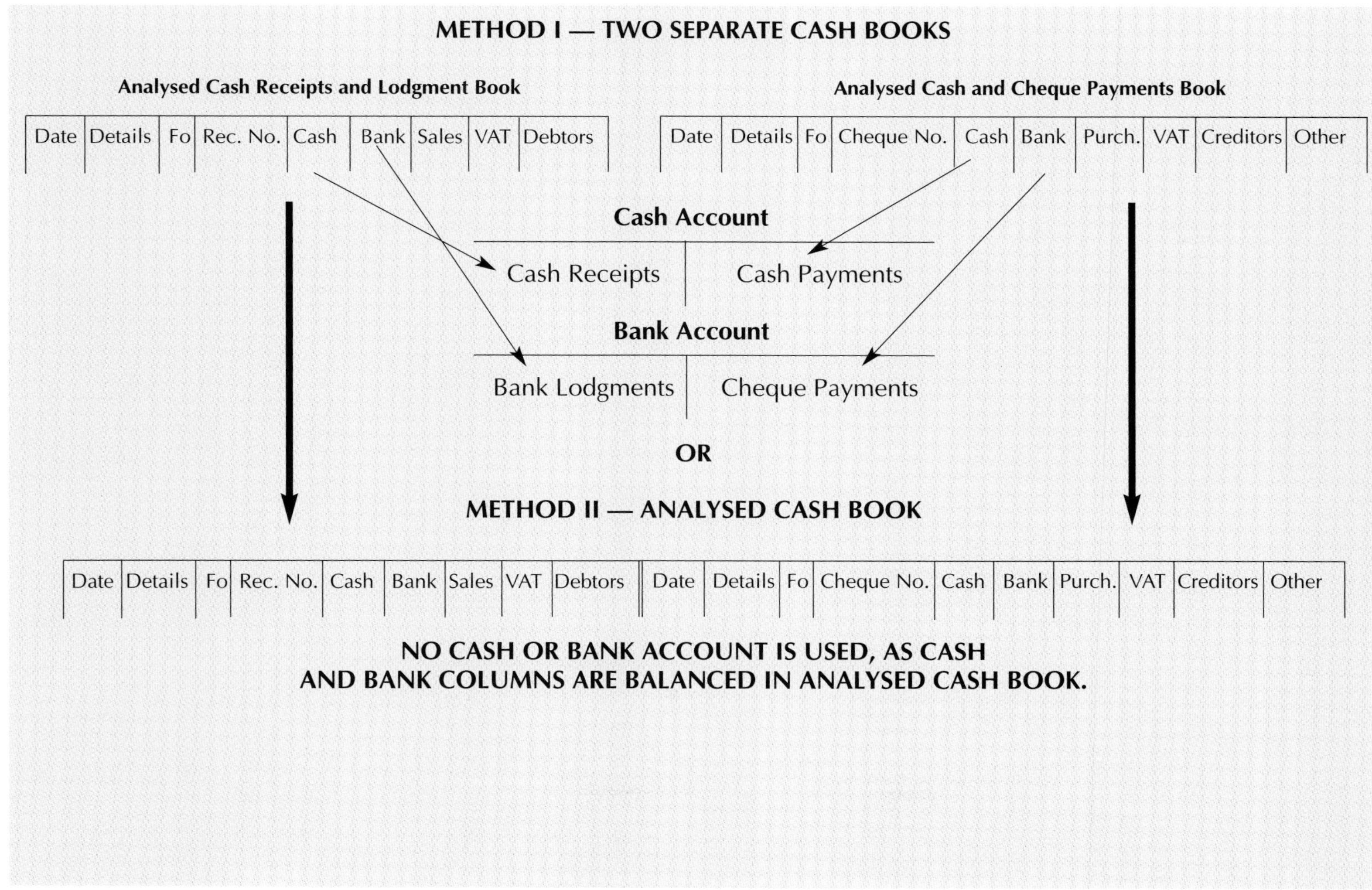
METHOD I — TWO SEPARATE CASH BOOKS
Analysed Cash Receipts and Lodgment Book
Date | Details | Fo | Rec. No. | Cash | Bank | Sales | VAT | Debtors
Analysed Cash and Cheque Payments Book
Date | Details | Fo | Cheque No. | Cash | Bank | Purch. | VAT | Creditors | Other
Cash Account
Cash Receipts
Cash Payments
Bank Account
Bank Lodgments
Cheque Payments
OR
METHOD II — ANALYSED CASH BOOK
Date | Details | Fo | Rec. No. | Cash | Bank | Sales | VAT | Debtors
Date | Details | Fo | Cheque No. | Cash | Bank | Purch. | VAT | Creditors | Other
NO CASH OR BANK ACCOUNT IS USED, AS CASH
AND BANK COLUMNS ARE BALANCED IN ANALYSED CASH BOOK.

Sample Question and Solution

Question

Record the following transactions for the month of June in the appropriate books of first entry, post relevant figures to the ledger, extract a trial balance as on 30 June.

NOTE

Analyse the cash and bank transactions using the following money column headings:

Debit (Receipts) Side: Cash, Bank, Sales, VAT, Debtors.
Credit (Payments) Side: Cash, Bank, Purchases, VAT, Creditors, Wages, Other.

Transactions

1 June Cash balance €3,000, Bank balance €10,000
4 June Cash sales lodged €6,000, this includes VAT of €1,000 (receipt No. 1)
10 June Paid wages cheque No. 41 €900
12 June Purchased goods cheque No. 42 €807 + VAT @ 20%
15 June D. Creedon Ltd (debtor) settled his account of €8,000 by cheque and it was lodged (receipt No. 2)
20 June Paid J. Shorthall Ltd (creditor) by cheque No. 43 €2,000
23 June Paid office expenses by cash €200
28 June Cash sales €10,000. This includes VAT of €1,667 (receipt No. 3)

Solution

METHOD I — TWO CASH BOOKS

Analysed Cash Receipts and Lodgment Book **Page 1**

Date 2014	Details	Fo	Rec. No.	Cash €	Bank €	Sales €	VAT €	Debtors €
4 June	Sales		1		6,000	5,000	1,000	
15 June	D. Creedon Ltd	DL1	2		8,000			8,000
28 June	Sales		3	10,000		8,333	1,667	
30 June	Debit Cash and Bank A/Cs			10,000	14,000	13,333	2,667	8,000
				GL1	GL2	GL3	GL5	GL4

Analysed Cash and Cheque Payment Book **Page 1**

Date	Details	Fo	Chq. No.	Cash €	Bank €	Purch. €	VAT €	Cred.s €	Wages €	Other €
2014										
10 June	Wages	GL/7	41		900				900	
12 June	Purchases		42		968	807	161			
20 June	J. Shorthall Ltd	CL/1	43		2,000			2,000		
23 June	Office Expenses	GL/8		200						200
30 June	Credit Cash and Bank A/Cs			200	3,868	807	161	2,000	900	200
				GL/1	GL/2	GL/6	GL/5			

Rules for Posting Cash Book to Ledger

(1) Any item in the analysed cash receipts and lodgment book, i.e. debit side of analysed cash book, is posted to the credit side of ledger.

(2) Any item in the analysed cash and cheque payment book, i.e. credit side of analysed cash book, is posted to debit side of ledger.

GENERAL LEDGER

Cash Account **No. 1**

Date	Details	Fo	Total €	Date	Details	Fo	Total €
2014				2014			
1 June	Balance		3,000	30 June	Payments	CB1	200
30 June	Receipts	CB1	10,000	30 June	Balance	C/d	12,800
			13,000				13,000
30 June	Balance	B/d	12,800				

Bank Account **No. 2**

Date	Details	Fo	Total €	Date	Details	Fo	Total €
2014				2014			
1 June	Balance		10,000	30 June	Payments	CB1	3,868
30 June	Receipts	CB1	14,000	30 June	Balance	C/d	20,132
			24,000				24,000
30 June	Balance	B/d	20,132				

Sales Account **No. 3**

Date	Details	Fo	Total	Date	Details	Fo	Total €
				2014			
				30 June	Cash Book	CB1	13,333

Capital Account **No. 4**

Date	Details	Fo	Total	Date	Details	Fo	Total €
				2014			
				1 June	Cash Book		13,000

VAT Account **No. 5**

Date	Details	Fo	Total	Date	Details	Fo	Total
2014			€	2014			€
30 June	Cash Purchases	CB1	161	30 June	Cash Sales	CB1	2,667
30 June	Balance	C/d	2,506				
			2,667				2,667
				30 June	Balance	B/d	2,506

Purchases Account **No. 6**

Date	Details	Fo	Total	Date	Details	Fo	Total
2014			€	2014			€
12 June	Bank	CB1	807				

Wages Account **No. 7**

Date	Details	Fo	Total	Date	Details	Fo	Total
2014			€	2014			€
10 June	Bank	CB1	900				

Office Expenses Account **No. 8**

Date	Details	Fo	Total	Date	Details	Fo	Total
2014			€				
23 June	Cash	CB1	200				

DEBTORS LEDGER

D. Creedon Ltd Account **No. 1**

Date	Details	Fo	Total	Date	Details	Fo	Total
				2014			€
				15 June	Bank	CB1	8,000

CREDITORS LEDGER

J. Shorthall Ltd Account **No. 1**

Date	Details	Fo	Total	Date	Details	Fo	Total
2014			€				
20 June	Bank	CB1	2,000				

NOTES

(i) Cash balance and bank balance are entered in the cash account and bank account on the debit side (overdrawn balance is entered on credit side).

(ii) The credit entry for these balances is in the capital account.

Trial Balance

Debit Balance → Debit Column

Credit Balance → Credit Column

Trial Balance as on 30 June 2014

Date	Details	Fo	Debit €	Credit €
	Cash		12,800	
	Bank		20,132	
	Sales			13,333
	Capital			13,000
	VAT			2,506
	Purchases		807	
	Wages		900	
	Office Expenses		200	
	D. Creedon Ltd			8,000
	J. Shorthall Ltd		2,000	
			36,839	36,839

METHOD II — ANALYSED CASH BOOK

Debit **Analysed Cash Book** **Credit**

Date	Details	Fo	Rec. No.	Cash €	Bank €	Sales €	VAT €	Debtors €	Date	Details	Fo	Chq. No.	Cash €	Bank €	Purch. €	VAT €	Crs €	Wages €	Other €
2014									2014										
1 June	Balance	GL4		3,000	10,000				10 June	Wages	GL/7	41		900				900	
4 June	Sales	GL3	1		6,000	5,000	1,000		12 June	Purchases	GL/6	42		968	807	161			
15 June	D. Creedon Ltd	DL1	2		8,000			8,000	20 June	J. Shorthall Ltd	CL/1	43		2,000			2,000		
28 June	Sales	GL3	3	10,000		8,333	1,667		23 June	Office Exp.	GL/8		200						200
									30 June	Balance	C/d		12,800	20,132					
				13,000	24,000	13,333	2,667	8,000					13,000	24,000	807	161	2,000	900	200
						↑ GL /3	↑ GL/5								↑ GL/6	↑ GL/5			
30 June	Balance	B/d		12,800	20,132														

Note

The analysed cash book will contain the same figures as in (1) the analysed cash receipts and lodgments book and (2) the analysed cash and cheque payments book, as well as the opening and closing balances in the cash account and bank account in the ledger, i.e. cash and bank accounts are balanced in the analysed cash book.

C. Opening Balances

(1) The opening balance in the cash account must be on the debit side.
(2) The opening balance in the bank account can be on the debit side (i.e. business has money in the bank), **OR** it can be on the credit side (i.e. business has an overdraft).

N.B. Opening balances are not posted to the ledger.

D. Contra Entries

A Contra Entry is where
(1) Cash is being lodged to the bank.

OR

(2) Cash is being withdrawn from the bank for use in office.

(1) Lodged cash in bank	Take money from cash. Credit cash. Put money into bank. Debit bank.
(2) Withdrew cash from bank	Take money from bank. Credit bank. Put money into cash. Debit cash.

N.B. A contra entry involves cash account and bank account only. A contra entry is not posted to the ledger. To denote a contra entry, a 'c' is put in the folio column.

E. Overheads of a Business

Overheads are the expenses involved in the running of a business. **When they are paid, they are recorded in the analysed cash and cheque payments book/credit side of analysed cash book.** To complete the double entry, **debit the appropriate ledger account**. The main overheads of a business are:

Rent	**Postage and Stationery**	**Wages and Salaries**
Rates	**Telephone**	**Interest on Loans**
Insurance	**Advertising**	**Light and Heat**

Practice Question

Record the following transactions for the month of July in the appropriate books of first entry, post relevant figures to the ledger, extract a trial balance as on 31 July.

Note
Analyse the cash and bank transactions using the following money column headings:

Debit (Receipts) Side: Cash, Bank, Sales, VAT, Debtors.
Credit (Payments) Side: Cash, Bank, Purchases, VAT, Creditors, Wages, Other.
Transactions

1 July Cash balance €5,000, Bank balance €15,000
3 July Cash sales lodged €8,000, this includes VAT of €1,333 (receipt No. 1)
4 July Paid wages cheque No. 80 €1,200
8 July Purchased goods cheque No. 81 €1,500 + VAT @ 20%
12 July Kennedy Ltd (debtor) settled its account of €10,000 by cheque and it was lodged (receipt No. 2)
15 July Paid Horgan Ltd (creditor) by cheque No. 82 €600
23 July Paid office expenses by cash €600
25 July Cash sales €9,000. This includes VAT of €1,500 (receipt No. 3)
26 July Purchased equipment by cheque No. 83 €6,000

Chapter 33 — Petty Cash Book

A. Introduction

The petty cash book is used to record small cash payments, e.g. postage stamps, bus fares, envelopes. It has a debit side that records the petty cash float, and the credit side records payments. The credit side is analysed to give a breakdown of the payments.

B. Imprest System

The petty cash book operates on the Imprest System, which works as follows:

(1) Chief cashier gives Petty cashier a sum of money called Float, which it is estimated will cover petty cash expenses for the month. It is shown on the debit side of the petty cash book.
(2) During the month this float is used to pay small expenses. A petty cash voucher is completed by the person requiring the money. Payments are recorded on the credit side of petty cash book.
(3) At the end of month, the petty cash book is balanced, and amount spent is calculated.
(4) Chief cashier gives petty cashier a sum equivalent to amount spent to restore imprest to original level so that petty cashier can start next month with the same float.

C. Advantages of Using the Imprest system

(1) It saves on bank charges – fewer cheques used.
(2) It is a record of small payments.
(3) It sets an upper limit to small office expenses.
(4) It highlights excessive expenses.
(5) The voucher is proof of payment.
(6) It reduces entries in Cash Book/Bank a/c.

D. Petty Cash Voucher

If an employee needs money to purchase something small, he will complete a petty cash voucher giving:

(1) Date
(2) Amount
(3) Reason for money required
(4) Signature of claimant
(5) Signature of supervisor

The payment is recorded in the credit side of the petty cash book.

Examination-Style Question and Solution

Question 1.

Answer (a), (b) and (c). This is a Petty Cash Question.

Mary Sweeney is the Office Manager in a company called Waldorf Ltd. She uses a Petty Cash Book to keep an account of small office expenses. At the beginning of each month, she starts off with an imprest of €100.

Here is what happened in May 2013:

- 1 May Balance (imprest) on hand €100.
- 2 May She paid €3 for postage — Petty Cash Voucher No. 101
- 4 May She bought envelopes for €2 — Petty Cash Voucher No. 102
- 6 May She paid €12 to Mr John Power to repair a broken typewriter — Petty Cash Voucher No. 103
- 7 May She bought writing paper (stationery) for €7 — Petty Cash Voucher No. 104
- 8 May She paid train fare €11 for sales representative — Petty Cash Voucher No. 105
- 9 May She paid the office cleaner €16 — Petty Cash Voucher No. 106
- 11 May She paid €6 for postage — Petty Cash Voucher No. 107
- 14 May She paid €5 out of petty cash to a local charity for a sponsored walk — Petty Cash Voucher No. 108
- 17 May She posted a parcel — the stamp cost €3 — Petty Cash Voucher No. 109
- 19 May She paid €4 taxi fare for sales manager — Petty Cash Voucher No. 110
- 23 May She paid the office cleaner €13 — Petty Cash Voucher No. 111
- 28 May She purchased computer paper (stationery) for €14 — Petty Cash Voucher No. 112

1. (a) A blank Petty Cash Voucher (No. 103) is supplied at the end of the question. Use it to enter the transaction of 6 May (only). (15)

1. (b) In your answer book, write up the Petty Cash Book for the month of May, using the following analysis columns:

POSTAGE STATIONERY CLEANING TRAVEL SUNDRIES

Total each analysis column, and balance the Petty Cash Book at the end of May. (40)

1. (c) How much money will Mary receive from the chief cashier to enable her to start next month with an imprest of €100? (5)

1. (a) Document for Question 1. (a) PETTY CASH VOUCHER

WALDORF LTD			
PETTY CASH VOUCHER		No. 103	
Details		Amount	
		€	c
Signature			
Date			

Source: Junior Certificate Ordinary Level. **(60 marks)**

Solution to Question 1.

1. (a) Document for Question 1. (a) PETTY CASH VOUCHER

WALDORF LTD			
PETTY CASH VOUCHER		No. 103	
Details		Amount	
John Power *Repairs to broken typewriter*		€	c
		12	*00*
Signature	*Mary Sweeney*		
Date	*6 May 2013*		

1. (b) PETTY CASH BOOK Page 1

Date	Details	Total €	Date	Details	Voucher No.	Total €	Postage €	Stationery €	Cleaning €	Travel €	Sundries €
2013			2013								
1 May	Balance	100.–	2 May	Postage	101	3.00	3.00				
			4 May	Envelopes	102	2.00		2.00			
			6 May	J. Power	103	12.00					12.00
			7 May	Writing Paper	104	7.00		7.00			
			8 May	Train Fare	105	11.00				11.00	
			9 May	Office Cleaner	106	16.00			16.00		
			11 May	Postage	107	6.00	6.00				
			14 May	Sponsored Walk	108	5.00					5.00
			17 May	Parcel Post	109	3.00	3.00				
			19 May	Taxi	110	4.00				4.00	
			23 May	Office Cleaner	111	13.00			13.00		
			28 May	Computer Paper	112	14.00		14.00			
						96.00	12.00	23.00	29.00	15.00	17.00
							GL/1	GL/2	GL/3	GL/4	GL/5
			31 May	Balance	C/d	4.00					
		100.–				100.00					
31 May	Balance B/d	4.–									
1 June	Bank	96.–									

1. (c) *Mary will receive from chief cashier €96.00.*

D. Posting Petty Cash Book to Ledger

At the end of month, the analysis columns are totalled and the Petty Cash Book is balanced. An account for each analysis column is opened in the general ledger and the total of each account is posted to the **debit side** of the relevant account.

GENERAL LEDGER

Postage Account No. 1

Date	Details	Fo	Total	Date	Details	Fo	Total
2013			€				
31 May	Petty Cash Book	PCB1	12.00				

Stationery Account No. 2

Date	Details	Fo	Total	Date	Details	Fo	Total
2013			€				
31 May	Petty Cash Book	PCB1	23.00				

Cleaning Account No. 3

Date	Details	Fo	Total	Date	Details	Fo	Total
2013			€				
31 May	Petty Cash Book	PCB1	29.00				

Travel Account No. 4

Date	Details	Fo	Total	Date	Details	Fo	Total
2013			€				
31 May	Petty Cash Book	PCB1	15.00				

Sundries Account No. 5

Date	Details	Fo	Total	Date	Details	Fo	Total
2013			€				
31 May	Petty Cash Book	PCB1	17.00				

PRACTICE QUESTIONS

(i) Answer **(a)**, **(b)** and **(c)**. This is a Petty Cash Question.

Mary Murphy is office manager in a company called Sherwood Ltd. She uses a petty cash book to keep an account of small office expenses. At the beginning of each month she starts off with an Imprest of €150.

Here is an account of transactions for March 2016.

- 1 March Balance (Imprest) on hand €150.
- 3 March She paid €2 for postage stamps — Petty Cash Voucher No. 201
- 5 March She purchased envelopes for €2 — Petty Cash Voucher No. 202
- 8 March She paid for cleaning office €5 — Petty Cash Voucher No. 203
- 10 March She paid bus fares €6 — Petty Cash Voucher No. 204
- 16 March She purchased copying paper €12 — Petty Cash Voucher No. 205
- 18 March She purchased stationery €6 — Petty Cash Voucher No. 206
- 22 March She paid for cleaning office €5 — Petty Cash Voucher No. 207
- 25 March She donated €6 to charity — Petty Cash Voucher No. 208
- 29 March She paid for bus fares €6 — Petty Cash Voucher No. 209
- 30 March Purchased postage stamps €10 — Petty Cash Voucher No. 210

(i) (a) On the blank Petty Cash Voucher No. 203 supplied below, enter the transaction of 8 March (only).

SHERWOOD LTD			
PETTY CASH VOUCHER		No. 203	
Details		Amount	
		€	c
Signature			
Date			

(i) (b) In your answer book, write up the petty cash book for the month of March, using the following analysis columns:

POSTAGE STATIONERY CLEANING TRAVEL SUNDRIES

Total each analysis column, and balance the petty cash book at end of March.

(i) (c) How much money will Mary receive from the chief cashier to enable her to start next month with an Imprest of €150?

(i) (d) Post the totals of the analysis columns to the appropriate ledger accounts.

Chapter 34 — General Journal

A. Introduction

The General Journal is used to record transactions that cannot be recorded in any other book of first entry.

These transactions are:
(1) Opening entries.
(2) Purchase and sale of fixed assets on credit.
(3) Bad debts written off.
The General Journal is also posted to the Ledger.

B. Layout of General Journal

GENERAL JOURNAL

Date	Details	Fo	Debit	Credit
	Names of Accounts and Narration (Explanation of Transaction)		A/C to be Debited	A/C to be Credited

(1) OPENING ENTRIES
A list of **Assets** and **Liabilities** at the start of the trading period.

Assets — Debit Column
Liabilities — Credit Column

The difference is called Share Capital and is entered in the Credit Column, i.e. money owed to owners/shareholders.

Assets – Liabilities = Share Capital

Narration — a brief explanation of the transaction.

Sample Question and Solution

Question
Kavanagh Ltd had the following Assets and Liabilities on 1 January. Enter these in the General Journal and post to the ledger.

Assets: Cash €10,000 Bank €20,000 Buildings €150,000
Debtor: Seamus McCarthy €6,000
Liabilities Creditor: Patrick Hennessey €3,000
Share Capital: €183,000

Solution

GENERAL JOURNAL **Page 1**

Date	Details	Fo	Debit €	Credit €
2014				
1 Jan.	Assets			
	Cash	CB1	10,000	
	Bank	CB1	20,000	
	Buildings	GL1	150,000	
	Debtor: Seamus McCarthy	DL1	6,000	
	Liabilities			
	Creditor: Patrick Hennessey	CL1		3,000
	Share Capital	GL2		183,000
			186,000	186,000
	Assets, Liabilities and Share Capital of Kavanagh Ltd on 1 Jan.			

Posting opening entries to ledger

- *Assets that are in the Debit Column of the General Journal are Debit Balances in the Ledger.*
- *Liabilities and Share Capital that are in the Credit Column of the General Journal are Credit Balances in the Ledger.*

GENERAL LEDGER

Building Account **No. 1**

Date	Details	Fo	Total	Date	Details	Fo	Total
2014			€				
1 Jan.	Balance	GJ1	150,000				

Share Capital Account **No. 2**

Date	Details	Fo	Total	Date	Details	Fo	Total
				2014			€
				1 Jan.	Balance	GJ1	183,000

DEBTORS LEDGER

Seamus McCarthy Account No. 1

Date	Details	Fo	Total	Date	Details	Fo	Total
2014			€				
1 Jan.	*Balance*	*GJ1*	*6,000*				

CREDITORS LEDGER

Patrick Hennessey Account No. 1

Date	Details	Fo	Total	Date	Details	Fo	Total
				2014			€
				1 Jan.	*Balance*	*GJ1*	*3,000*

CASH BOOK

Date	Details	Fo	Cash €	Bank €	Date	Details	Fo	Cash	Bank
2014 *1 Jan.*	*Balance*	*GJ1*	*10,000*	*20,000*					

(2) PURCHASE AND SALE OF FIXED ASSETS ON CREDIT

Sample Question and Solution

Question

- 2 Jan. Purchased office equipment on credit from Munster Business Equipment for €3,000 + VAT @ 20%
- 3 Jan. Sold office equipment on credit to Frank Boland for €500 + VAT @ 20%

Solution — Explanation

- *2 Jan. Debit office equipment account €3,000 — receiving account*
  Debit VAT account €600
  Credit Munster Business Equipment — €3,600 — giving account
- *3 Jan. Debit Frank Boland account — €600 — receiving account*
  Credit office equipment account — €500 — giving account
  Credit VAT account — €100

GENERAL JOURNAL				Page 1
Date	Details	Fo	Debit €	Credit €
2015				
2 Jan.	Office Equipment A/C	GL1	3,000	
	VAT A/C	GL2	600	
	Munster Business Equipment A/C	CL1		3,600
	Purchase of Office Equipment on Credit			
3 Jan.	Frank Boland A/C	DL1	600	
	Office Equipment A/C	GL1		500
	VAT A/C	GL2		100
	Sale of Office Equipment on Credit			

GENERAL LEDGER

Office Equipment Account

Date	Details	Fo	Total	Date	Details	Fo	Total
2015			€	2015			€
2 Jan.	Munster Business Equipment	GJ1	3,000	3 Jan.	Frank Boland	GJ1	500

VAT Account

Date	Details	Fo	Total	Date	Details	Fo	Total
2015			€	2015			€
2 Jan.	Munster Business Equipment	GJ1	600	3 Jan.	Frank Boland	GJ1	100

DEBTORS LEDGER

Frank Boland Account

Date	Details	Fo	Total	Date	Details	Fo	Total
2015			€				
3 Jan.	Office Equipment	GJ1	600				

CREDITORS LEDGER

Munster Business Equipment Account

Date	Details	Fo	Total	Date	Details	Fo	Total
				2015			€
				2 Jan.	Office Equipment	GJ1	3,600

(3) BAD DEBTS WRITTEN OFF

A bad debt arises when goods are sold on credit to a debtor and the debtor fails to pay the money owed. The business will then write the figure off as a bad debt.

Sample Question and Solution

Question

5 Feb. Jim Lawlor (debtor) owes €600 and has been declared bankrupt and can pay only €200. The remaining €400 is to be written off as a bad debt.

Solution

Debit bank account with €200 — amount received.
Debit bad debts account €400 — amount of bad debt.
Credit Jim Lawlor — €600 — to close his account.

GENERAL JOURNAL — **Page 2**

Date	Details	Fo	Debit €	Credit €
2016				
5 Feb.	*Bank A/C*	*CB1*	*200*	
	Bad Debts A/C	*GL1*	*400*	
	Jim Lawlor A/C	*DL1*		*600*
	Jim Lawlor declared bankrupt. Paid €200, balance owed written off as a bad debt.			

CASH BOOK — **Page 1**

Date	Details	Fo	Cash €	Bank	Date	Details	Fo	Cash	Bank
2016									
5 Feb.	*Jim Lawlor*	*GJ2*	*200*						

GENERAL LEDGER

Bad Debts Account — **No. 1**

Date	Details	Fo	Total €	Date	Details	Fo	Total
2016							
5 Feb.	*Jim Lawlor*	*GJ2*	*400*				

DEBTORS LEDGER

Jim Lawlor Account **No. 1**

Date 2016	Details	Fo	Total €	Date 2016	Details	Fo	Total €
1 Feb.	Balance	GJ2	600	5 Feb.	Bank	GJ2	200
				5 Feb.	Bad Debts	GJ2	400
			600				600

PRACTICE QUESTION

Colour Printing Ltd runs a small business. Enter the following opening balances and transactions in the general journal, and post to the ledger.

1 MAR.

Assets

Cash €5,000, Bank €10,000
Stock €290,000 Motor Vehicles, €25,000
Debtors: Print and Design Ltd €200
Graphic Print Ltd €800

Liabilities

Creditors: Kerry Printers Ltd €2,000
ABC Printers Ltd €1,000
Share Capital €48,000

3 MAR. Purchased printing equipment on credit from Kerry Printers Ltd for €15,000 + VAT @ 20%.

5 MAR. Sold printing equipment on credit to Graphic Print Ltd for €2,000 + VAT @ 20%.

10 MAR. Print and Design Ltd (debtor) has been declared bankrupt, owes €200 and can pay only €50. Remaining €150 to be written off as a bad debt.

Higher Level

Chapter 35 — Book-Keeping Revision

In this chapter we will summarise briefly the books of first entry and work a question from a Junior Certificate paper (Higher Level).

BOOKS OF FIRST ENTRY — SUMMARY

Books of First Entry	Type of Transaction Book Is Used For	Source Documents	Rules for Posting to Ledger
Purchases day book	Goods purchased on credit	Invoices received	DR — Purchases A/C Net DR — VAT A/C — VAT CR — Personal A/C — Total
Purchases returns day book	Returns of goods purchased on credit	Credit notes received	DR Personal A/C — Total CR Purch. Ret. A/C — Net CR VAT A/C — VAT
Sales day book	Goods sold on credit	Invoices sent	DR Personal A/C — Total CR Sales A/C — Net CR Vat A/C — VAT
Sales returns day book	Return of goods previously sold on credit	Credit notes sent	DR Sales Ret. A/C — Net DR VAT A/C — VAT CR Personal A/C — Total
Cash book	Cash receipts → Bank lodgments →	Cash register/+ receipts given Lodgment counterfoils/ + bank statements	Debit side of cash book → Credit side of ledger
	Cash payments → Cheque payments →	Cash vouchers Cheque counterfoils/ + bank statements	Credit side of cash book → Debit side of ledger
Petty cash book	Small items of expenditure	Petty cash vouchers	Total of each analysis column is posted to Debit side of ledger A/C
General journal	(1) Opening entries	Relevant invoices, etc.	(1) DR Assets — CR Liabilities
	(2) Purchase of assets on credit		(2) DR — Asset A/C DR — VAT A/C CR — Personal A/C
	(3) Sale of assets on credit		(3) DR — Personal A/C CR — Asset A/C CR — VAT A/C
	(4) Bad debts written off		(4) DR — Bank A/C DR — Bad Debts A/C CR — Personal A/C

Examination-Style Question and Solution

Question 1.

Answer (a), (b) and (c). This is a book of First Entry and Ledger Question.
Sunshine Paints Ltd had the following balances in its General Journal on 1 May 2013.

GENERAL JOURNAL				
Date	**Details**	**F**	**Dr** €	**Cr** €
2013				
1 May	Premises	GL1	70,000	
	Motor Vans	GL2	30,000	
	Bank		5,000	
	Debtor: J.J. Builders Ltd	DL1	3,000	
	Creditor: Throne Paints Ltd	CL1		48,000
	Ordinary Share Capital	GL3		60,000
			108,000	108,000

The following transactions took place during the month of May 2013:

CREDIT TRANSACTIONS

4/5/13	Purchased paint for resale on credit from Throne Paints Ltd	Invoice No. 361 €40,000 + VAT 20%
10/5/13	Sold paint on credit to Brushwell Ltd	Invoice No. 120 €5,000 + VAT 20%
17/5/13	Sold paint on credit to J.J. Builders Ltd	Invoice No. 121 €25,000 + VAT 20%

BANK TRANSACTIONS

6/5/13	Cash sales lodged		€9,000 (This includes €1,500 VAT.)
8/5/13	Paid wages	(Cheque No. 75)	€1,050
15/5/13	Purchased paint	(Cheque No. 76)	€1,200 + VAT 20%
22/5/13	J.J. Builders Ltd settled their account in full by cheque and it was lodged.		
28/5/13	Paid Throne Paints Ltd	(Cheque No. 77)	€35,000

You are required to:

1. (a) Post the balances on 1 May given in the General Journal to the relevant accounts. (7)

1. (b) Record the transactions for the month of May in the appropriate books of first entry. Post relevant figures to the ledger.

NOTE

Analyse the bank transactions using the following money column headings:
Debit (Receipts) Side: Bank, Sales, VAT, Debtors.
Credit (Payments) Side: Bank, Purchases, VAT, Creditors, Wages. (25)

1. (c) Balance the accounts on 31 May 2013 and extract a Trial Balance as on that date. (8)

Source: Junior Certificate Higher Level. **(40 marks)**

Solution to Question 1.

PURCHASES DAY BOOK

Date	Details	Inv. No.	Fo	Net €	VAT €	Total €
4/5/13	Throne Paints Ltd	361	CL9	40,000	8,000	48,000
31/5/13	Debit Purchases and VAT A/Cs			40,000	8,000	48,000

SALES DAY BOOK

Date	Details	Inv. No.	Fo	Net €	VAT €	Total €
10/5/13	Brushwell Ltd	120	DL2	5,000	1,000	6,000
17/5/13	J.J. Builders Ltd	121	DL1	25,000	5,000	30,000
31/5/13	Credit Sales and VAT A/Cs			30,000	6,000	36,000

Analysed Cash Book (1)

Date	Details	Fo	Bank €	Sales €	VAT €	Debtors €	Date	Details	Fo No.	Chq.	Bank €	Purch. €	VAT €	Crs €	Wages €
1/5/13	Balance	GJ1	5,000				8/5/13	Wages	GL4	75	1,050				1,050
6/5/13	Sales	GL1	9,000	7,500	1,500		15/5/13	Purch.	GL2	76	1,440	1,200	240		
22/5/13	J.J. Builders	DL1	33,000			33,000	28/5/13	Throne Paints	GL9	77	35,000			35,000	
							31/5/13	Bal.	C/d		9,510				
			47,000	7,500	1,500	33,000					47,000	1,200	240	35,000	1,050
31/5/13	B/d		9,510												

OR

Analysed Cash Receipts and Lodgments Book

Date	Details	Fo	Bank €	Sales €	VAT €	Debtors €
6/5/13	Sales	GL1	9,000	7,500	1,500	
22/5/13	J.J. Builders	DL1	33,000			33,000
31/5/13	Debit Bank A/C		42,000	7,500	1,500	33,000

AND

Analysed Cheque Payments Book								
Date	Details	Fo	Ch. No.	Bank €	Purch. €	VAT €	Cdts €	Wages €
8/5/13	Wages	GL4	75	1,050				1,050
15/5/13	Purchases	GL2	76	1,440	1,200	240		
28/5/13	Throne Paints	GL9	77	35,000			35,000	
31/5/13	Credit Bank A/C			37,490	1,200	240	35,000	1,050

AND

Bank Account No. 1

Date	Details	Fo	Total €	Date	Details	Fo	Total €
1/5/13	Balance	GJ1	5,000	31/5/13	Cheque Payments Book	CPB1	37,490
31/5/13	Cash Receipts and Lodgments	CRLB1	42,000	31/5/13	Balance	C/d	9,510
			47,000				47,000
31/5/13	Balance	B/d	9,510				

GENERAL LEDGER

Premises Account

Date	Details	Fo	Total €	Date	Details	Fo	Total
1/5/13	Balance	GJ1	70,000				

Motor Vans Account

Date	Details	Fo	Total €	Date	Details	Fo	Total
1/5/13	Balance	GJ1	30,000				

Ordinary Share Capital Account

Date	Details	Fo	Total	Date	Details	Fo	Total €
				1/5/13	Balance	GJ1	60,000

Wages Account

Date	Details	Fo	Total €	Date	Details	Fo	Total
8/5/13	Bank	CB1	1,050				

Sales Account

Date	Details	Fo	Total	Date	Details	Fo	Total €
				31/5/13	Sales Day Book	SB1	30,000
				31/5/13	Bank	CB1	7,500
							37,500

Purchases Account

Date	Details	Fo	Total €	Date	Details	Fo	Total
31/5/13	Purchases Day Book	PB1	40,000				
31/5/13	Bank	CB1	1,200				
			41,200				

VAT Account

Date	Details	Fo	Total €	Date	Details	Fo	Total €
31/5/13	Credit Purchases	PB1	8,000	31/5/13	Credit Sales	SB1	6,000
31/5/13	Cash Purchases	CB1	240	31/5/13	Cash Sales	CB1	1,500
				31/5/13	Balance	C/d	740
			8,240				8,240
1/6/13	Balance	C/d	740				

DEBTORS LEDGER

J.J. Builders Ltd Account

Date	Details	Fo	Total €	Date	Details	Fo	Total €
1/5/13	Balance	GJ1	3,000	22/5/13	Bank	CB1	33,000
17/5/13	Sales	SB1	30,000				
			33,000				33,000

Brushwell Ltd Account

Date	Details	Fo	Total €	Date	Details	Fo	Total
10/5/13	Sales	SB1	6,000				

CREDITORS LEDGER

Throne Paints Ltd Account

Date	Details	Fo	Total €	Date	Details	Fo	Total €
28/5/13	Bank	CB1	35,000	1/5/13	Balance	GJ1	48,000
31/5/13	Balance	C/d	61,000	4/5/13	Purchases	PB1	48,000
			96,000				96,000
				1/6/13	Balance	B/d	61,000

Trial Balance as on 31/5/03

Date	Details	Fo	Debit (€)	Credit(€)
31/5/13	Premises		70,000	
	Motor Vans		30,000	
	Ordinary Share Capital			60,000
	Wages		1,050	
	Sales			37,500
	Purchases		41,200	
	VAT		740	
	Brushwell Ltd		6,000	
	Throne Paints Ltd			61,000
	Bank		9,510	
			158,500	158,500

Higher Level

Chapter 36 — Control Accounts

We can check on the accuracy of the debtors and creditors ledger — by Control accounts (Total accounts).

A. Principles of Control Accounts

(1) Entries in a control account are exactly the same as in personal accounts, **but they are in total**.
(2) Items **debited** in a personal account are **debited** in total in a control account. Items **credited** in a personal account are **credited** in total in a control account.
(3) The control account is prepared by taking the **totals from the day books**.

B. Types of Control Account

(1) Debtors Control Account	**(2)** Creditors Control Account
↓	↓
Checks Debtors (Sales) Ledger	Checks Creditors (Purchases) Ledger

There are two types:

(1) DEBTORS CONTROL ACCOUNT

The debtors control account is a total account and is prepared by taking totals of sales day book, sales returns book and total cash/cheques received from debtors. The balance in the debtors control account should be equal to the total of the balances on **all** personal accounts in the debtors ledger, thus providing evidence of the accuracy of the debtors ledger.

Consider the entries in the personal account of a debtor.

Debit		**A Debtor A/C**			**Credit**
	ENTRIES	**SOURCE**		**ENTRIES**	**SOURCE**
	Balance (amount due from debtor) →	General Journal		Sales returns →	Sales Returns Day Book
	Credit sales →	Sales Day Book		Cash/cheques received from debtor →	Cash Book
				Balance C/d (amount due from debtor)	

And now look at the control account.

DEBTORS CONTROL (TOTAL) ACCOUNT					
	ENTRIES	SOURCE		ENTRIES	SOURCE
	Balance (total amount due from all debtors) →	General Journal		Total sales returns →	Sales Returns Day Book
				Total cash/cheques received from debtors →	Cash Book
	Total credit sales →	Sales Day Book		Balance C/d (balance due from all debtors)	

NB Total debtors account is prepared from totals of books of first entry (SDB, SRDB, CB).

Sample Question and Solution

Question

Complete and balance the debtors control account from the following data.

- Balance as on 1 June 2016 €2,000
- Total cash received from debtors in June €10,000
- Total sales on credit in June €15,000
- Total sales returns in June €1,000

Solution

'T' ACCOUNT FORMAT

Debtors Control Account

Date 2016	Details	Fo	Total €	Date 2016	Details	Fo	Total €
1 June	*Balance B/d*	*GJ*	*2,000*	*30 June*	*Cash rec. from debtors*	*CB*	*10,000*
30 June	*Credit sales*	*SB*	*15,000*	*30 June*	*Sales returns*	*SRB*	*1,000*
				30 June	*Balance*	*C/d*	*6,000*
			17,000				*17,000*
30 June	*Balance*	*B/d*	*6,000*				

OR

CONTINUOUS BALANCING FORMAT

Debtors Control A/C					
Date	**Details**	**Fo**	**Debit (€)**	**Credit (€)**	**Balance (€)**
2016					
1 June	*Balance B/d*	*GJ*			*2,000*
30 June	*Credit sales*	*SB*	*15,000*		*17,000*
30 June	*Cash received from debtors*	*CB*		*10,000*	*7,000*
30 June	*Sales returns*	*SRB*		*1,000*	*6,000*

(2) CREDITORS CONTROL ACCOUNT

The creditors control account is also a total account and is prepared by taking the totals of purchases day book, purchases returns book and total cash/cheques paid to creditors from the cash book. The balance in the creditors control account should be equal to the total of the balances on **all** personal accounts in the creditors ledger, thus providing evidence of the accuracy of the creditors ledger.

Consider the entries in a personal account of a creditor.

Debit		**A Creditor A/C**			**Credit**
	ENTRIES	**SOURCE**		**ENTRIES**	**SOURCE**
	Purchases returns →	Purchases Returns Book		Balance (amount due to creditor) →	General Journal
	Cash/cheques paid to creditor →	Cash Book		Credit purchases →	Purchases Day Book
	Balance C/d (amount due to creditor)				

And now look at the control account.

CREDITORS CONTROL (TOTAL) ACCOUNT					
	ENTRIES	**SOURCE**		**ENTRIES**	**SOURCE**
	Total purchases returns →	Purchases Ret. Book		Balance (total amount due to all creditors) →	General Journal
	Total cash/cheques paid to creditors →	Cash Book		Total credit purchases →	Purchases Day Book
	Balance C/d (amount due to all creditors)				

N.B. Total creditors account is prepared from totals of books of first entry (PDB, PRDB, CB).

Sample Question and Solution

Question

Complete and balance the creditors control account from the following data.

- Balance as on 1 July 2016 €4,000
- Total purchases on credit in July €20,000
- Total payments (by cheque) during July to creditors €15,000
- Total payments (by cash) during July to creditors €1,000
- Total purchases returns during July €3,000

Solution

'T' ACCOUNT FORMAT

Creditors Control Account

Date	Details	Fo	Total	Date	Details	Fo	Total
2016			€	2016			€
31 July	*Payments to creditors — cheques*	*CB*	*15,000*	*1 July*	*Balance B/d*	*GJ*	*4,000*
31 July	*Payments to creditors — cash*	*CB*	*1,000*	*31 July*	*Total credit purchases*	*PB*	*20,000*
31 July	*Purchases returns*	*PRB*	*3,000*				
31 July	*Balance*	*C/d*	*5,000*				
			24,000				*24,000*
				31 July	*Balance B/d*		*5,000*

OR

CONTINUOUS BALANCING FORMAT

Creditors Control A/C

Date	Details	Fo	Debit (€)	Credit (€)	Balance (€)
2016					
1 July	*Balance*	*GJ*			*4,000*
31 July	*Credit purchases*	*PB*		*20,000*	*24,000*
31 July	*Payments to creditors — cheques*	*CB*	*15,000*		*9,000*
31 July	*Payments to creditors — cash*	*CB*	*1,000*		*8,000*
31 July	*Purchases returns*	*PRB*	*3,000*		*5,000*

Higher Level

Chapter 37 — Continuous Presentation of Ledger Accounts

A. Types of Presentation

There are two ways of presenting ledger accounts.

(1) 'T' ACCOUNT FORMAT

This has the debit side on the left and the credit side on the right.

(2) CONTINUOUS BALANCING FORMAT

This has a debit column, a credit column and a balance column. The balance column is adjusted after each transaction so we can see immediately the balance on a particular day.

NB Students may opt to do ledger accounts using either the 'T' account format or the continuous balancing format. But Higher Level students must be able to convert from 'T' account format to continuous balancing format or vice versa.

Conversion of a Debtor's Account from 'T' Account Format to Continuous Balancing Format

Sample Question and Solution

Question

Convert the following account in the debtors ledger into continuous balancing format.

DEBTORS LEDGER

DR ↑		**Patrick Gallagher Account**					**CR ↓**
Date	**Details**	**Fo**	**Total**	**Date**	**Details**	**Fo**	**Total**
2015			€	2015			€
1 Jan.	Balance	GJ	2,000	15 Jan.	Cash	CB	2,000
10 Jan.	Sales	SB	15,000	18 Jan.	Bank	CB	9,000
22 Jan.	Sales	SB	11,000	25 Jan.	Sales returns	SRB	1,000
				31 Jan.	Balance	C/d	16,000
			28,000				28,000
31 Jan.	Balance	B/d	16,000				

Solution

DEBTORS LEDGER

Patrick Gallagher A/C					
Date	**Details**	**Fo**	**Debit + (€)**	**Credit – (€)**	**Balance (€)**
2015					
1 Jan.	*Balance*	*GJ*			*2,000*
10 Jan.	*Sales*	*SB*	*15,000*		*17,000*
15 Jan.	*Cash*	*CB*	—	*2,000*	*15,000*
18 Jan.	*Bank*	*CB*	—	*9,000*	*6,000*
22 Jan.	*Sales*	*SB*	*11,000*	—	*17,000*
25 Jan.	*Sales Returns*	*SRB*	—	*1,000*	*16,000*

N.B. In Debtors Ledger

Figures in Debit column increase the balance.
Figures in Credit column reduce the balance.

Conversion of a Creditor's Account from 'T' Account Format to Continuous Balancing Format

Sample Question and Solution

Question
Convert the following account in the creditors ledger into continuous balancing format.

CREDITORS LEDGER

DR ↓		John Molloy Account					CR ↑
Date	**Details**	**Fo**	**Total**	**Date**	**Details**	**Fo**	**Total**
2015			€	2015			€
10 Feb.	Cash	CB	3,000	1 Feb.	Balance	GJ	10,000
15 Feb.	Bank	CB	6,000	6 Feb.	Purchases	PB	15,000
24 Feb.	Purchases returns	PRB	3,000	17 Feb.	Purchases	PB	2,000
28 Feb.	Balance	C/d	15,000				
			27,000				27,000
				28 Feb.	Balance	B/d	15,000

Solution

CREDITORS LEDGER

John Molloy A/C					
Date	**Details**	**Fo**	**Debit – (€)**	**Credit + (€)**	**Balance (€)**
2015					
1 Feb.	Balance	GJ			10,000
6 Feb.	Purchases	PB		15,000	25,000
10 Feb.	Cash	CB	3,000		22,000
15 Feb.	Bank	CB	6,000		16,000
17 Feb.	Purchases	PB		2,000	18,000
24 Feb.	Purchases returns	PRB	3,000		15,000

N.B. In Creditors Ledger

Figures in the Credit column increase the balance.
Figures in the Debit column reduce the balance.

FINAL ACCOUNTS OF A PRIVATE LIMITED COMPANY

Chapter 38 — Trading Account

A. Purpose of a Trading Account

The purpose of a trading account is to find the gross profit or gross loss made by a business in the trading period.

B. Trading Period

The trading period is the account period. It is usually twelve months (i.e. 1 January 2005–31 December 2005), but it could also be for six months.

C. Gross Profit/Gross Loss

The gross profit/gross loss is the difference between sales and cost of sales.

D. Contents of a Trading Account

(1) **Sales** — Value of all sales during the year/turnover.
(2) **Sales Returns/Returns Inwards** — Goods returned to us by debtors.
(3) **Opening Stock** — Value of stock at start of year.
(4) **Purchases** — Goods bought for resale during the year.
(5) **Purchases Returns/Returns Outwards** — Goods returned to our suppliers.
(6) **Carriage Inwards** — Transport costs of purchases for resale.
(7) **Customs Duty/Import Duty** — Tax on goods coming into the country.
(8) **Manufacturing Wages/Direct Wages** — Wages paid to manufacturing workers.
(9) **Closing Stock** — Value of stock at end of year.

Net Sales/Turnover = Sales – Sales Returns.

Net Purchases = Purchases – Purchases Returns.

Cost of Sales = Opening Stock + Purchases + Carriage Inwards + Customs Duty + Manufacturing Wages – Closing Stock.

Gross Profit = Net Sales – Cost of Sales.

Sample Question and Solution

Question

From the following information, prepare the trading account of Bobbit Enterprises Ltd for year ending 31 December 2015.

- Sales €200,000
- Purchases €80,000
- Carriage inwards €6,000
- Manufacturing wages €3,000
- Sales returns €1,000
- Purchases returns €2,000
- Opening stock (1 January 2015) €10,000
- Closing stock (31 December 2015) €15,000
- Import duty €2,000

Solution

Trading Account of Bobbit Enterprises Ltd for Year Ending 31 December 2015				
			€	€
	Sales	*200,000*		
	Less sales returns		*1,000*	
	Net sales/turnover			*199,000*
	Deduct Cost of Sales			
	Stock 1/1/15		*10,000*	
	Purchases	*80,000*		
	Less purchases returns	*2,000*	*78,000*	
	Carriage inwards		*6,000*	
	Import duty		*2,000*	
	Manufacturing wages		*3,000*	
	Cost of goods available for sale		*99,000*	
	Less closing stock 31/12/15		*15,000*	
	Cost of Sales			*84,000*
	Gross Profit			*115,000*

E. Interpretation of Information Presented in a Trading Account

The trading account gives the owner(s) of a business a lot of valuable information. (Refer to trading account of Bobbit Enterprises Ltd.)

(1) NET SALES/TURNOVER

€199,000

(2) COST OF SALES

€84,000

(3) RATE OF STOCK TURNOVER

This tells us how many times the stock is replaced in the business during the year.

$$\text{Formula} = \frac{\text{Cost of Sales}}{\text{Average Stock}} \qquad \frac{€84,000}{€12,500} = 6.72 \text{ Times}$$

$$\text{Average Stock} = \frac{\text{Opening Stock} + \text{Closing Stock}}{2}$$

$$\frac{€10,000 + €15,000}{2}$$

$$= \frac{€25,000}{2} = €12,500 = \text{Average Stock}$$

This business has a stock turnover of 6.72 times, which means that it replaces its stock every 54 days approx. (365 ÷ 6.72).

(4) GROSS PROFIT MARGIN/GROSS PROFIT PERCENTAGE

This rate shows how much gross profit was made on each €1.00 of sales.

$$\text{Formula} = \frac{\text{Gross Profit x } 100\%}{\text{Sales}} \qquad \frac{€115,000 \text{ x } 100\%}{€199,000} = 57.78\%$$

This firm is making a gross profit of 57.78c on every €1.00 of sales. The gross profit percentage can be compared with

(a) Previous year's gross profit margin.
(b) Other firms in the same industry.
(c) The industry average.

F. Trading and Non-Trading Stock

Trading stock is the stock of goods for resale to customers. Non-trading stock is stock of goods not for resale to customers, e.g. stock of heating, stock of stationery, stock of packing materials.

G. Stocktaking — Higher Level

The aim of stocktaking is to find out the value of goods in the business on a particular day. Stocktaking involves only trading stock.

(1) REASONS FOR STOCKTAKING

(a) To find the value of closing stock required for the trading account and balance sheet.
(b) To identify slow-moving items and damaged goods.
(c) To find out whether goods have been stolen.
(d) To check stock records, and for stock control purposes.
(e) To identify goods that need to be ordered.
(f) To cross-check computer records.

(2) MANUAL STOCKTAKING PROCEDURE

(a) Close business on the day. Ensure that stock is low on the day.
(b) Divide store into sections. Arrange all stock in its correct place.
(c) Assign two stocktakers to each section: one will count the goods, the other will record the information on the stock sheets.
(d) Note all damaged or obsolete stock.
(e) On completion of task, stocksheets will be returned to the accounts department for valuation of stock on hand.

(3) VALUATION OF STOCK

Stock is valued at the **lowest** of (a) cost price or (b) replacement price or (c) selling price.

(4) STOCKTAKING REPORT

STOCKTAKING REPORT DECEMBER 2016

To: Declan O'Brien Accounts Department
From: George Sutton Stock Supervisor
Date: 10 January 2017

Introduction: I was asked by you to report on the stocktaking on 31 December 2016.

Body of Report:
(a) Stocktaking took place on 31 December 2016 commencing at 10.00 a.m. and finishing at 5.00 p.m. The store was closed for business on the day.
(b) The task was performed accurately, a number of spot checks were taken, and all stock sheets were accurate.
(c) Some items of stock are slow-moving (see stock sheets Nos. 6 and 10). Some stock is also damaged (see stock sheet No. 14). This stock needs urgent attention.
(d) I am satisfied that this stock count is correct.

I am available to discuss this report if required.

Signed: George Sutton, Stock Supervisor.

Chapter 39 — Profit and Loss Account

A. Purpose of a Profit and Loss Account

The purpose of a profit and loss account is to find the net profit or net loss made by a business in the trading period — profit after all expenses are deducted.

Net Profit/Net Loss = Gross Profit + Gains – Expenses

B. Gains

Gains are income other than trading income received by a business, e.g. rent received, discount received, interest received, insurance received, bad debt recovered.

C. Expenses/Overheads

Overheads are the expenses involved in the running of a business on a daily basis, e.g. rent, insurance, wages, telephone.

D. Finding Net Profit/Net Loss

(1) Add gains to gross profit.
(2) Subtract total expenses.

E. Monitoring Overheads — Higher Level

Firms must curtail overheads as much as possible otherwise their net profit will be substantially reduced. All overheads must be recorded carefully.
(1) Establish whether the expense is necessary.
(2) Record the payment carefully.
(3) Check all bills for accuracy before payment.
(4) Eliminate wastage in the business, i.e. unnecessary telephone calls.

Examination-Style Question and Solution

Question
Answer all sections. This is a Monitoring of Overhead (Expenses) Question.

(A) Give **two** reasons why it is important for a business to monitor its overheads.
(B) The following table shows the Budget and Actual figures for a business's overheads for 2015.
(i) List the overheads whose actual figures are **greater than** the budgeted figures, and give one possible reason per overhead, for the difference.
(ii) List the overheads whose actual figures are **less than** the budgeted figures, and give one possible reason, per overhead, for the difference. (15)

Business overheads for 2015

Overheads	**Budgeted €**	**Actual €**
Rent	40,000	65,000
Advertising	20,000	15,000
Light and Heat	6,000	8,500
Insurance	8,000	10,000
Bank loan interest	7,000	5,000

Source: Junior Certificate Higher Level.

Solution:

A (i) To identify the main overheads of a business, i.e. to see what the money is spent on.
(ii) To help in the planning process. Accurate figures are needed to make projections.
(iii) To compare the actual figures with budgeted figures to make sure the business is on target.
(iv) To identify areas where overruns take place.
(v) To make any necessary changes as soon as possible.

B (i) *Rent* — the landlord increased the rent.
Light and Heat — the winter was colder than expected.
Insurance — the premium was increased
(ii) *Advertising* — in order to save, the business reduced its advertising expenditure.
Bank loan interest — the rate of interest fell.

F. Recording Overheads — Higher Level

All overheads when paid are entered in the analysed cash book **credit side**. The relevant account is **debited** in the ledger.

Example

10 Jan. Paid insurance €2,000 by cheque.

Analysed Cash Book

Date	Details	Fo	Cash	Bank	Date	Details	Fo	Cash	Bank
					2014				€
					10 Jan.	Insurance			2,000

Insurance A/C

Date	Details	Fo	Bank	Date	Details	Fo	Bank
2014			€	2014			€
10 Jan.	Bank		2,000	31 Jan.	P + L A/C		2,000

At end of year all overheads are closed off to the profit and loss account.

Debit P + L A/C (show under expenses).
Credit Overhead A/C (Insurance in above example).

Profit and Loss Account for year ending 31/1/2014

	Expenses		
	Insurance		2,000

G. Difference between a Trading A/C and a Profit and Loss A/C

Trading A/C shows	Profit and Loss A/C shows
(1) Sales (2) Opening stock, purchases and closing stock (3) Purchasing expenses (4) Gross profit/gross loss	(1) Gains (2) All expenses (3) Net profit/net loss

H. Capital Expenditure and Revenue Expenditure — Higher Level

Capital Expenditure — Purchasing fixed assets which will last a number of years, e.g. equipment, machinery, premises, motor vehicles. These assets are recorded in the **balance sheet** and not in the profit and loss account.

Revenue Expenditure — Expenses involved in the day-to-day running of the business, e.g. wages, rent, insurance, advertising, telephone. These expenses are recorded in the **profit and loss account.**

Examination-Style Question

Question 1.

Classify the following items of expenditure under Capital or Revenue for a Delivery Van manufacturing business:

A. Stock of Heating Oil; **B.** Machinery; **C.** Wages; **D.** Repairs to Machinery; **E.** Delivery Vans for Resale; **F.** Repayment of Bank Term Loan; **G.** Carriage Outwards; **H.** Factory Extension.

Place appropriate letter under Capital or Revenue Expenditure in table below.

CAPITAL EXPENDITURE	REVENUE EXPENDITURE

Source: Junior Certificate Higher Level. (4)

Sample Question and Solution

Question

From the following, prepare a profit and loss account of Bobbit Enterprises Ltd for year ending 31 December 2015.

Gross profit	€115,000	Advertising	€1,600
Postage and telephone	€8,150	Audit fees	€4,000
Rent received	€6,800	Insurance received	€4,600
Bank charges	€200	Marketing expenses	€1,500
Loan interest	€6,500	Carriage outwards	€900
Bad debts w/o	€2,000	Sales staff's salaries	€10,400
Packing materials	€8,000	Travelling expenses	€9,000
Rent	€200	Showroom expenses	€2,500
Insurance	€2,500		

Solution

Profit and Loss Account of Bobbit Enterprises Ltd for Year Ending 31 December 2015

		€	€
	Gross Profit		115,000
	Add Gains		
	Insurance received	4,600	
	Rent received	6,800	11,400
			126,400
	Less Expenses		
	Postage and telephone	8,150	
	Bank charges	200	
	Loan interest	6,500	
	Bad debts W/o	2,000	
	Packing materials	8,000	
	Rent	200	
	Insurance	2,500	
	Advertising	1,600	
	Audit fees	4,000	
	Marketing expenses	1,500	
	Carriage outwards	900	
	Sales staff's salaries	10,400	
	Travelling expenses	9,000	
	Showroom expenses	2,500	57,450
	Net Profit		68,950

I. Interpretation of Information Presented in a Profit and Loss Account

The profit and loss account gives the owner(s) of a business a lot of valuable information. (Refer to profit and loss account of Bobbit Enterprises Ltd.)

(1) TOTAL EXPENSES

€57,450

(2) NET PROFIT

€68,950

(3) NET PROFIT MARGIN/NET PROFIT PERCENTAGE

This ratio shows how much net profit was made on each €1.00 of sales.

$$\text{Formula} = \frac{\text{Net Profit x 100\%}}{\text{Sales}} \qquad \frac{€68{,}950 \text{ x } 100\%}{€199{,}000} = 34.64\%$$

This firm is making a net profit of 34.64c on every €1.00 of sales. The net profit percentage can be compared with

(a) Previous year's net profit margin.
(b) Other firms in the same industry.
(c) The industry average.

Chapter 40 — Profit and Loss Appropriation Account

A. Purpose of Profit and Loss Appropriation Account

The purpose of the profit and loss appropriation account is to show how the profit made is distributed (shared out). The board of directors will recommend to the shareholders how the profit should be shared.

B. Ordinary Share Dividend

Profit made in a company belongs to the shareholders. Profit distributed to shareholders is called ordinary share dividend.

C. Retained Earnings

It is normal practice to retain some profit for future use in the business. This is called retained earnings.

Ordinary Share Dividend is amount of profit given to shareholders.

Retained Earnings is amount of profit retained by the company for future use.

D. Calculation of Ordinary Share Dividend — Higher Level

The dividend is calculated as a percentage of the issued share capital of the company and not a percentage of net profit.

Sample Question and Solution

Question

Bobbit Enterprises Ltd has an issued capital of €100,000 ordinary shares @ €1 each. Net profit for year ending 31 December 2015 was €68,950. The directors declared a dividend of 10%.

(1) Calculate the ordinary share dividend.
(2) Prepare the profit and loss appropriation account.

Solution

(1) *Calculation of ordinary share dividend*

Dividend = 10% of €100,000 (issued share capital) = €10,000

N.B. The balance of the profit, i.e. €58,950, is retained by the company for future use.

Each shareholder will get 10c per share owned, e.g. John, who owns 2,000 shares, will get a dividend cheque of (2,000 × 10c) = €200.

(2) Profit and Loss Appropriation Account of Bobbit Enterprises Ltd for Year Ending 31 December 2015

				€
	Net profit			68,950
	Ordinary share dividend			10,000
	Retained earnings			58,950

E. Ledger Account to Record Ordinary Share Dividend and Retained Earnings

Ordinary Share Dividend Account

Date	Details	Fo	Total	Date	Details	Fo	Total €
				31/12/15	Profit and Loss App. A/C		10,000

Retained Earnings Account

Date	Details	Fo	Total	Date	Details	Fo	Total €
				31/12/15	Profit and Loss App. A/C		58,950

(1) The ordinary share dividend is a **liability** of the business until it is paid — it will be entered in the balance sheet under current liabilities.

When the dividend is paid

Debit ordinary share dividend account.

Credit bank account.

When the dividend is paid, there is no liability — thus there will be no entry in the balance sheet.

(2) The retained earnings will be entered in the balance sheet in the financed by section under the heading 'Reserves'.

F. Why Would a Company Retain Profits at the End of a Financial Year?

(1) To finance expansion.
(2) To finance the purchase of fixed assets.
(3) To be able to pay dividends in years when losses are made.
(4) To save for the future.

Chapter 41 — Balance Sheet

A. Balance Sheet

A balance sheet is a statement of assets, liabilities and share capital of a business on a particular day.

Assets — Property or things that a business owns.
Liabilities — Debts that a business owes.
Share Capital — Money invested in the company by its owners/shareholders (money owed to shareholders).

B.

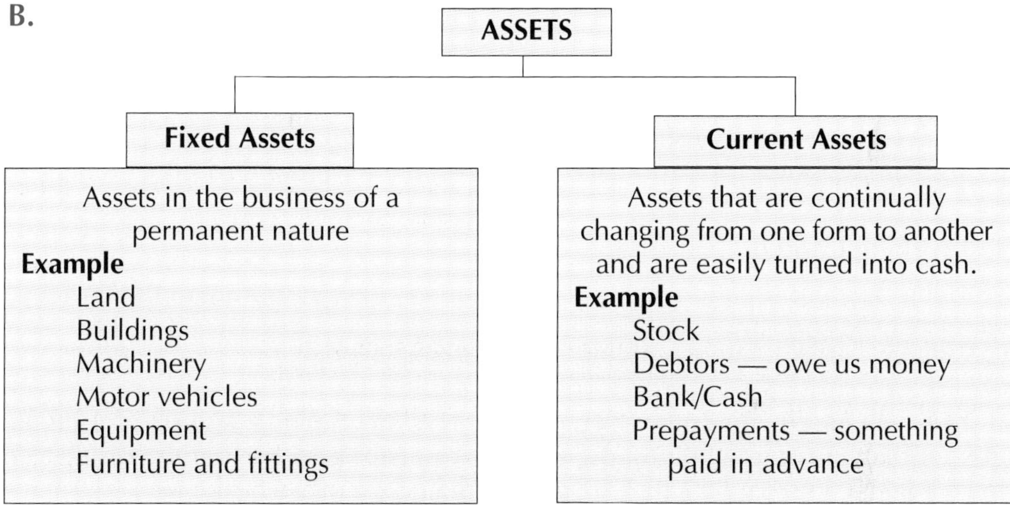

C.

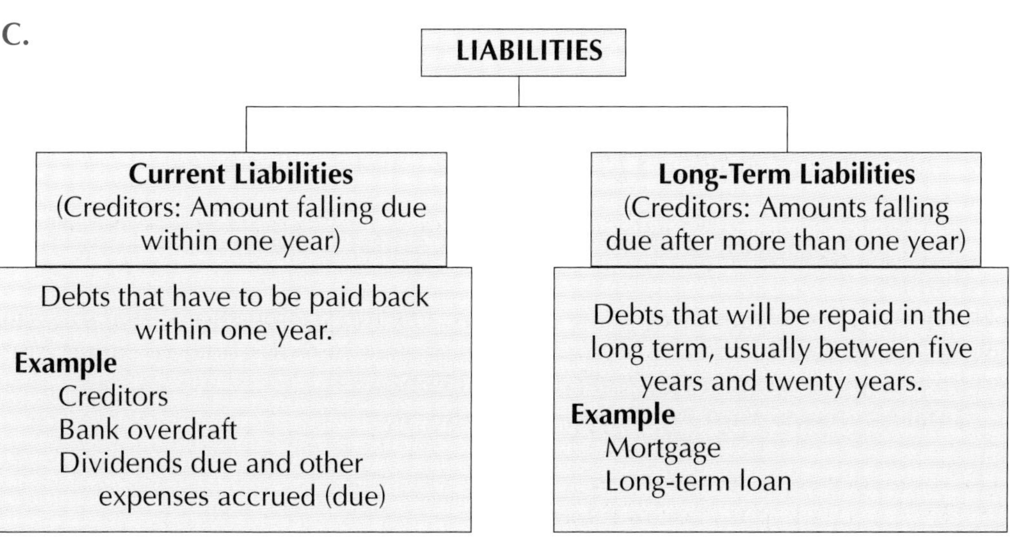

D.

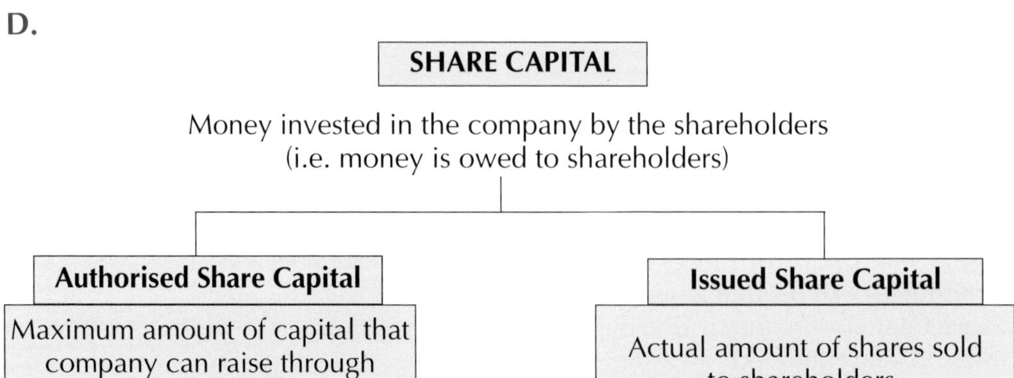

E. Reserves/Retained Earnings

Amount set aside out of profits and retained by the company for future use (balance in profit and loss appropriation account). This money is owed to shareholders.

F. Working Capital

Working capital is the money available for the day-to-day running of the business.

(Current assets – Current Liabilities = Working Capital)

It shows whether the business can pay its debts as they fall due. If current assets are greater than current liabilities, the working capital is **positive** and the firm is said to be **liquid**. If current liabilities are greater than current assets, the working capital is **negative** and the firm is said to have a **liquidity problem** and to be **overtrading** (i.e. it cannot pay its debts as they arise).

G. Total Net Assets = Fixed Assets + Working Capital

H. Shareholders' Funds = Ordinary Share Capital + Reserves

I. Capital Employed = Ordinary Share Capital + Reserves + Long-Term Liabilities

The balance sheet is made up of two sections. The top section shows what the **total net assets are worth**, and the bottom section shows where the finance comes from to finance these assets. This is called **Capital Employed**.

Total Net Assets Must Equal Capital Employed.

Sample Question and Solution

Question

From the following information prepare the balance sheet of Bobbit Enterprises Ltd as on 31 December 2015.

FB	Authorised share capital	€200,000	Ordinary shares at €1 each
FB	Issued share capital	€100,000	Ordinary shares at €1 each
FA	Land	€115,950	
CA	Closing stock	€15,000	
CL	Bank overdraft	€6,000	
CA	Debtors	€18,000	
FA	Buildings	€60,000	
FA	Machinery	€20,000	
RES	Retained earnings	€58,950	
CA	Bank	€6,000	
CL	Creditors	€10,000	
CA	Cash	€2,000	
CA	Prepayments	€1,000	
FA	Motor vehicles	€10,000	
CL	Dividends due	€10,000	
CL	Wages due	€3,000	
LTL	Long-term loan	€60,000	

Key
FB = Financed By
FA = Fixed Asset
CA = Current Asset
CL = Current Liability
RES = Reserves
LTL = Long-Term Liability

Solution

Balance Sheet of Bobbit Enterprises Ltd as on 31 December 2015

	Cost €	Depre-ciation €	Net Book Value €
Fixed Assets			
Land	115,950		115,950
Buildings	60,000		60,000
Machinery	20,000		20,000
Motor vehicles	10,000		10,000
	205,950		205,950
Current Assets			
Closing stock	15,000		
Debtors	18,000		
Bank	6,000		
Cash	2,000		
Prepayments	1,000	42,000	
Less Current Liabilities (Creditors: Amounts falling due within one year)			
Bank overdraft	6,000		
Creditors	10,000		
Dividends due	10,000		
Wages due	3,000	29,000	
Working capital			+13,000
Total net assets			218,950
FINANCED BY			
Authorised share capital			
200,000 ordinary shares @ €1 each			200,000
Issued Share Capital			
100,000 ordinary shares @ €1 each			100,000
Reserves			
Retained earnings			58,950
Long-Term Liabilities (Creditors: Amounts falling due after more than one year)			
Long-term loan			60,000
Capital employed			218,950

J. Business Terms

Accruals Expenses due at end of trading period.
Appreciation Assets increasing in value.
Assets Items of value owned by a business.
Balance Sheet A summary of assets and liabilities on a particular date.
Capital Employed Total money used in business. It is ordinary shares + reserves + long-term liabilities.
Carriage Inwards Cost of transport on purchases for resale. It is shown in the Trading Account as part of the cost of sales.
Carriage Outwards Delivery cost of goods sold. It is shown as a selling expense in the Profit and Loss Account.
Current Assets Assets easily converted into cash.
Current Liabilities Debts that must be repaid within one year.
Depreciation Reduction in the value of fixed assets due to usage, wear and tear, and age.
Dividends Profit distributed to shareholders.
Fixed Assets Assets of a permanent nature in the business not for resale.
Liability A debt the business owes.
Liquidity Ability of firm to pay debts as they fall due.
Long-Term Liabilities Amount borrowed by a business that will be repaid in the long term.
Net Worth Fixed assets + (current assets – current liabilities).
Overtrading Negative working capital.
Prepayments Expenses paid in advance at end of year.
Retained Earnings Amount of profit retained by company.
Secured Loan Some asset is given as security/collateral for the loan.
Share Capital Money invested by owners of a company.
Term Loan A medium-term loan repayable over a one- to five-year period.
Working Capital Current assets – current liabilities.

Chapter 42 — Revision Trading, Profit and Loss Account, Appropriation Account and Balance Sheet (Without Adjustments)

A. Type of Question on Final Accounts at Ordinary Level

This question on the Junior Certificate examination requires the preparation of a full set of final accounts from information presented in a trial balance with closing stock listed underneath the trial balance. There also may be one or two other theory questions included.

PROCEDURE

(1) Examine each item in the trial balance, and establish where it will go in the accounts.

> **N.B.** Debit column contains Assets and Expenses.
> Credit column contains Liabilities and Gains.

(2) Write down on the question where each item goes, i.e. T (Trading A/C), P & L (Profit and Loss A/C), App. (Appropriation A/C), B/S (Balance Sheet).
(3) Tick off each item as you enter it in the accounts.

Examination-Style Question and Solution

Question 1.
Answer (a), (b) and (c). This is a Final Accounts and Balance Sheet Question.

➢ Furnish Ltd is a company that sells furniture. Its Authorised Capital is 150,000 Ordinary Shares at €1 each.

➢ The following Trial Balance has been taken from the books of Furnish Ltd as at 31 December 2014 — the end of the financial year.

		Dr €	Cr €
B/S	Issued Share Capital in €1 Shares		120,000
T	Cash Sales		480,000
T	Cash Purchases for Resale	312,000	
T	Opening Stock at 1/1/2014	22,000	
T	Carriage Inwards	4,500	
App.	Dividend Paid	25,000	
P&L	Insurance	13,150	
P&L	Wages and Salaries	49,500	
P&L	Interest on Bank Overdraft	850	
P&L	Light and Heat	15,300	
P&L	Telephone	1,200	
B/S	Bank Overdraft		18,000
B/S	Cash in Hand	9,500	
B/S	Premises	80,000	
B/S	Machinery	85,000	
		618,000	618,000

T, B/S Closing Stock at 31 December 2014 was €31,000

1. (a) From the above figures, prepare a Trading and Profit and Loss Account and an Appropriation Account for the year ended 31 December 2014, and a Balance Sheet at that date. (46)

1. (b) Explain what 'Bank Overdraft' means. (7)

1. (c) What is the main reason why a Profit and Loss Appropriation Account is prepared? (7)

Source: Junior Certificate Ordinary Level. **(60 marks)**

Solution to Question 1.

1. (a) Trading and Profit and Loss and Appropriation Account for Year Ending 31 December 2014

	Sales			480,000
	Deduct Cost of Sales			
	Opening stock 1/1/14		22,000	
	Purchases		312,000	
	Carriage Inwards		4,500	
	Cost of Goods Available for Sale		338,500	
	Less Closing Stock 31/12/14		31,000	
	Cost of Sales			307,500
	Gross Profit			172,500
	Less Expenditure			
	Insurance		13,150	
	Wages and Salaries		49,500	
	Interest on Bank Overdraft		850	
	Light and Heat		15,300	
	Telephone		1,200	80,000
	Net Profit			92,500
	Less Dividends			25,000
	Reserves/Retained Earnings (Profit and Loss Balance)			67,500

Balance Sheet as on 31 December 2014

		Cost	Depre-ciation	Net Book Value
	Fixed Assets			
	Premises	*80,000*	—	*80,000*
	Machinery	*85,000*	—	*85,000*
		165,000	—	*165,000*
	Current Assets			
	Closing stock	*31,000*		
	Cash	*9,500*	*40,500*	
	Less Current Liabilities (Creditors: Amounts falling due within one year)			
	Bank overdraft		*18,000*	
	Working capital			*22,500*
	Total Net Assets			*187,500*
	FINANCED BY			
	Authorised Share Capital 150,000 Ordinary Shares @ €1 ea.			*150,000*
	Issued Share Capital 120,000 Ordinary Shares @ €1 ea.			*120,000*
	Reserves			
	Profit and Loss A/C balance			*67,500*
	Capital employed			*187,500*

1. (b) Bank Overdraft
A short-term loan whereby a bank gives permission to a current account holder to write cheques and withdraw more money than there is in the account up to a certain limit.

1. (c) A profit and loss appropriation account is prepared in order to show how the net profit was distributed.

Higher Level

Chapter 43 — Adjustments to Final Accounts

The aim of final accounts is to give a 'true and fair picture' of the business, i.e. finding true figures for gross profit and net profit. To do this, certain adjustments must be made.

➢ Accruals (amounts due).
➢ Prepayments (amounts paid in advance).
➢ Bad debts written off.
➢ Depreciation — straight line.
➢ Dividends.
➢ Closing stocks.

Because these adjustments are not in the trial balance, they are not therefore in the books of account and must be included in the accounts twice, once debit/once credit. One entry will be in the **trading or profit and loss account**.

The second entry will be in the **balance sheet**.

A. Accruals (Amounts Due)

(1) ACCRUED EXPENSES (EXPENSES DUE BY A FIRM)

All expenses relating to the trading period must be included in the accounts, whether paid or not.

Question

O'Flynn Ltd paid €10,000 insurance by cheque on 1 January 2016, but on 31 December there was still €1,000 due for the year 2016.

Solution **Bank Account**

Date	Details	Fo	Total	Date	Details	Fo	Total
				2016			€
				1 Jan.	*Insurance*		*10,000*

Insurance Account

Date	Details	Fo	Total	Date	Details	Fo	Total
2016			€	2016			€
1 Jan.	*Bank*		*10,000*	*31 Dec.*	*Profit and Loss A/C*		*11,000*
31 Dec.	*Balance (Ins. Due)*	*C/d*	*1,000*				
			11,000				*11,000*
				31 Dec.	*Balance (Ins. Due) (Current Liability)*	*B/d*	*1,000*

Entries in the Profit and Loss Account and Balance Sheet

RULES

(i) Add amount due on to amount paid in profit and loss account.
(ii) Show amount due as a current liability in balance sheet.

Profit and Loss Account (Extract) for Year Ending 31 December 2016

	Expenses				
	Insurance		10,000		
	Add insurance due		1,000	11,000	

Balance Sheet (Extract) as on 31 December 2016

	Current Liabilities				
	Insurance due		1,000		

(2) ACCRUED INCOME (EXPENSES DUE TO THE FIRM)

This is income for the period in question but not yet received, e.g.

- Rent receivable due.
- Commission receivable due.
- Insurance receivable due.

RULES

Add amount due to the amount received in the gains section of the profit and loss account. Show amount due as a current asset in balance sheet.

Question

Insurance received €15,000 for year ending 31 December 2017.
Insurance received due €2,000 at the end of December 2017.

Solution

Profit and Loss Account (Extract) for Year Ending 31 December 2017

	Gains				
	Insurance received			*15,000*	
	Add insurance received due			*2,000*	*17,000*

Balance Sheet (Extract) as on 31 December 2017

	Current Assets				
	Insurance received due		*2,000*		

B. Prepayments (Amounts Paid in Advance)

(1) PREPAYMENT MADE BY OUR BUSINESS

This occurs when an amount is paid in this trading period, but it is for the next trading period (i.e. paid in advance). Since we can put only expenses that belong to a trading period into the profit and loss account, prepayments must be deducted.

RULES

(i) Deduct amount prepaid from expense figure in profit and loss account.
(ii) Show amount prepaid as a current asset in Balance Sheet.

Question

O'Callaghan Ltd rented a warehouse on 1 February 2016 for €500 per month. It paid €6,000 rent for the year ended 31 January 2017 (twelve months).

N.B. We can charge only eleven months rent to the profit and loss account for 2016 because one month's rent is paid for January 2017.

Solution

Bank Account

Date	Details	Fo	Total	Date	Details	Fo	Total
				2016			€
				1 Feb.	*Rent*		*6,000*

Rent Account

Date	Details	Fo	Total	Date	Details	Fo	Total
2016			€	2016			€
1 Feb.	*Bank*		*6,000*	*31 Dec.*	*P & L A/C*		*5,500*
				31 Dec.	*Balance (Rent P/p)*	*C/d*	*500*
			6,000				*6,000*
31 Dec.	*Balance (Rent P/p) (Current asset in balance sheet)*	*B/d*	*500*				

Profit and Loss Account (Extract) for Year Ending 31 December 2016

	Expenses				
	Rent		*6,000*		
	Less rent prepaid		*500*	*5,500*	

Balance Sheet (Extract) as on 31 December 2016

	Current Assets				
	Rent prepaid		*500*		

(2) PREPAYMENTS MADE TO OUR BUSINESS

If a business has surplus storage space, it may (sublet) rent some of it to another business. The rent we get is called rent receivable. Sometimes this rent receivable is prepaid to us (i.e. it is received before it is due).

RULES

(i) Subtract amount prepaid from amount received in the gains in profit and loss account.

(ii) Show amount prepaid as a current liability in balance sheet.

Question

Rent received €1,000 for year ending 31 December 2017.
Rent receivable prepaid €100 at end of December 2017.

Solution

Profit and Loss Account (Extract) for Year Ending 31 December 2017

	Gains				
	Rent received			1,000	
	Subtract rent receivable prepaid			100	900

Balance Sheet (Extract) as on 31 December 2017

	Current Liabilities				
	Rent receivable prepaid			100	

C. Bad Debts Written Off

A bad debt arises when a debtor is declared bankrupt and cannot pay what is owed. The business must then write the amount off as a bad debt (loss to the business).

Question

1/1/16 Debtors €10,000.

Adjustment 31.12.16 Bad debts to be written off €1,000.

Solution

Debtors Account

Date	Details	Fo	Total	Date	Details	Fo	Total
1/1/16	*Balance*		10,000	31/12/16	*Bad debts*		1,000
				31/12/16	*Balance*	c/d	9,000
			10,000				10,000
31/12/16	*Balance*	B/d	9,000				

Bad Debts Account

Date	Details	Fo	Total	Date	Details	Fo	Total
31/12/16	*Debtors*		*1,000*	31/12/16	*Profit and Loss A/C*		*1,000*

WRITING UP PROFIT AND LOSS ACCOUNT AND BALANCE SHEET

RULES
(i) Show bad debts written off as an expense in the profit and loss account.
(ii) Deduct bad debts from debtors in the balance sheet.

Profit and Loss Account (Extract) for year ending 31/12/2016

	Expenses Bad debts		1,000		

Balance Sheet (Extract) as on 31/12/2016

	Current Assets				
	Debtors		10,000		
	Less bad debts written off		1,000	9,000	

N.B. Bad debts figure in trial balance — show as expense in P & L A/C. Do not deduct from debtors in balance sheet. (It is already deducted.)

D. Depreciation — Straight Line

Depreciation is the reduction in the value of an asset due to usage, wear and tear, and age.

Depreciation is calculated by getting a percentage of the cost of the asset — the figure will be the same every year. This is called straight line depreciation.

RULES
(i) Show depreciation as an expense in the profit and loss account.
(ii) Deduct depreciation from the cost of the asset in the fixed assets section of the balance sheet.

Question
Machinery 1 January 2017 €10,000.
Adjustment Depreciate machinery by 20%.

Solution

Machinery Account

Date	Details	Fo	Total €	Date	Details	Fo	Total €
1/1/17	Balance		10,000	31/12/17	Depreciation		2,000
				31/12/17	Balance	C/d	8,000
			10,000				10,000
31/12/17	Balance	B/d	8,000				

Depreciation Account

Date	Details	Fo	Total €	Date	Details	Fo	Total €
31/12/17	Machinery		2,000	31/12/17	Profit and Loss A/C		2,000

Profit and Loss Account (Extract) for Year Ending 31 December 2017

	Expenses				
	Depreciation of machinery			2,000	

Balance Sheet (Extract) as on 31 December 2017

			Cost €	Deprec. €	Net Bk Val. €
	Fixed Assets				
	Machinery		10,000	2,000	8,000

E. Dividends

Dividends can be paid or proposed.

(1) DIVIDENDS PAID

Dividends paid will appear in the debit column of the trial balance. Since they are paid, there is no liability in the balance sheet. **Dividends paid are entered in the profit and loss appropriation account only.**

(2) DIVIDENDS PROPOSED

Dividends proposed will appear as an adjustment. Dividends proposed are calculated as a percentage of the issued share capital of the company.

RULES

(i) Calculate the dividend, and enter it as a deduction from net profit in the profit and loss appropriation account.

(ii) Show dividend due as a current liability in the balance sheet.

F. Closing Stocks

(1) CLOSING STOCK OF GOODS

Closing stock is entered in the trading account and as a current asset in the balance sheet.

(2) CLOSING STOCKS OF OIL, STATIONERY, ETC., I.E. NON-TRADING STOCKS.

RULES

(i) Subtract closing stock from appropriate expenses in the profit and loss account.

(ii) Show closing stock as a current asset in the balance sheet.

Higher Level

Chapter 44 — Revision Final Accounts and Balance Sheet (Including Adjustments)

A. Type of Exam Question

This question is given in the form of a trial balance, i.e. figures in the debit column and credit column.

Debit Column Assets/Expenses	Credit Column Liabilities/Gains

B. Adjustments

Adjustments will be given under the totals of the trial balance, and items in the trial balance that must be adjusted should be marked with '*'.

C. Summary of Adjustments

Adjustment	How Adjustment Is Treated in Profit and Loss Account	How Adjustment Is Treated in Balance Sheet
(1) Accruals (a) Due by firm (b) Due to firm	 Add to amount paid Add to amount received	 Current liability Current asset
(2) Prepayments (a) Made by us (b) Made to us	 Deduct from expense Deduct from amount received	 Current asset Current liability
(3) Bad debt written off	Show as expense	Deduct from debtors
(4) Depreciation	Show as expense	Deduct from fixed asset
(5) Dividends (a) Paid (b) Proposed	 Enter in profit and loss appropriation account Enter in profit and loss appropriation account	 No entry Current liability
(6) Closing Stock (a) Goods (b) Non-trading stock	 Trading account Deduct from expense	 Current asset Current asset

Examination-Style Question and Solution

Question 1.

Answer (a) and (b). This is a Final Accounts and Balance Sheet Question.

1. (a) The following Trial Balance was extracted from the books of Paintwell Ltd on 31 May 2016. You are required to prepare the company's Trading, Profit and Loss and Appropriation Accounts for the year ended 31/5/16, and a Balance Sheet as at that date. The Authorised Share Capital is 200,000 €1 Ordinary Shares.

FB

		DR €	CR €
T	Purchases and Sales T	189,000	290,000
CA	Debtors and Creditors CL	56,000	45,300
T	Sales Returns and Purchases Returns T	11,000	4,000
E	Bad Debts	2,500	
E	Insurance	8,500	
G	Rent Receivable *		7,800
T	Carriage Inwards	4,600	
FA	Buildings at Cost *	120,000	
T	Opening Stock 1/6/15	14,400	
LTL	15 Year Loan		20,000
CA	Cash	2,500	
FA	Equipment at Cost *	80,000	
CL	Bank Overdraft		3,000
E	Wages and Salaries *	30,000	
E	Bank Interest	1,600	
FB	Issued Share Capital: 150,000 €1 shares		150,000
		520,100	520,100

You are given the following additional information as on 31/5/16:

(i) Closing Stock €18,000; [T + CA]
(ii) Wages and Salaries due €6,000; [E + CL]
(iii) Dividends Declared 10%; (App. A/C + CL)
(iv) Rent receivable prepaid €200; [G + CL]
(v) Depreciation: Buildings 5%; Equipment 15%. [E + FA] (35)

(b) Write a brief note on how the company might reduce bad debts in the future. (5)

Source: Junior Certificate Higher Level. **(40 marks)**

*	=	Adjust figure
T	=	Trading account
E	=	Expense — profit and loss account
G	=	Gain — profit and loss account
App.	=	Appropriation account
FA	=	Fixed assets
CA	=	Current assets
CL	=	Current liabilities
FB	=	Financed By

Solution

PAINTWELL LTD

Trading and Profit and Loss Account for Year Ending 31 May 2016

(A)	**Sales**		290,000	
	Less Sales Returns		11,000	279,000
	Deduct Cost of Sales			
	Stock 1/6/15 (opening)		14,400	
	Purchases	189,000		
	Less Purchases Returns	4,000	185,000	
	Carriage Inwards		4,600	
	Cost of Goods Available for Sale		204,000	
	Less Stock 31/5/16 (closing)		18,000	
	Cost of Sales			186,000
	Gross Profit			93,000
	Add Gains			
	Rent receivable		7,800	
	Less rent receivable prepaid		200	7,600
				100,600
	Less Expenses			
	Bad Debts		2,500	
	Insurance		8,500	
	Wages and Salaries	30,000		
	Add Wages Due	6,000	36,000	
	Bank Interest		1,600	
	Depreciation — Equipment	12,000		
	Depreciation — Buildings	6,000	18,000	66,600
	Net Profit			34,000
	Less 10% Dividend			15,000
	Reserves (Retained Earnings)			19,000

PAINTWELL LTD

Balance Sheet as at 31 May 2016

		Cost	Depreciation	NBV
Fixed Assets				
Buildings		120,000	6,000	114,000
Equipment		80,000	12,000	68,000
		200,000	18,000	182,000
Current Assets				
Closing Stock		18,000		
Debtors		56,000		
Cash		2,500	76,500	
Less Current Liabilities				
(Creditors: Amounts falling due within one year)				
Creditors		45,300		
Bank Overdraft		3,000		
Dividends due		15,000		
Rent Receivable Prepaid		200		
Wages Due		6,000	69,500	
Working Capital				7,000
Total Net Assets				189,000
FINANCED BY				
Authorised Share Capital				
200,000 Ordinary Shares @ €1 each				200,000
Issued Share Capital				
150,000 Ordinary Shares @ €1 each				150,000
Reserves				
Retained Earnings				19,000
Long-Term Liabilities				
(Creditors: Amounts falling due after more than one year)				
15-yr loan				20,000
Capital Employed				189,000

1. (b) *How Company Might Reduce Bad Debts in the Future*

(i) Get a reference from customer's bank.
(ii) Get a reference from another firm that customer deals with.
(iii) Give less credit in future.
(iv) Give cash discounts to encourage prompt payment.
(v) Charge interest on overdue accounts.
(vi) Have a better credit control system in operation.

Higher Level

REPORTING ON ACCOUNTS

Chapter 45 — Assessing a Business

A. Introduction

It is important that accounts are interpreted or made clear for the benefit of interested parties.

This is done by the use of **ratios** that show the relationships between figures. These figures are then compared with

(1) Previous year's figures.
(2) Other firms in the same industry.

B. Parties Interested in the Accounts of a Company

(1) Banker — Can loans and overdrafts be repaid?
(2) Creditors — Can business pay for goods supplied on credit?
(3) Shareholders — How much profit does the company make, and what will the dividend per share be?
(4) Employees — Is employment secure?
(5) Investors — Is company a good investment?
(6) Management — Is company performing better or worse than last year?
(7) Revenue Commissioners — How much profit is company making for tax purposes?

C. Interpretation of Accounts Using Ratios

A company can be assessed by using the following headings or areas:

➢ Profitability
➢ Liquidity
➢ Activity
➢ Solvency
➢ Dividend Policy

(1) PROFITABILITY

The profitability ratios show how successful the management of the business was in making profit in the company.

The profitability ratios are as follows:

Ratio	Formula	Ans.	Information Given by Ratio
(a) Return on share capital	$\frac{\text{Net Profit x 100\%}}{\text{Issued Share Capital}}$	Percentage %	Shows return shareholders are getting on their own investment and should be compared with return from banks or other firms.
(b) Return on capital employed	$\frac{\text{Net Profit x 100\%}}{\text{Capital Employed}}$	Percentage %	Shows return on total amount invested in company and should be compared with return from banks or other firms.
(c) Gross profit percentage/ margin	$\frac{\text{Gross Profit x 100\%}}{\text{Sales}}$	Percentage %	Tells us how much gross profit was made on each €1.00 of sales. Compare with last year or other firms.
(d) Net profit percentage/ margin	$\frac{\text{Net Profit x 100\%}}{\text{Sales}}$	Percentage %	Tells us how much net profit was made on each €1.00 of sales. Compare with last year or other firms.

(2) LIQUIDITY

Liquidity is the ability of the company to pay its debts as they fall due. Liquidity is measured by subtracting current liabilities from current assets. This is called working capital.

Working Capital = Current Assets – Current Liabilities

If the working capital is positive, the firm is said to be liquid. If the working capital is negative, the firm is said to be **overtrading**.

The Liquidity Ratios are

Ratio	Formula	Ans.	Information Given by Ratio
(a) Current ratio or working capital ratio	Current Assets: Current Liabilities	Ratio	Tells us if the company has enough current assets to pay its current liabilities. A company should have a current ratio of 2:1, i.e. current assets should be double current liabilities.
(b) Quick asset ratio or acid test ratio	Current Assets – Closing Stock: Current Liabilities	Ratio	Omits closing stock, as stock may not be quickly turned into cash. The recommended ratio is 1:1, i.e. a healthy firm should be able to pay its current liabilities out of liquid assets (i.e. CA – stock).

(3) ACTIVITY

The ratios tell us how active the company was during the year.
The Activity Ratios are

Ratio	Formula	Ans.	Information Given by Ratio
(a) Rate of stock turnover	$\frac{\text{Cost of Sales}}{\text{Average Stock}}$	Times	Tells us how many times the stock is replaced in the business during the year.
(b) Period of credit given to debtors	$\frac{\text{Debtors x 365}}{\text{Credit Sales}}$	Days	Tells us how many days credit the firm gives debtors **OR** how long it takes debtors to pay.
(c) Period of credit received from creditors	$\frac{\text{Creditors x 365}}{\text{Credit Purchases}}$	Days	Tells us how much credit the firm receives from creditors or how long it takes the firm to pay its creditors.

(4) SOLVENCY

A firm is **solvent** if total assets are greater than outside liabilities, so that it can continue in business.

Total Assets = Fixed Assets + Current Assets
Outside Liabilities = Current Liabilities + Long-Term Liabilities

If outside liabilities are greater than total assets, the firm is said to be **insolvent** or **bankrupt.** (Firm cannot continue in business.)

Ratio	Formula	Ans.	Information Given by Ratio
Solvency	Total Assets: Outside Liabilities	Ratio	Tells us whether business is solvent or insolvent.

(5) DIVIDEND POLICY

Dividend is the amount of profit given to shareholders. It is the board of directors which decides how much of a dividend will be paid to shareholders. The rate of dividend ratio tells us how much dividends are paid to shareholders.

Ratio	Formula	Ans.	Information Given by Ratio
Rate of dividend	$\frac{\text{Dividend Paid x 100\%}}{\text{Issued Share Capital}}$	Percentage %	Rate of dividend paid to shareholders.

Sample Question and Solution

Question

Scott Ltd has an authorised share capital of 400,000 €1 ordinary shares. Its accounts for year ended 31 December 2016 are as follows.

Trading and Profit and Loss Account for Year Ending 31 December 2016

	Sales		100,000
	Deduct Cost of Sales		
	Opening stock	6,000	
	Purchases	44,000	
	Cost of goods available	50,000	
	Less closing stock	10,000	
	Cost of Sales		40,000
	Gross Profit		60,000
	Less expenses		10,000
	Net Profit		50,000
	Less dividend 10%		20,000
	Retained earnings		30,000

Balance Sheet as on 31 December 2016

	FIXED ASSETS			260,000
	Current Assets			
	Closing stock	10,000		
	Debtors	10,000		
	Bank	60,000	80,000	
	Current Liabilities			
	(Creditors: Amounts falling due within one year)			
	Creditors	8,000		
	Dividend due	20,000		
	Accruals	12,000	40,000	
	Working capital			40,000
	Total Net Assets			**300,000**
	FINANCED BY			
	Authorised Share Capital			400,000
	Issued share capital			200,000
	Retained Earnings			30,000
	Long-Term Liabilities			
	(Creditors: Amounts falling due after more than one year)			
	Long-term loan			70,000
	Capital Employed			**300,000**

Calculate and comment on:

(1) Return on share capital
(2) Return on capital employed
(3) Gross profit margin
(4) Net profit margin
(5) Working capital ratio
(6) Acid test ratio
(7) Rate of stock turnover
(8) Period of credit given to debtors
(9) Period of credit received from creditors
(10) Solvency ratio
(11) Rate of dividend.

Solution

Ratio	Formula	Figures	Answer	Comment
1. Return on share capital	Net Profit x 100% / Issued Share Capital	50,000 x 100% / 200,000	25%	This rate of return is very satisfactory when compared with rate that could be earned by investing the same amount in a bank or building society.
2. Return on capital employed	Net Profit x 100% / Capital Employed	50,000 x 100% / 300,000	16.66%	Satisfactory when compared with rates of return from bank or building society.
3. Gross profit margin	Gross Profit x 100% / Sales	60,000 x 100% / 100,000	60%	This business is making a gross profit of 60c on every €1.00 of sales.
4. Net profit margin	Net Profit x 100% / Sales	50,000 x 100% / 100,000	50%	This business is making a net profit of 50c on each €1.00 of sales.
5. Working capital ratio	Current Assets : Current Liabilities	80,000:40,000	2:1	This ratio is ideal because the recommended working capital ratio is 2:1. Firm can pay debts as they fall due from current assets. Firm has no liquidity problem.
6. Acid test ratio	CA – Closing Stock:CL	80,000 – 10,000:40,000 70,000:40,000	1.75:1	This ratio is very satisfactory as the recommended acid test ratio is 1:1. Firm can pay current liabilities from liquid assets.
7. Rate of stock turnover	Cost of Sales / Average Stock	40,000 / 8,000	5 times	Stock is being replaced 5 times a year in business. (New stock is purchased every 10.5 weeks.)
8. Period of credit given to debtors	Debtors x 365 / Credit Sales	10,000 x 365 / 100,000	36.5 days	This firm is giving debtors 36.5 days credit, or it is taking 36.5 days to get money from debtors.
9. Period of credit received from creditors	Creditors x 365 / Credit Purchases	8,000 x 365 / 44,000	66 days	This firm paid its creditors in 66 days.
10. Solvency ratio	Total Assets : Outside Liabilities	340,000:110,000	3.09:1	This business is solvent, as total assets are greater than outside liabilities.
11. Rate of dividend	Dividend Paid x 100% / Issued Share Capital	20,000 x 100% / 200,000	10%	Firm paid a 10% dividend to shareholders.

COMPARISON OF ACCOUNTS AND BALANCE SHEET AND PREPARATION OF A REPORT

To get an accurate picture of any business, it is necessary to compare the accounts and balance sheets of a number of trading periods. Once the accounts have been assessed and the ratios prepared, a report on the performance of the company is compiled for interested parties.

Examination-Style Question and Solution

Question 1.

This question is about Reporting on the Performance of a Business.

Assume you are Joe Cronin, Financial Consultant, of 10 Cork Road, Waterford. Study the Final Accounts and Balance Sheets of King Ltd, Waterford, set out below, for the years 2013 and 2014. Prepare a Report, using today's date, for the shareholders of King Ltd comparing the performance of the company in the two years under the following three headings:

(a) Profitability; (b) Liquidity; (c) Dividend Policy.

2013			2014		
Trading, Profit and Loss and Appropriation Accounts for Year Ending 31/5/2013			**Trading, Profit and Loss and Appropriation Accounts for Year Ending 31/5/2014**		
		€			€
Sales		140,000	Sales		270,000
Less Cost of Sales		84,000	Less Cost of Sales		108,000
Gross Profit		56,000	**Gross Profit**		162,000
Less Expenses		44,600	Less Expenses		133,500
Net Profit		11,400	**Net Profit**		28,500
Less Dividends		1,400	Less Dividends		10,500
Reserves		10,000	Reserves		18,000
Balance Sheet as at 31/5/2013			**Balance Sheet as at 31/5/2014**		
	€	€		€	€
Fixed Assets		105,000	Fixed Assets		95,000
Current Assets	20,000		Current Assets	30,000	
Less Current Liabilities	30,000	–10,000	Less Current Liabilities	15,000	15,000
		95,000			110,000
Financed By			**Financed By**		
Ordinary Share Capital		70,000	Ordinary Share Capital		70,000
Reserves		10,000	Reserves		28,000
Long-Term Loan		15,000	Long-Term Loan		12,000
		95,000			110,000

Source: Junior Certificate Higher Level. **(40 marks)**

Solution to Question 1. Reporting on the Performance of a Business

10 Cork Road
Waterford

15 June 2014

Title: *Report Comparing Performance of King Ltd in the Years 2013 and 2014*

To *Shareholders*
King Ltd
Waterford

Introduction

I was asked on your behalf to prepare a report comparing the performance of King Ltd in the years 2013 and 2014 under the headings profitability, liquidity and dividend policy. I used all the relevant ratios, which are also attached to my report. My main findings are laid out below.

Body of Report

1. (a) Profitability

The company is profitable. The profit in 2014 is bigger than in 2013.

	2013	2014
Gross margin	40.00%	60.00%
Net margin	8.14%	10.56%
Return on share capital	16.29%	40.71%
Return on capital employed	12.00%	25.90%

It can be seen from the above figures that King Ltd is profitable and this profitability is on the increase. Return on share capital and return on capital employed compare very well with what is available from banks or building societies.

1. (b) Liquidity

The company had a minus working capital in 2013. Thus it had a liquidity problem. In 2014 the working capital is positive. Thus the company has no liquidity problem.

	2013	2014
Working capital ratio	0.66:1	2:1

The liquidity position of King Ltd is improving, and in 2014 it is at the recommended level of 2:1.

1. (c) Dividend Policy

The company paid dividends in both years. The 2014 dividend was greater than the 2013 dividend.

	2013	2014
Rate of dividend	2%	15%

The shareholders received a big increase in dividends in 2014 in line with the increase in profits.

I am available to discuss this report if required.

Signed
Joe Cronin
Financial Consultant

RATIO ANALYSIS

Ratio	Formula	Figures		Answers	
		2013	2014	2013	2014
Gross margin	Gross Profit x 100% / Sales	56,000 x 100% / 140,000	162,000 x 100% / 270,000	40%	60%
Net margin	Net Profit x 100% / Sales	11,400 x 100% / 140,000	28,500 x 100% / 270,000	8.14%	10.56%
Return on share capital	Net Profit x 100% / Issued Share Capital	11,400 x 100% / 70,000	28,500 x 100% / 70,000	16.29%	40.71%
Return on capital employed	Net Profit x 100% / Capital Employed	11,400 x 100% / 95,000	28,500 x 100% / 110,000	12%	25.9%
Working capital ratio	CA:CL	20,000:30,000	30,000:15,000	0.66:1	2:1
Rate of dividend	Dividend Paid x 100% / Issued Share Capital	1,400 x 100% / 70,000	10,500 x 100% / 70,000	2%	15%

REASONS WHY A BUSINESS WOULD USE RATIO ANALYSIS

(1) To assess its performance against
- Previous years
- Other enterprises
- Other forms of investment

(2) To calculate its level of profitability through
- Gross profit margin
- Net profit margin
- Return on capital employed

(3) To calculate its level of liquidity through
- Working capital ratio
- Acid test ratio

(4) To help management make informed decisions.

(5) To present additional information about itself in reports for interested parties.

LIMITATION OF FINAL ACCOUNTS IN ASSESSING A BUSINESS

The final accounts of a business give us financial information only. The following are not taken into account.

(1) Experienced and efficient staff. Management/staff relationships. Loyal staff and customers.

(2) Balance sheet holds only for a particular day.

(3) Assets may not be shown at their current values — some assets may have appreciated over the years, e.g. premises.

(4) The accounts of a business are a record of past transactions and can be used only as an estimate of future performance.

(5) Final accounts only give information about a particluar year.

APPLIED ACCOUNTS

Chapter 46 — Club Accounts

A. Introduction

A club is an organisation set up for the benefit of its members. Members elect officers at its AGM to run the club.

All clubs must keep a record of their financial activities during the year. They are non-profit-making organisations.

B. Functions of Club Officers

Chairperson	Secretary	Treasurer
1. Runs club.	1. Calls meetings.	1. Collects subscriptions.
		2. Issues receipts for all money received.
2. Chairs meetings.	2. Sends agenda to members.	3. Lodges money received to bank account.
3. Keeps order at meetings.	3. Arranges the meetings.	4. Makes all club payments.
4. Follows agenda.	4. Takes notes at meetings and writes up minutes.	5. Keeps records.
5. Puts motions to a vote.		6. Prepares annual accounts.
		7. Prepares a financial report for AGM.

C. Annual General Meeting (AGM)

Members attend, speak and vote on various items on the agenda (programme for meeting).

The treasurer presents his report to the members at the AGM.

(1) PURPOSE OF TREASURER'S REPORT

(a) To inform members of the club's cash position at the end of the year.
(b) To inform members if the club had a surplus or deficit for the year.
(c) To give details of the club's assets and liabilities.
(d) To provide a basis for future financial decisions, i.e. subscriptions, borrowings, fundraising, expansion, etc.

(2) AGENDA

The agenda is the programme for the meeting sent by the secretary to all members, outlining the items to be discussed at the meeting.

Agenda for AGM of Manchester United FC

The AGM of Man Utd FC will be held on 10 March 2015 at 8 pm at Old Trafford. The agenda is as follows:

(a) Minutes of last AGM
(b) Matters arising from minutes
(c) Chairperson's Report
(d) Secretary's Report
(e) Treasurer's Report
(f) Election of Officers
(g) AOB.

Peter Kenyon
Secretary

(3) MINUTES OF MEETINGS

Minutes are a written record of discussions and decisions taken at meetings. They are prepared by the secretary of the club.

D. Accounts Kept by a Club

The following accounts are usually kept by the treasurer of a club.

- ☛ Analysed cash book/analysed receipts and payments book, usually written up on a monthly basis.
- ☛ Receipts and payments account for the year.
- ☛ Income and expenditure account for the year.
- ☛ Balance sheet on the last day of the year.

ANALYSED CASH BOOK/ANALYSED RECEIPTS AND PAYMENTS BOOK

- ☛ It is the same as a cash book for business.
- ☛ Receipts on the debit side.
- ☛ Payments on the credit side.
- ☛ It is analysed into suitable columns to meet the requirements of the club.

Examination-Style Question and Solution

Question 1.

The Hightown Girls Football Club play all their games in the summer. In the winter, they practise in a local indoor sports centre, which they use as their clubhouse. They have to pay rent for the use of the sports centre. They sell drinks (minerals) and run a disco every two weeks in order to raise money for playing gear. They also collect the subscriptions (membership fees) for the year.

Here is what happened in January 2015 (all dealings are in cash):

- ➢ 1 Jan. Cash on hand since last year €300
- ➢ 2 " Received subscriptions €50
- ➢ 3 " Paid for cans of drinks €30
- ➢ 5 " Disco night: received €350 at the door
- ➢ 5 " Received €45 from sale of drinks
- ➢ 6 " Paid disc-jockey (DJ) €50 for running the disco
- ➢ 8 " Received subscriptions €60
- ➢ 9 " Bought drinks for €70 and paid for them
- ➢ 10 " Paid €10 for posters for next disco
- ➢ 11 " Paid for rent of sports centre €25
- ➢ 12 " Received subscriptions €25
- ➢ 14 " Sold drinks €30
- ➢ 16 " Paid local radio for advertising disco €15
- ➢ 17 " Bought and paid for more drinks €40
- ➢ 19 " Disco night: received €400 at the door and €150 for sale of all drinks
- ➢ 20 " Paid disc-jockey €50 for running the disco
- ➢ 25 " Paid for rent of sports centre €25
- ➢ 30 " Received more subscriptions €55

1. (a) Using your answer book, write up and balance the Receipts and Payments Account of the club for the month of January 2015.
Use the following headings for Receipts and Payments and total each column:
Receipts: Total, Subscriptions, Disco, Drinks.
Payments: Total, Disco, Drinks, Rent. (50)
1. (b) What is the title given to the person who keeps the books for the club? (5)
1. (c) What profit (surplus) did the club make on discos for the month? (5)

Source: Junior Certificate Ordinary Level. **(60 marks)**

Solution to Question 1.

1. (a) Hightown Girls Football Club

Receipts and Payments Account Analysed for Month of January 2015

Receipts | Payments

Date	Details	Total €	Subscriptions €	Disco €	Drinks €	Date	Details	Total €	Disco €	Drinks €	Rent €
1 Jan.	Cash on hand	300				3 Jan.	Drink purchases	30		30	
2 Jan.	Subscriptions	50	50			6 Jan.	Disc-jockey (DJ)	50	50		
5 Jan.	Disco receipts	350		350		9 Jan.	Drink purchases	70		70	
5 Jan.	Drink sales	45			45	10 Jan.	Posters	10	10		
8 Jan.	Subscriptions	60	60			11 Jan.	Rent	25			25
12 Jan.	Subscriptions	25	25			16 Jan.	Advertising	15	15		
14 Jan.	Drink sales	30			30	17 Jan.	Drink purchases	40		40	
19 Jan.	Disco receipts	400		400		20 Jan.	Disc-jockey (DJ)	50	50		
19 Jan.	Drink sales	150			150	25 Jan.	Rent	25			25
30 Jan.	Subscriptions	55	55			31 Jan.	Balance C/d	1,150			
		1,465	190	750	225			1,465	125	140	50
31 Jan.	Balance B/d	1,150									

1. (b) Treasurer.
1. (c) Profit made on discos for month = €625 (Receipts €750 – Payments €125).

(2) RECEIPTS AND PAYMENTS ACCOUNT (CASH BOOK)

A receipts and payments account is prepared at the end of the year using totals from analysis columns.

It shows

(a) Cash balance at **start** of year.
(b) **Receipts** — on the debit side.
(c) **Payments** — on the credit side.
(d) Cash balance at **end** of year.

Rule for Receipts and Payments Account
Debit — Receipts
Credit — Payments

SAMPLE RECEIPTS AND PAYMENTS ACCOUNT

Receipts and Payments Account of Killeen GAA Club for Year Ending 31/12/14

		€		€
1/1/14	Balance B/f	13,200	Caretaker's wages	4,200
	Subscriptions	3,300	Travel expenses	2,910
	Bar sales	34,400	Insurance	1,290
	Gate receipts	4,250	Bar purchases	30,150
			Secretary expenses	850
			Purchase of equipment	9,800
			Balance C/d	5,950
		55,150		55,150
31/12/14	Balance B/f	5,950		

Club has €5,950 cash on hand on 31 December 2014. This will be shown as a current asset in balance sheet.

(3) INCOME AND EXPENDITURE ACCOUNT

An income and expenditure account for a club is the same as a profit and loss account used in business. It shows all the club's **income** and all the club's **expenditure** for the year.

Expenditure	Income
Cleaning	Subscriptions
Repairs	Bar profit
Insurance	Catering profit
Light and heat	Competition receipts
Depreciation of assets	Dance receipts
Telephone and stationery	Raffle profit
Secretarial expenses	
Wages	

If income is greater than expenditure, it is called excess of income over expenditure. If expenditure is greater than income, it is called excess of expenditure over income.

HOW TO PREPARE AN INCOME AND EXPENDITURE ACCOUNT

From a given receipts and payments account with adjustments included:

(i) Exclude opening and closing balances.
(ii) Exclude purchase or sale of assets.
(iii) Include adjustments.

(4) BALANCE SHEET

The balance sheet of a club is exactly the same as the balance sheet of a business. It shows assets and liabilities as usual.

There are two differences in the 'Financed By' section:
Capital is called **Accumulated Fund**.
Net Profit is called **Excess of Income over Expenditure**, which is added to accumulated fund.

E. Adjustments in Club Accounts — Higher Level

(1) BAR TRADING ACCOUNT

If the club operates a bar, it will be necessary to prepare a bar trading account. The profit or loss on the bar is transferred to the income and expenditure account.

Example

	€
Bar sales	10,000
Bar purchases	6,000
Bar stock at start	2,000
Bar stock at end	1,800

Bar Trading Account

	€	€
Bar sales		10,000
Deduct Cost of Sales		
Opening stock	2,000	
Bar purchases	6,000	
Cost of goods available for sale	8,000	
Less closing stock	1,800	
Cost of Sales		6,200
Bar profit		3,800

(2) FUNCTIONS

Most clubs run functions such as dances, dinners, concerts, competitions. A profit or loss must be worked out on these functions and entered in the income and expenditure account.

Profit ⇛ Income
Loss ⇛ Expenditure

Example

Dance receipts	€2,000
Dance expenses	€1,200
Profit on dance	€800 ⇛ Income

(3) SUBSCRIPTIONS

Clubs get their finance mainly from members' subscriptions. We must include in the income and expenditure account only subscriptions for the period of account we are dealing with. Thus subscriptions will need to be adjusted.

Rule for Adjusting Subscriptions

— Start with subscriptions received.
— Add subscriptions due at end.
— Deduct subscriptions prepaid at end.

Balance Sheet

Subscriptions due at end
⇛ **Current Assets**
Subscriptions prepaid at end
⇛ **Current Liability**

Example
Subscriptions received €2,000
Subscriptions due at end €100
Subscriptions prepaid at end €300

Solution

Subscriptions received	€2,000
Add subscriptions due end	€100
	€2,100
Less subscriptions prepaid end	€300
Income and expenditure account	€1,800
Balance Sheet	
Subscriptions due	€100 ⇛ CA
Subscriptions prepaid	€300 ⇛ CL

(4) DEPRECIATION OF FIXED ASSETS

(a) Calculate percentage depreciation on the cost figure at end of year. Enter figure in **expenditure** section.
(b) **Deduct depreciation from cost of asset** in the fixed assets section of balance sheet.

(5) ACCRUALS AT END OF YEAR (AMOUNTS DUE)

(a) **Add** to expenditure figure in income and expenditure account.
(b) Show amount due as **current liability** in balance sheet.

(6) AMOUNTS PAID IN ADVANCE AT END OF YEAR

(a) **Deduct** prepaid amount from expenditure in income and expenditure account.
(b) Show prepaid amount as **current asset** in balance sheet.

(7) CALCULATION OF ACCUMULATED FUND IF NOT GIVEN

Add up all assets in club at start of year. Add up all liabilities in club at start of year. Subtract liabilities from assets. Difference is accumulated fund.

Examination-Style Question and Solution

Question 1.

Answer (a) and (b). This is a Club Account Question.

1. (a) The Treasurer of the local Social Club has been taken ill, and you have been asked to prepare accounts for the Annual General Meeting next week. You are required to prepare:

- ➢ An Income and Expenditure Account for the year ended 31/5/2015. (15)
- ➢ A separate Trading Account for the canteen for the same period. (6)
- ➢ A Balance Sheet as at 31/5/2015. (15)

The Trial Balance at 31/5/2015 is as shown:

Trial Balance	**Dr** €	**Cr** €
Clubhouse	15,000	
Equipment	4,200	
Canteen Sales		8,500
Members' Subscriptions		4,600
Canteen Purchases	6,850	
Light and Heat	800	
Telephone	350	
Postage and Stationery	70	
Wages	3,200	
Repairs to Equipment	530	
Furniture	2,500	
Profit on Raffle		900
Canteen Stock (1/6/14)	440	
Accumulated Fund (1/6/14)		19,940
	33,940	33,940

The following matters must also be taken into consideration:

(i) Subscriptions due €310;
(ii) Canteen Stock (31/5/2015) €490;
(iii) Telephone due €40;
(iv) Depreciate equipment by 10% and furniture by 5%.

1. (b) Calculate the gross profit percentage on the canteen sales and make a comment on it. (4)

Source: Junior Certificate Higher Level. **(40 marks)**

Solution to Question 1.

1. (a) **Income and Expenditure Account for Year Ending 31 May 2015**

	€	€	€
Income			
Members' Subscriptions	4,600		
Add Subscriptions Due	310	4,910	
Profit on Raffle		900	
Profit on Canteen		1,700	7,510
Less Expenditure			
Light and Heat		800	
Telephone	350		
Add Telephone Due	40	390	
Postage and Stationery		70	
Wages		3,200	
Repairs		530	
Depreciation			
Equipment 10%	420		
Furniture 5%	125	545	5,535
Excess Income over Expenditure			1,975

Trading Account Canteen for Year Ending 31 May 2015

	€	€
Canteen Sales		8,500
Deduct Cost of Sales		
Stock 1/6/14	440	
Canteen Purchases	6,850	
Cost of Goods Available for Sale	7,290	
Less Closing Stock 31/5/15	490	
Cost of Sales		6,800
Canteen Profit		1,700

Balance Sheet as at 31 May 2015

	Cost €	Deprec. €	NBV €
Fixed Assets			
Clubhouse	15,000		15,000
Equipment	4,200	420	3,780
Furniture	2,500	125	2,375
	21,700	545	21,155
Current Assets			
Stock (Canteen)	490		
Subscriptions Due	310	800	
Less Current Liabilities (Creditors: Amounts falling due within one year)			
Telephone Due		40	
Working Capital			760
Total Net Assets			21,915
Financed By			
Accumulated Fund 1/6/91		19,940	
Add Excess Income over Expenditure		1,975	
			21,915

1. (b)

$$\frac{\text{Gross Profit x 100\%}}{\text{Sales}} \quad \frac{1{,}700 \text{ x } 100\%}{8{,}500} = 20\%$$

Comment: *Satisfactory margin before expenses but lower than a business percentage.*

F. Treasurer's Report

The treasurer will present the treasurer's report at the AGM. It informs the members of the financial situation of the club.

Treasurer's Report on Local Social Club — Refer to Accounts and Solution above (Higher Level Question)

LOCAL SOCIAL CLUB
Treasurer's Report

To All Club Members 3 June 2015
From Ryan Giggs, Treasurer

Please find attached with this report final accounts and balance sheet of club.

Body of Report

1. Canteen profit was €1,700 as shown in canteen trading account.
2. The income and expenditure shows that the club had a surplus of €1,975 for the year.
3. There is €310 owing in subscriptions at end of year.
4. To improve facilities for members for the future I recommend that members' subscriptions be increased from €5 to €10 per year.

I am available to discuss this report if required.

Signed

Ryan Giggs
Treasurer

G. Business Terms

Accumulated Fund = Capital (assets – liabilities).
Agenda Programme for meeting.
AGM Annual General Meeting.
Deficit Loss made by a club.
Excess/Surplus Profit made by a club.
Income and Expenditure Account Profit and loss account
Minutes of Meeting Record of meeting.
Receipts and Payments Account Cash account for a club.
Subscriptions Amount of money paid each year to a club in order to remain a member.

Chapter 47 — Farm Accounts

A. Introduction

Farming in Ireland is a big and important business. Farmers, like any other business, must keep proper accounts.

B. Purpose of Farm Accounts

(1) To find out whether the farm made a **profit** or **loss**.
(2) To find out **which sections** of farming are most profitable.
(3) For submission to **Revenue Commissioners** for tax liability.
(4) To provide information to **bank manager** when making a loan application.
(5) To provide information if applying for **government** or **EC grants**.

C. Farm Accounts

(1) Most farmers will keep an **analysed cash book** to record daily receipts and payments.
(2) At the end of the year an **income and expenditure account** is prepared to find profit or loss made.
(3) A **balance sheet** is also prepared to show the farmer's assets, liabilities and capital.

ANALYSED CASH BOOK

This book is used to record the daily receipts and payments of the farmer.

Receipts — Debit side. **Payments — Credit side.**

Sample Question and Solution on Analysed Cash Book

Question

John and Mary Keane run a farm in Co. Meath. The following is a list of their receipts and payments for the month of October 2015.

1 Oct. Balance at bank	€1,500
5 Oct. Contractors for beet Ch. No. 1	€700
7 Oct. Tractor insurance Ch. No. 2	€560
10 Oct. Sales of potatoes	€1,600
12 Oct. Sales of vegetables	€1,200
14 Oct. Wages, potato picking Ch. No. 3	€200
15 Oct. Purchase of vegetable bags Ch. No. 4	€260
19 Oct. Sales of sugar beet	€6,000
20 Oct. Sales of vegetables	€1,400
20 Oct. Wages, vegetable packing Ch. No. 5	€180
21 Oct. Contractors for beet Ch. No. 6	€600
22 Oct. Haulage of beet to factory Ch. No. 7	€300
23 Oct. Diesel and oil for tractor Ch. No. 8	€400

24 Oct.	Wages, potato picking Ch. No. 9	€290
25 Oct.	Sales of potatoes	€2,000
26 Oct.	Sales of sugar beet	€2,600
27 Oct.	Receipt of EC grant	€1,500
27 Oct.	Repairs to potato digger Ch. No. 10	€170
29 Oct.	Purchase of potato bags Ch. No. 11	€700
30 Oct.	Telephone bill Ch. No. 12	€180

Prepare an analysed cash book for the Keanes using the following headings.

Receipts: Total, Potatoes, Vegetables, Sugar Beet, Other.
Payments: Total, Potatoes, Vegetables, Sugar Beet, Other.

Solution

ANALYSED CASH BOOK

Date	Details	Total	Potatoes	Veg. Beet	Sugar	Other	Date	Details No.	Chq.	Total	Potatoes	Veg. Beet	Sugar	Other
2015		€	€	€	€	€	2015			€	€	€	€	€
1 Oct.	Balance	1,500					5 Oct.	Contractors — beet	1	700			700	
10 Oct.	Sales — potatoes	1,600	1,600				7 Oct.	Tractor — insurance	2	560				560
12 Oct.	Sales — vegetables	1,200		1,200			14 Oct.	Wages — potato picking	3	200	200			
19 Oct.	Sales — sugar beet	6,000			6,000		15 Oct.	Purchases — veg. bags	4	260		260		
20 Oct.	Sales — vegetables	1,400		1,400			20 Oct.	Wages — veg. packing	5	180		180		
25 Oct.	Sales — potatoes	2,000	2,000				21 Oct.	Contractors — beet	6	600			600	
26 Oct.	Sales — sugar beet	2,600			2,600		22 Oct.	Haulage — beet to factory	7	300			300	
27 Oct.	EC — grant	1,500				1,500	23 Oct.	Diesel, oil — tractor	8	400				400
							24 Oct.	Wages — potato picking	9	290	290			
							27 Oct.	Repairs — potato digger	10	170	170			
							29 Oct.	Purchases — potato bags	11	700	700			
							30 Oct.	Telephone bill	12	180				180
		17,800	3,600	2,600	8,600	1,500				4,540	1,360	440	1,600	1,140
							31 Oct.	Balance C/d		13,260				
		17,800								17,800				
31 Oct.	Balance B/d	13,260												

Sample Question and Solution on Income and Expenditure Account and Balance Sheet

Denis and Mary O'Leary run a farm. The following figures are taken from their books.

Gross Income	€
Potatoes	7,000
Vegetables	9,000
Sugar beet	6,000
Fruit	8,000

Expenditure	€
Interest on loan	1,500
Wages	4,500
Light and heat	700
Hire of equipment	600
Rent	550
Seeds	1,200
Plants	2,500
Telephone	1,300
Insurance — tractor	650
Diesel and oil	700
Fertiliser	1,500
Repairs to machinery	120
Contractors — beet	700

Assets and Liabilities	€
Land	100,000
Buildings	50,000
Stock	3,000
Debtors	5,000
Creditors	2,650
ACC loan	28,000
Tractors	20,000
Equipment	10,000
Cash	700
Bank	2,900
Capital	150,000
Drawings	2,530

The following information is also available on 31 December 2016.

- Light and heat due €50
- Rent prepaid €100
- Depreciate tractors by 5% of cost.

Prepare:

(1) Income and expenditure account for the year ending 31 December 2016.
(2) Balance sheet as at 31 December 2016.

Solution

(1) Income and Expenditure Account for Year Ending 31 December 2016

	€	€	€
Income			
Potatoes		7,000	
Vegetables		9,000	
Sugar beet		6,000	
Fruit		8,000	30,000
Less Expenditure			
Interest on loan		1,500	
Wages		4,500	
Light and heat	700		
Add light and heat due	50	750	
Hire of equipment		600	
Rent	550		
Less rent prepaid	100	450	
Seeds		1,200	
Plants		2,500	
Telephone		1,300	
Insurance — tractor		650	
Diesel and oil		700	
Fertiliser		1,500	
Repairs to machinery		120	
Contractors — beet		700	
Depreciation of tractors		1,000	17,470
Farm net profit/excess income over expenditure			12,530

(2) **Balance Sheet as at 31 December 2016**

	Cost	Deprec.	NBV
Fixed Assets			
Land	*100,000*	—	*100,000*
Buildings	*50,000*	—	*50,000*
Tractors	*20,000*	*1,000*	*19,000*
Equipment	*10,000*	—	*10,000*
	180,000	*1,000*	*179,000*
Current Assets			
Stock	*3,000*		
Debtors	*5,000*		
Cash	*700*		
Bank	*2,900*		
Rent prepaid	*100*	*11,700*	
Less Current Liabilities (Creditors: Amounts falling due within one year)			
Creditors	*2,650*		
Light and heat due	*50*	*2,700*	
Working capital			*9,000*
Total net assets			*188,000*
Financed By			
Capital	*150,000*		
Add farm profit	*12,530*	*162,530*	
Less drawings		*2,530*	*160,000*
Long-Term Liabilities (Creditors: Amounts falling due after more than one year)			
ACC loan			*28,000*
Capital employed			*188,000*

D. Farm Report

To Denis and Mary O'Leary
From J.P. Kiely, Teagasc Farm Advisor

High Street
Kerry

10 January 2017

Introduction
I was asked by you to assess the performance of your farm.

Having visited your farm and examined your account the following are my findings.

Body of Report:

1. Farm profit was €12,530 for year ending 31 December 2016.
2. Return on capital invested was 8.3%

   i.e. $\frac{\text{Net Profit x 100\%}}{\text{Capital Invested}}$ $\frac{\text{€12,530 x 100\%}}{\text{€150,000}}$ = 8.3%

   a reasonably satisfactory return comparable to bank interest rates.
3. The net profit margin was 42.76%

   $\frac{\text{Net Profit x 100\%}}{\text{Sales}}$ = $\frac{\text{€12,530 x 100\%}}{\text{€30,000}}$ = 41.76%
4. The working capital ratio was 4.3:1

   CA:CL
   €11,700:€2,700
   4.3:1

   Very satisfactory and well above the recommended ratio of 2:1.
5. There is €2,900 in the bank deposit account and €700 in cash.

I am available to discuss this report if required.

Signed

J.P. Kiely
Teagasc Adviser

Chapter 48 — Service Firms

A. Introduction

Service firms supply and sell a service rather than a product.

Examples: Travel agencies, hairdressing, accounting, banking, insurance, cleaning, secretarial, horse training.

B. Accounts Prepared by Service Firms

- **Analysed cash book** to record daily receipts and payments.
- **Operating statement** (profit and loss account) for year.
- **Balance sheet** as at last day of the year.

(1) ANALYSED CASH BOOK

Most service firms will keep an analysed cash book as their main financial record.

Sample Question and Solution

Question

Jim Coppell Ltd trains horses. The following is a list of his receipts and payments for the month of July 2015.

1 July	Cash on hand	€800
1 July	Training fees received	€2,900
2 July	Vet's fees paid Ch. No. 1	€740
4 July	Rates Ch. No. 2	€2,100
7 July	Race winnings	€2,400
10 July	Hay sales	€3,800
11 July	Insurance Ch. No. 3	€1,890
13 July	Postage and telephone Ch. No. 4	€700
16 July	Wages Ch. No. 5	€4,000
17 July	Hay sales	€2,600
18 July	Training fees received	€1,800
19 July	Light and heat Ch. No. 6	€1,780
20 July	Race winnings	€1,900
21 July	Vet's fees Ch. No. 7	€900
22 July	Wages Ch. No. 8	€2,540
24 July	Race winnings	€2,400
25 July	Light and heat Ch. No. 9	€2,600
28 July	Hay sales	€2,900
29 July	Vet's fees Ch. No. 10	€900
30 July	Training fees received	€750
31 July	Wages Ch. No. 11	€640

Prepare an analysed cash book for Jim Coppell Ltd using the following headings.
Receipts: Total, Training Fees, Race Winnings, Hay Sales.
Payments: Total, Rates and Insurance, Wages, Postage and Telephone, Light and Heat, Vet's Fees.

Solution

ANALYSED CASH BOOK

Date	Details	Total	Trg Fees	Race Wngs	Hay Sales	Date	Details	Chq. No.	Total	Rates & Insur.	Wages	Postage & Phone	Light & Heat	Vet's Fees
2015			€	€	€	2015			€	€	€	€	€	€
1 July	Balance	800				2 July	Vet's fees	1	740					740
1 July	Training fees	2,900	2,900			4 July	Rates	2	2,100	2,100				
7 July	Race winnings	2,400		2,400		11 July	Insurance	3	1,890	1,890				
10 July	Hay sales	3,800			3,800	13 July	Post and telephone	4	700			700		
17 July	Hay sales	2,600			2,600	16 July	Wages	5	4,000		4,000			
18 July	Training fees	1,800	1,800			19 July	Light and heat	6	1,780				1,780	
20 July	Race winnings	1,900		1,900		21 July	Vet's fees	7	900					900
24 July	Race winnings	2,400		2,400		22 July	Wages	8	2,540		2,540			
28 July	Hay sales	2,900			2,900	25 July	Light and heat	9	2,600				2,600	
30 July	Training fees	750	750			29 July	Vet's fees	10	900					900
						31 July	Wages	11	640		640			
		22,250	5,450	6,700	9,300				18,790	3,990	7,180	700	4,380	2,540
						31 July	Balance	C/d	3,460					
		22,250							22,250					
31 July	Balance B/d	3,460												

(2) FINAL ACCOUNTS OF SERVICE FIRMS

(a) Service firms will prepare an **operating statement** (profit and loss account) to find out whether the firm made a profit or a loss.

(b) Service firms will also prepare a **balance sheet** and it is the same as any other balance sheet.

Examination-Style Question and Solution

Question 1.

Answer (a) and (b). This is a question on Final Accounts and Balance Sheet of a Service Firm.

(To be completed in your Answerbook.)

Jim Coppell Ltd trains horses. He prepares an Operating Statement (Profit and Loss A/C) and Balance Sheet at the end of each year.

The following Trial Balance was taken from the books on 31 December 2016.

Trial Balance as at 31 December 2016		
	Dr €	**Cr €**
Sales income from:		
– Training Fees		116,405
– Race Winnings		44,600
– Sale of Hay		5,000
Rates	4,630	
Insurance	12,310	
Wages	37,950	
Postage and Telephone	2,540	
Light and Heat	4,635	
Vet's Fees	2,775	
Bank Overdraft		14,720
Cash on Hand	6,385	
Ordinary Share Capital (50,000 €1 shares)		50,000
Land	80,000	
Stables	59,500	
Motor Vehicles	20,000	
	230,725	230,725

1. (a) Prepare an Operating Statement for Jim Coppell Ltd for the year ended 31 December 2016 and a Balance Sheet as on that date. (50)

1. (b) State **one** reason why Jim Coppell Ltd should keep accounts. (10)

Source: Junior Certificate Ordinary Level. **(60 marks)**

Solution to Question 1.

JIM COPPELL LTD

Operating Statement for Year Ending 31 December 2016

	€	€
Sales Income		
Training Fees	116,405	
Race Winnings	44,600	
Sale of Hay	5,000	
Total Income		166,005
Less Expenditure		
Rates	4,630	
Insurance	12,310	
Wages	37,950	
Postage and Telephone	2,540	
Light and Heat	4,635	
Vet's Fees	2,775	
Total Expenditure		64,840
Net Profit		101,165

Balance Sheet as on 31 December 2016

	Cost	Deprec.	NBV
Fixed Assets	€	€	€
Land	80,000	—	80,000
Stables	59,500	—	59,500
Motor Vehicles	20,000	—	20,000
	159,500		159,500
Current Assets			
Cash		6,385	
Less Current Liabilities (Creditors: Amounts falling due within one year.)			
Bank Overdraft		14,720	
Working Capital			– 8,335
Total Net Assets			151,165
Financed By			
50,000 Ordinary Shares @ €1 each			50,000
Reserves			
Net Profit			101,165
Capital Employed			151,165

1. (b) *Reasons Why Jim Coppell Should Keep Accounts*

- *To find out whether he is making a profit or loss.*
- *To see how much tax he has to pay.*
- *To help him plan for the future.*
- *To provide information for bank if making a loan application.*

PRACTICE QUESTIONS

(i) (Higher Level only)

Redo the Jim Coppell Ltd question — operating statement and balance sheet — taking the following adjustments into account on 31 December 2016.

- Wages due €1,300.
- Insurance prepaid €770.
- Depreciate motor vehicles by 10%.
- Stock of postage stamps on hand €100.
- Vet's fees due €250.

SECTION FOUR — INFORMATION TECHNOLOGY

Chapter 49 — Modern Information Technology

A. Introduction

Information Technology (IT) is a modern term applied to the processing of knowledge and data using computers and other electronic advances.

Data Processing (DP) is the operation of collecting, storing, processing and transmitting data.

B. Computers

A computer is a device capable of solving problems by accepting data, performing mathematical operations on the data, and giving out results.

C. Types of Computer System

(1) MAINFRAME COMPUTERS

Large, powerful and expensive computers that are used for processing information in large businesses and organisations, e.g. Eircom, ESB.

(2) MINI COMPUTERS

Smaller and more compact systems. Found in medium-sized businesses or in government departments.

(3) MICRO COMPUTERS

The smallest and cheapest class of computer. They are used in many homes as personal computers; operated by one person, they fit on a desk. They are widely used in schools and businesses for word processing, databases and spreadsheets.

D. Hardware and Software

HARDWARE

Physical part of a computer system, e.g. monitor, keyboard, disk drive, printer.

SOFTWARE

Programs or instructions that tell a computer what to do. Software may be built into the computer's ROM or can be stored on disk and loaded into the computer when required.

E. Hardware/Computer Equipment

A computer is made up of many parts called hardware, and includes monitor, keyboard and system unit. The system unit holds the computer's processor (CPU), memory and disk drives.

F. Parts of a Computer

The **Keyboard** is used to get the information into the computer.

The **CPU** is used to process the information, i.e. do calculations.

The **Monitor** displays the result.

The **Printer** produces a hard copy of this display.

The **Disk Drive** makes it possible for the information to be stored on disk for use in the future.

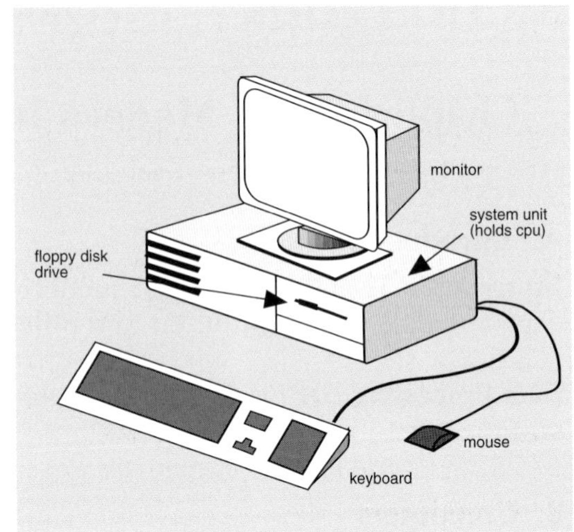

G. Main Components of a Computer

(1) Input devices — hardware used to enter data.
(2) Processor — hardware that produces results.
(3) Output devices — hardware that displays results.
(4) Storage — hardware used to store information.

H. Input Devices

(1) KEYBOARD

A device for entering data and programs into the computer. It is a display of keys that produce characters on display when pressed.

(2) MOUSE

A small device with a ball underneath. When moved, it guides a pointer across the screen. Used in many programs, especially graphics.

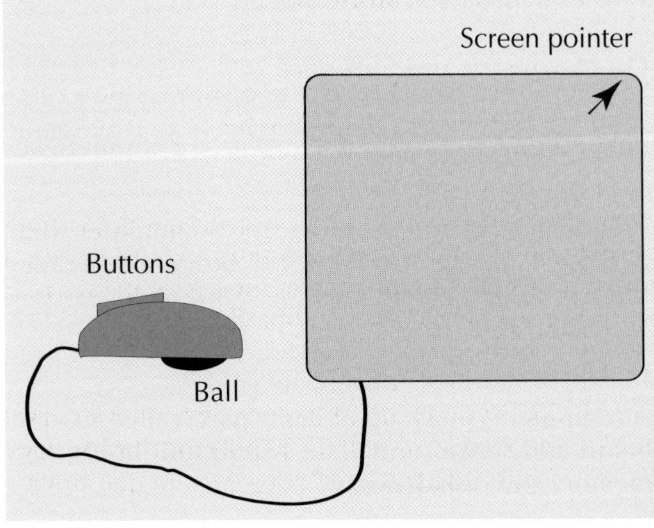

(3) SCANNER

A scanner is used to copy text, pictures, drawings, etc, into the computer.

(4) LIGHT PEN

A device resembling a pen connected to the computer by cable, it can be used to write or draw on the screen. Used mainly in graphics.

(5) MAGNETIC CARD READER

This machine reads data from the magnetic strip on a plastic card, e.g. cash dispensing machines reading ATM plastic card.

(6) TOUCH SCREEN

The screen displays choices and the user touches the desired choice. Used mainly in banks.

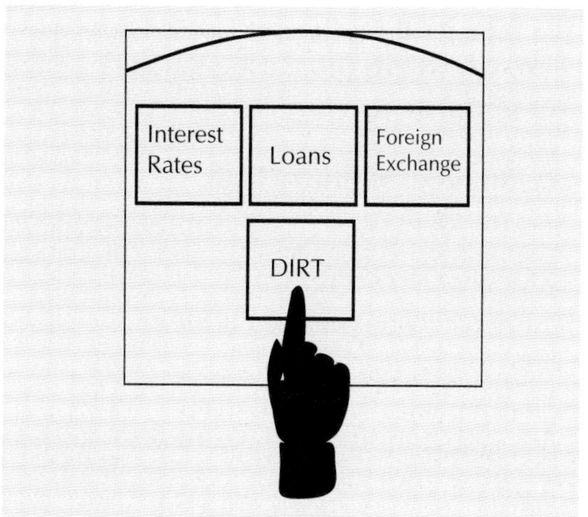

(7) MICROPHONE/VOICE ENTRY DATA (VDE)

A microphone is connected to the computer. The information put into the computer is interpreted by a special program. Can be used for the physically handicapped.

(8) MODEM (**MO**DULATOR/**DEM**ODULATOR)

This is a device for connecting two computers by a telephone line. It is used to transfer information from one computer to another.

(9) JOYSTICK

This is a device attached to the computer by a cable. It is a hand-held lever, and when moved, it sends signals to the CPU. It is used for playing computer games.

(10) MAGNETIC INK CHARACTER RECOGNITION (MICR)

This is used in banking. The numbers along the bottom of each cheque are printed in magnetic ink. The bank staff write the amount of the cheque in magnetic ink and with the use of a magnetic ink character reader linked to a computer, the customer's bank account is updated.

(11) OPTICAL MARK READER (OMR)

The device is connected to a computer and detects the presence or absence of a mark in a given position, each position having a value known to the computer. Used in Lotto, and multiple choice exam questions.

I. Processing Hardware

CENTRAL PROCESSING UNIT (CPU)

This is the brain of the computer, where all calculations on the data are carried out. It is the place where the computer interprets and processes information.

There are three main areas in the CPU.

(1) The Control Unit

The part that makes the computer carry out each instruction of a program in sequence. It controls the operation of the computer.

(2) The Arithmetic and Logic Unit (ALU)

The part where the mathematical calculations are carried out and logic operations are performed.

(3) Storage/Memory Unit

The part where the data and programs are stored. It is like our own memory.

MEMORY AND STORAGE

There are two types of memory.

(1) Random Access Memory (RAM)

The instructions your computer gets and information it processes are kept in RAM during your work session. RAM is not a permanent storage place for information, as it is active only while your computer is on. When you turn off your computer, information is deleted from RAM, so always save it on a disk before switching off your computer.

(2) Read Only Memory (ROM)

This memory holds the data and instructions permanently needed by the computer, e.g. the instructions needed for the operation of the computer. This information is entered at the time of manufacture and cannot be altered by the user. When the computer is turned off, this information is not lost.

MEASURING COMPUTER MEMORY

(1) Byte is the amount of storage needed to hold one character (character is any keyboard symbol, e.g. digit 0 1 2; letter A B C; punctuation mark , : ?; sign + − =.
(2) Kilobyte (KB) one kilobyte = 1,024 bytes.
(3) Megabyte (MB) one megabyte = 1,048,576 bytes.
(4) Gigabyte (GB)

Memory capacity is the number of bytes that a computer can hold in RAM at one time, e.g. a computer with 4MB RAM will hold 4 × 1,048,576 bytes.

The more RAM available in a computer, the more data it can handle and the bigger the programs it can accommodate.

Secondary storage

This storage supplements the main storage of a computer: for instance, floppy disks and hard disks.

(1) Diskette or floppy disk — a thin flexible disk inside a protective plastic cover, it is removed from the disk drive when not in use. Floppy disks are normally 3 1/2" and vary in the amount of information that they hold.

(2) CD Rom (Compact Disc Read Only Memory) — can store large amounts of written, audio or graphical data.

(3) Memory stick or flash drive — known as a USB mass storage device.

(4) Fixed disk — hard disk — permanently installed inside the case of the computer. It can store very large amounts of information, which can be accessed much more quickly.

J. Output Hardware

Output devices allow you to see the information entered and processed.

(1) MONITOR/VDU

A monitor (Visual Display Unit) is the most common method of displaying information. There are many types of monitor. Monochrome screens display only one colour, i.e. black on white or green on black. Colour screens can display many colours.

(2) PRINTER

A printer is a device that allows you to put the information on paper. This is a permanent copy, sometimes called a 'printout' or 'hard copy'.

TYPES OF PRINTER

(1) Dot matrix printers

These form characters on paper by printing a pattern of dots. They are cheap but slow and do not produce high-quality copies.

(2) Daisy wheel printers

The hammer strikes the character, which in turn strikes the paper through the ribbon. The output of these printers is 'letter quality', i.e. the characters are fully formed, and continuous lines are produced similar to a typewriter.

(3) Laser printers

Similar to photocopying. Capable of very high speeds, top-quality copies, good graphics, good colour, but the printers are expensive.

(4) Ink jet printers

A fine jet of quick-drying ink is fired at the paper and forms characters as it lands. They are very quiet and produce high-quality copies. They can achieve speeds of up to 200 characters per second.

(5) Plotters

Devices for drawing lines on paper. Mainly used for diagrams and drawing plans, etc.

K. Computer Software/Packages

Software is the set of instructions that enables the computer to perform its functions. There are two types of software.

(1) OPERATING SYSTEM

The operating system gets your computer running and controls the operation of its activities. It looks after the internal running of the computer, i.e. reading disks, listing contents of disks, saving and loading programs, etc. A common operating system used with IBM is Microsoft Disk Operating System — MS DOS.

(2) PROGRAMS

A program is a coded set of instructions that interprets the information you give the computer. A wide variety of programs are used for different tasks, including word processing, e.g. Microsoft Word, Word Perfect; spreadsheets, e.g. Lotus 1-2-3; database management, e.g. dBASEIII; accounting, e.g. SAGE; graphics, e.g. Illustrator.

INTEGRATED SOFTWARE

Programs that can exchange data with each other, e.g. a software package that has a word processor, database, spreadsheet and communications program — like Microsoft Works.

L. Software Programs Used in Business

(1) WORD PROCESSING

A software system that allows you to write sentences and paragraphs. You can produce letters, documents and reports. Text can be moved, copied, replaced and checked for spelling, print sizes can be changed, and when finished, it can all be printed on paper.

(2) DATABASE

A database is a filing system on computer. It can be used in business for names and addresses of customers, in schools for students and class lists, in hospitals for patients, etc.

(3) SPREADSHEET

A spreadsheet is used for doing mathematical and financial calculations, e.g. budgets, accounts, stock records, payroll and business planning. The screen is divided into rows and columns and each intersection contains a cell. The big advantage of using a spreadsheet is that if you change one figure all other figures involved will be automatically adjusted.

(4) MAIL MERGE

This program allows you to produce personalised letters, i.e. they look as if they were written specially for a particular person. To do this you type out a letter on the word processor and merge with name and address from the database. The same letter can be addressed to a number of people.

(5) PAYROLL

A program used by business to calculate wages.

(6) COMPUTERISED ACCOUNTS

Used to prepare accounts in business.

(7) COMPUTER-AIDED DESIGN (CAD)

Used in the design of products.

(8) COMPUTER-AIDED MANUFACTURE (CAM)

A package used to assist in the manufacture of goods.

(9) GRAPHICS

This program allows the user to produce and print out pie charts and bar charts. Very useful in business when trying to illustrate figures or accounting information.

(10) DESKTOP PUBLISHING (DTP)

This program is used to produce professional-quality reports, booklets, magazines, brochures and other publications on computer. A high-quality printer is essential.

(11) SPELL CHECKER

Most word processing programs include a dictionary. It compares typed words with words in its dictionary and will highlight any words with incorrect spelling.

M. Use of Information Technology

(1) IN BUSINESS

(a) For **typing** letters, documents and reports using word processor.
(b) For **filing**, e.g. names and addresses of customers using database.
(c) For **doing accounts, payroll and wages slip, stock records** using spreadsheet.
(d) For **illustrating information** graphically.
(e) For **sending personalised letters** to people using mail merge.
(f) For **reading bar codes** in shops and controlling stock.
(g) Some firms use computers for **designing products** (CAD), and in **manufacturing** (CAM).
(h) For **communicating** with other firms and customers. e.g. e-mail, internet.

(2) IN COMMUNICATIONS

(a) Through **satellite TV** we can get immediate coverage of all major events throughout the world, e.g. World Cup soccer.
(b) **Mobile phones** can be used by reporters to send information back to radio or TV headquarters.
(c) **A modem** can be used to transfer information from one computer to another over a telephone line, e.g. foreign journalists can send information back to headquarters using a PC and modem.
(d) **Telecom call card**, where a computer in the phone can read the card.
(e) **Fax machine** can be used to transmit information; this is made up of a scanner, modem and printer.

(f) **Eircom** provides a wide range of services that are computer-based, e.g. video conferencing.
(g) **E-mail** is used extensively to communicate, and many businesses have **Internet websites** for advertising their products and services worldwide.

(3) IN THE HOME

There are many uses of information technology in the home.
(a) Internet access – reservations/home banking/reseach.
(b) E-mail for communications.
(c) Word processing – writing a letter.
(d) Spreadsheets/budgets/accounts.
(e) Database/filing/storing information.
(f) Security/remote control/sensors, e.g. fire alarms, burglar alarms.
(g) Timers in household appliances, e.g. central heating systems.
(h) Texting/e-mail/Internet access via mobile phone.

(4) IN BANKING

(a) All **deposit** accounts, **current** accounts, **loan accounts** and **overdrafts** are recorded on computer.
(b) **All information processed** through banks is done on computer — direct debits, standing orders, credit transfers and PayPath.
(c) **Bank statements** are prepared through computer.
(d) The **numbers** along the bottom of each **cheque** are printed in magnetic ink. The cheque is read by MICR linked to computer, and cheque is cleared.
(e) All **bank information** is kept on computer, e.g. interest rates on mortgages and term loans, deposit account rates of interest, rates of exchange of foreign currency.
(f) All **ATMs** are linked to computer and allow customers to withdraw, lodge, check balance, order a cheque book, order a statement twenty-four hours a day.
(g) **Electronic Funds Transfer at Point of Sale (EFTPOS):** the customer is given a plastic card, and when he comes to a shop checkout, the card is inserted into an electronic device, the PIN is keyed in and the amount of the bill is deducted from the customer's bank account and put into the shop's bank account, e.g. Laser.

N. Computerised Accounts

Computers have many uses in accounting.
(1) Day books, debtors, creditors and nominal ledger, cash book, and preparing trial balance.
(2) Business documents — invoicing, credit notes, etc. and printing statements for customers.
(3) VAT analysis.
(4) Trading and profit and loss account and balance sheet.
(5) Wages/pay roll/wages slips.
(6) Stock control/stock records.

Most accounting packages are 'integrated' — this means that when data is entered, all the records are updated at once. For example, a company sold goods for

€1,000 with VAT @ 21%, to O'Flynn Ltd. When this is entered in the computer
➢ Sales day book updated
➢ O'Flynn Ltd updated
➢ Debtors control account updated
➢ Sales account updated
➢ VAT account updated.

O. Keyboarding

The keyboard is used to type instructions for your computer and to type information you want your computer to process. Efficient keyboarding involves being able to type properly, i.e. resting fingers on home keys ASDF JKL, and moving around the keyboard without looking at keyboard. Here are some of the keys on a computer keyboard and their use.

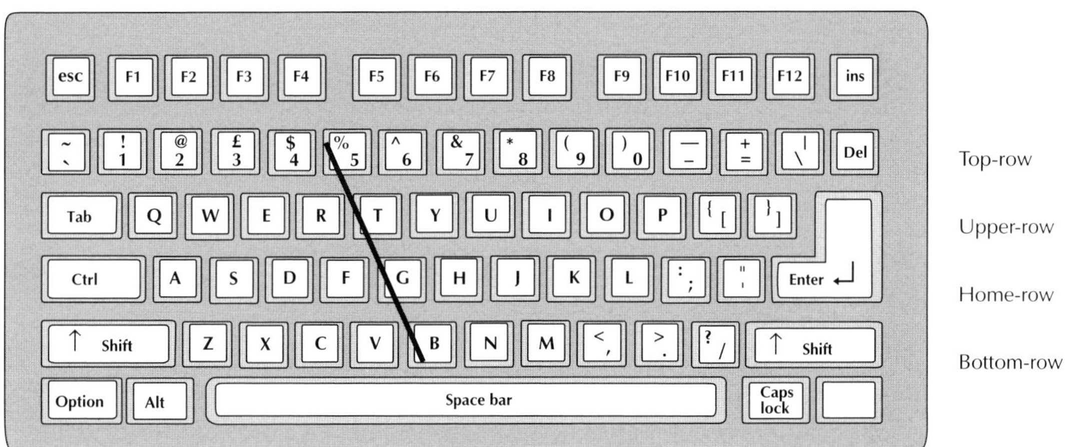

(1) **QWERTY** — First six letters on the second row.
(2) **Home Keys** — ASDF JKL.
(3) **Space Bar** — To move on one space, i.e. between words.
(4) **Shift Key** — To make capital letters.
(5) **Caps Lock Key** — To make a line of capital letters.
(6) **Enter/Return Key** — Moves cursor to next line, or when using a program, tells the computer to carry out instruction.
(7) **Function Keys** — To perform special functions within a program, e.g. F1 — Help.
(8) **Del (Delete)** — To eliminate data from screen.
(9) **Ins (Insert)** — To insert a character omitted.
(10) **Tab Key** — To set margins.
(11) **Esc (Escape)** — To cancel an operation.

P. Proofreading

Proofreading is checking your work for errors and making the necessary corrections before making a printout.

Q. Factors to Be Considered Before Purchasing a Computer System

(1) How much will the system cost and how will it be financed?
(2) Is a computer system required, and how will firm benefit from owning a computer?
(3) Size of system required and availability of software.
(4) Will employees have to be trained? How much will training cost? Will there be staff lay-offs?
(5) Where will computer system be located, and is the location suitable?

R. Recording Purchase of a Computer in the Books of a Company

(1) PURCHASE OF COMPUTER BY CHEQUE

Rule
Debit Computer Account
Credit Bank Account

(2) PURCHASE OF COMPUTER ON CREDIT

The purchase of an asset on credit is recorded in the **general journal** then posted to **ledger**.

Rule
Debit Computer Account
Credit Supplier's Account

Example

1 January 2016 Purchased computer system on credit from Lotus Ltd for €5,000.

General Journal — **Page 1**

Date	Particulars	Fo	Debit €	Credit €
1/1/16	Computer A/C	GL1	5,000	
	Lotus Ltd			5,000
	Purchase of computer system on credit			

Ledger

Computer A/C

Date	Particulars	Fo	Total €	Date	Particulars	Fo	Total
1/1/16	Lotus Ltd	GJ	5,000				

Lotus Ltd

Date	Particulars	Fo	Total	Date	Particulars	Fo	Total €
				1/1/16	Computer	GJ1	5,000

S. Dictionary of Information Technology Terms

Apple Brand name for a family of microcomputers manufactured by Apple.
Back-Up Copy Copy of the file kept for reference in case original data is lost or destroyed.
Backspace A keyboard operation that deletes the character one space to the left of the cursor.
Broadband Internet Access Broadband offers 'high speed always on' internet access. It is currently the fastest internet access available, 15 times faster than dial up, allowing downloading and other transactions to be completed more efficiently for internet users.
Business Graphics Pie chart, bar charts, graphs, etc.
Byte Amount of storage needed to hold one character.
Bug Mistake in a computer program or an error in the working of the computer.
Central Processing Unit (CPU) Part of computer system which interprets and carries out instructions.
COBOL Language developed for business data processing applications.
CD ROM (Compact Disk Read Only Memory) An optical disk on which data is recorded. It is five inches in diameter.
Computer-Aided Design (CAD) A program that converts rough sketches into a finished form.
Computer-Aided Manufacture (CAM) Using computers in manufacturing.
Cursor A symbol on the screen that indicates where the next character will appear.
Disk A magnetic device for storing information and programs.
Disk Operating System (DOS) Gets your computer running and controls the operation of computer.
E-Commerce Buying or selling on the Internet or making payment on the Internet.
Editing Correcting or changing programs or data.
Electronic Mail (E-mail) A way of sending typed messages and computer files directly from one computer to another over the Internet.
Facsimile/Fax Scanning of a document and transmission of it via wires. Copy is produced at destination.
File A collection of data on a particular topic.
Formatting Preparing a disk for holding information.
Internet An international network linking millions of computers in different countries through the telephone system. It is a means of communication and a source of information on supplies or services. It can also be used for banking, e-mail, reservations and ordering.
Internet Service Provider (ISP) A company that allows you access the Internet. e.g. Eircom, Indigo, Ireland on Line (IOL).
Java Computer programming language.
Kilobyte abbreviated K. = 1,024 bytes.
Lotus 123 An electronic spreadsheet program.
Megabyte 1,048,576 bytes or 1,024 kilobytes.
Menu A list of choices on screen.
Microsoft An American company producing software systems.
MS DOS Microsoft Disk Operating System.
Network Where many computers within an organisation are linked together, so that all of them can access information from the same source.

Programmer A person who designs and writes programs.

Programming Translating information into a language that the computer can understand.

Scrolling Continuous movement of data on the screen, i.e. one line appears on bottom and all lines move upwards, line on top disappears from view.

Software Package A prewritten program that can be purchased for specific use, e.g. word processing package.

Spell Checker A program that informs user of spelling mistakes.

Virus A program that damages files.

Web Browser A piece of software that allows your computer to surf the Internet and view websites, e.g. Netscape Navigator.

World Wide Web (www) A vast collection of linked documents available over the Internet.

Examination-Style Questions and Solutions

Question 1.

Answer (a) and (b). This is a Question on Information Technology.

Philip Ryan is a final year university student of architecture. He lives with his parents, who own and run a bar and disco. He is trying to convince his parents to buy a new computer that could be used by all the family.

1. **(a)** State **two** uses to which the new computer could be put by **each** of the following:

- **(i)** The Ryans in their business.
- **(ii)** Philip in his studies.
- **(iii)** The Ryans in running their home. (24)

1. **(b)** Philip shopped around for a computer and saw the following advertisement:

A P.C. with 17" VGA colour monitor
Colour ink jet printer, 128 Megabytes
RAM 30 GB H.D. storage fast
running speed, keyboard and
mouse including packages
work for word processing,
spread sheets, database.
All for the amazing price of

€ 2,614
incl. VAT

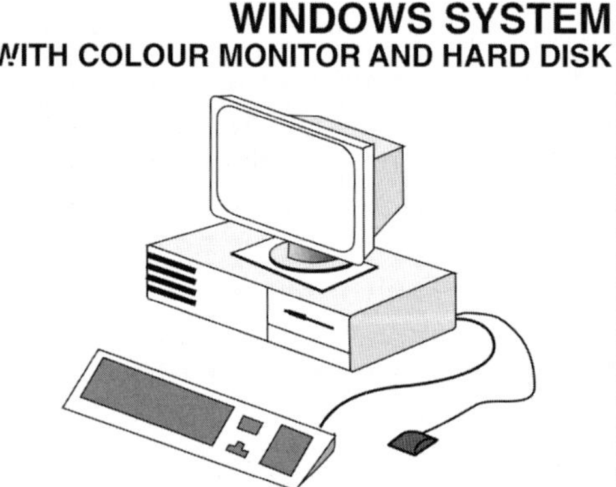

Explain any four of the words underlined in the above advertisement. (16)

Source: Junior Certificate Higher Level. **(40 marks)**

Solution to Question 1.

1. (a) *(i) Stock control, accounting, word processing, databases, communications, payroll.*

(ii) Mathematical calculation, writing reports, language learning, database.

(iii) Household budgets, household accounts, word processing, database.

1. (b) *Monitor*

A visual display unit or screen that shows information being inputted into the computer. It is also used for viewing output before printing a hard copy.

Megabyte

The measure of the RAM of the computer. It is 1,048,576 bytes. The bigger the RAM capacity, the larger the program the machine can operate.

Keyboard

The main input device for communicating information and instructions to the computer. It is similar to the keyboard of a typewriter but has additional special function keys and number pads.

Mouse

A hand-operated device that moves the cursor on the VDU.

Word Processing

This is a program used for typing letters, reports and documents. It is possible to insert, delete and rearrange the text until it is satisfactory before printing out a hard copy. Some programs have a spell checker built in.

Database

An electronic filing cabinet in which information can be inputted, stored and later retrieved when required.

Question 2.

Answer all sections. This is an Information Technology question.

The directors of P.J. Ltd, manufacturers and suppliers of household furniture, were very impressed with the quotation from Hiteck Computers. Hiteck Ltd were offering an 'all in' package, which included the computer system and a selection of business software, at a special price of €10,000.

2. (a) What are the three main hardware parts of a computer system? (6)

2. (b) Give three types of computer software suitable for the business. (6)

2. (c) State three ways in which P.J. Ltd may benefit from purchasing a computer system. (9)

2. (d) P.J. Ltd purchased the computer system from Hiteck Ltd on credit, on 25/5/15. Record this purchase in the appropriate book of first entry of P.J. Ltd and post the relevant figures to the ledger. (12)

2. (e) State two suitable outside sources of finance that P.J. Ltd could use to finance the computer system.

Give a brief explanation of any **one** of these **two** sources. (7)

Source: Junior Certificate Higher Level. **(40 marks)**

Solution to Question 2.

2. (a) *Visual display unit, keyboard, disk drive, printer, mouse.*
2. (b) *Since P.J. Limited manufacture and supply household furniture, the main type of software would be Computer-Aided Design (CAD), Computer-Aided Manufacture (CAM) plus any of the following: word processing, spreadsheet, database, payroll, accounts, stock control.*

2. (d)

General Journal

			€	€
25/5/15	Computer A/C	GL1	10,000	
	Hiteck Ltd A/C	GL1		10,000
	Purchase of computer system on credit			

LEDGER

Computer A/C

			€				
25/5/15	Hiteck Ltd	GJ1	10,000				

Hiteck Ltd A/C

							€
				25/5/15	Computer	GJ1	10,000

2. (c) *(i) Reduction in number of staff required.*
(ii) Speed in production.
(iii) Letter designs.
(iv) More accurate work.

2. (e) Leasing, Term Loan, Hire Purchase.

Leasing — *This is a form of renting where you obtain the use but never the ownership.*

Term Loan — *P.J. Ltd could get a loan from the bank of €10,000 and repay it over three to five years.*

Hire Purchase — *This is a system where you pay a deposit and the balance over an agreed number of instalments. P.J. Ltd would get immediate possession of the computer system but become the legal owner only when the last instalment was paid.*

Chapter 50 — Examination Format

Ordinary Level **1 Paper** **400 Marks** **2 1/2 Hours**

Section	Time Allocated	Description of Questions	Marks per Question	Total Marks
A	25 mins	20 short questions ranging over entire syllabus. Answer all 20 questions. Calculators may be used. Remember to include all of Section 'A' in your answer book.	5	100
B	25 mins per question	8 long questions given. Answer any 5 questions. These questions range over entire syllabus. Calculators may be used. Marks will be given for layout and presentation.	60	300

Higher Level **2 Papers** **400 Marks**

Paper I **240 Marks** **2 1/2 Hours**

Section	Time Allocated	Description of Questions	Marks per Question	Total Marks
A	30 mins	20 short questions ranging over the entire syllabus. Answer all questions. Calculators may be used. Remember to include all of Section 'A' in your answer book.	4	80
B	30 mins per question	6 long questions given. Answer any 4 questions. Questions in this section will deal mainly with the **personal** and **social** development to include **economics**, **club accounts** and practical **personal business** knowledge and skills. Calculators may be used. Marks will be given for layout and presentation.	40	160

Paper II		160 Marks	2 Hours	
Section	Time Allocated	Description of Questions	Marks per Question	Total Marks
No sections	30 mins per question	6 long questions given. Answer any 4 questions. Questions will focus on the syllabus from perspective of operating a business. Calculators may be used.	40	160

Chapter 51 — Examination Structure and Advice

Section A — Ordinary and Higher Level

All twenty short questions must be answered on the question paper.

Allow approx. twenty-five minutes for Section A.

These short questions can be chosen from any part of the syllabus.

Remember to return completed Section A with your answer book.

Remember **(a)** Short correct answers are required.
(b) Where one tick (✓) is required tick only **once**, otherwise no marks allowed.
(c) If more than one tick (✓) is required tick **required** number only.
(d) Rough work and calculations must be shown.
(e) Calculators are allowed — but show workings clearly.

SECTION A-TYPE QUESTIONS

Ordinary Level 20 Qs x 5 marks	Higher Level 20 Qs x 4 marks
1. Writing out in full initials used in business. 2. Writing most correct word in space provided. 3. Filling missing words in a sentence. 4. Tick (✓) appropriate box. 5. Multiple choice. 6. ESB meter reading calculation. 7. Currencies and countries of EU. 8. Currency exchange calculations. 9. True/False questions. 10. Definitions of business terms. 11. Putting names in alphabetical order. 12. Entering book-keeping transactions in accounts. 13. Balancing an account. 14. Questions on distance table — delivery systems. 15. Questions on business documents.	1. Writing out in full initials used in business. 2. Matching terms with explanations. 3. Mark-up and margin. 4. Tick (✓) appropriate box. 5. Multiple choice. 6. Converting 'T' A/Cs to continuous balance and vice versa. 7. Currencies and countries of EU. 8. Currency exchange calculations. 9. Source documents of day books. 10. Definitions of business terms. 11. Control accounts. 12. Double entry book-keeping questions. 13. Completing A/Cs, e.g. insurance.

Section B — Ordinary Level

Attempt any five out of eight questions given. There will be three or four parts to each question.

The first four questions usually deal with household budgets, household accounts, consumer/letter of complaint, money and banking. The remaining questions may deal with business documents, final A/Cs, information technology, economic issues, delivery systems, insurance, communications, marketing, etc.

Allow about twenty-two minutes for each long question. This will ensure that you have time to read the paper carefully at the beginning of the exam and time to read back on your answer at the end of the exam.

ANALYSIS OF PAST EXAM PAPERS
Section B — Ordinary Level

	1996	1997	1998	1999	2000	2001	2002	2003	2004	2005	2006
Household budget	Q1	Q1	Q1	Q1	Q1	Q1	Q1	Q1	Q1	Q1	Q1
Household a/cs/analysed cash book						Q6					Q6
Consumer/letter of complaint				Q3				Q3			
Money and banking (i) cheque, lodgment, withdrawal						Q4		Q4	Q4		
(ii) bank statement/bank rec.	Q4				Q4						
Credit and borrowing/HP and letter writing		Q7			Q7			Q8			
Insurance			Q4			Q3		Q7			
Economic framework/inflation	Q7(a)										Q8
National budgeting/foreign trade			Q7			Q8			Q8		Q8
Forms of business							Q7			Q8	Q7
Communications/bar chart/sales											
Chain of production and channels of distribution	Q8								Q8		
People at work/Being an Employer/Wages	Q7	Q4		Q4, Q7		Q7	Q4		Q3	Q4	Q4
Bar chart/pie chart/advertising/Marketing			Q8						Q7		
Delivery systems/Transport				Q8			Q8			Q7	
Letter writing	Q3		Q3		Q3						Q3
Business documents	Q5	Q5	Q5	Q5	Q5	Q5	Q5	Q5	Q5	Q5	Q5
Petty cash	Q2		Q6				Q6			Q6	
Final A/Cs — business		Q2	Q2	Q2		Q2	Q2	Q2		Q2	Q2
Club A/Cs		Q6			Q6			Q6			
Final A/Cs — service firm	Q6				Q2				Q2		
Information technology					Q8					Q3	
Farm Accounts/Letter writing		Q3		Q6			Q3		Q6		

Paper I Section B — Higher Level

Attempt any four out of six questions given.

Paper I Section B will examine business of living and economic awareness sections of the course.

Questions may deal with household budgeting/household accounts, consumer, money and banking, credit and borrowing, personal insurance, economic framework/inflation, national budgeting, foreign trade, club A/Cs, people at work and information technology.

Allow about twenty-eight minutes for each question.

ANALYSIS OF PAST EXAM PAPERS

Paper I Section B — Higher Level

	1996	1997	1998	1999	2000	2001	2002	2003	2004	2005	2006
Household budget	Q1	Q1	Q1	Q1	Q1 B,C	Q1	Q1	Q1	Q1	Q1	Q1
Household A/Cs/analysed cash book					Q1 A						
Consumer/Letter writing			Q2	Q4	Q5		Q3	Q5		Q5 C,D	
Money and banking											
(i) Bank A/C/bank st/bank rec		Q2		Q2 A	Q2	Q3		Q2		Q4	
(ii) Saving, investing, interest calculations	Q6						Q2 B,C,D				Q6 A
(iii) Methods of payment				Q2 C			Q2 A				
(iv) Cheques				Q2 B							Q6 B
Credit and borrowing											
(i) Hire purchase											
(ii) Cost of borrowing		Q4	Q4						Q5	Q5 A,B	Q6 C
Insurance	Q5		Q6			Q2			Q4		Q5
Economic framework/inflation		Q5 A	Q5 C	Q3 A,B	Q3		Q6 D			Q6 A,B	Q3 AB
National budgeting	Q4	Q5 A				Q4	Q6 A,B,C		Q3	Q6 C	
Foreign trade		Q5 B	Q5 A,B	Q3 C,D				Q4			Q3 C
People at work								Q6			Q4 B
Being an employer/Wages	Q2			Q6	Q6				Q6	Q3	
Petty cash/club account	Q3										
Club accounts		Q3	Q3	Q5	Q4	Q5	Q5	Q3	Q2	Q2	Q2
Information technology		Q6				Q6					
Industrial Relations							Q4				Q4 A

Paper II — Higher Level

Attempt any four out of six questions given.

Paper II will examine enterprise and information technology. However, there may be some overlap between Paper I and Paper II at Higher Level.

Questions may deal with forms of business, financial planning and cash flow statements, insurance for business, being an employer, marketing, delivery systems/cost of transport, business documents, books of first entry and ledger, final accounts including adjustments, reporting on financial accounts, information technology.

Allow about twenty-eight minutes for each question.

ANALYSIS OF PAST EXAMINATION PAPERS

Paper II — Higher Level

	1996	1997	1998	1999	2000	2001	2002	2003	2004	2005	2006
Bank statement/bank account/bank rec.	Q6										
Forms of business		Q6 C	Q2				Q3			Q6	
Finance for business	Q5 C				Q5		Q4			Q5	
Financial planning/ cash flow forecast			Q5	Q5				Q6			
Insurance for business					Q4					Q3	
Being an employer						Q5					Q3
Industrial relations	Q4							Q3			
Marketing			Q6			Q3			Q3		Q6 A
Delivery systems/cost of transport	Q5 A,B	Q5		Q6		Q6		Q5			Q5 C,D
Business documents	Q2	Q2			Q2	Q2	Q5	Q2	Q2	Q2	Q2 B
Selling on credit and bad debts											Q2 A
Books of first entry and ledger	Q1	Q1	Q1	Q1	Q1	Q1	Q1	Q1	Q1	Q1	Q1
Trading A/C and stocktaking				Q2							
Depreciation	Q5 D										
Final A/C incl. adjustments	Q3	Q3	Q3	Q4	Q3	Q4	Q2	Q4	Q4	Q4	Q4
Reporting on accounts		Q4					Q6		Q5		
Information technology			Q4								
Farm Accounts		Q6 A,B									
Service Firm				Q3							Q6 C
Monitoring overheads					Q6 A,B				Q6 A		
Petty Cash book/Analysed Cash Book					Q6 C				Q6 B		
Chain of Production and Channels of Distribution											Q5 A,B

General Advice

(i) Read paper carefully before you start.

(ii) Begin with Section A: these questions are easier and will build up your confidence for the remainder of the paper.

(iii) When dealing with long questions
→ do the questions you know best first
→ look at the breakdown of marks for each part of the question
→ attempt all parts of questions chosen and divide your time according to the marks available for each part.

(iv) Write the number of each question clearly alongside the answer, and label each part (a) (b) (c), etc.

(v) Use blank documents supplied with the questions, and return them with your answer book.

(vi) Marks are given for layout and presentation, so accuracy and neatness are vitally important, especially when answering book-keeping and business document questions.

(vii) Calculators may be used, but you must show your workings. Make sure your calculator is in good working order and be familiar with it. Be careful of the decimal point. The Examination Commission will not supply calculators on day of exam.

(viii) A specially designed and suitably ruled answer book is available to all candidates. The main benefit in using this stationery is that it saves considerable time during the examination in ruling various columns for answering questions. It is clearly stated on the front cover of the answer book what each page is suitable for.

(ix) Allow a few minutes at end of exam for reading back over your answers.

(x) Good luck in the exam.

Examination Papers

Coimisiún na Scrúduithe Stáit
State Examinations Commission

JUNIOR CERTIFICATE EXAMINATION, 2007

BUSINESS STUDIES – HIGHER LEVEL – PAPER I

WEDNESDAY, 13 JUNE 2007 – MORNING, 9.30 to 12.00 noon

SECTION A
(80 Marks)

Answer all 20 questions. Each question carries 4 marks. Calculators may be used.

1. Tick (✓) whether the following forms of communication are Oral, Written or Visual:

FORM OF COMMUNICATION	ORAL	WRITTEN	VISUAL
Telephone calls			
Report			
Bar Chart			
Radio			

2. The following initials relate to income and expenditure. What do they stand for?

PRSI	
PAYE	
VAT	
DIRT	

3. Outline **two** reasons why market research is important to a business:

(i) ______________________________

____

(ii) ______________________________

____

4. Answer *either* **(A)** *or* **(B)**:

(A) Enter the following transaction in the Sales Day Book of Harty Ltd:

On 8 June 2007, Harty Ltd sold goods on credit to Petrol Ltd (Invoice No. 26) for €45,000. The VAT rate on these goods is 21%.

Harty Ltd – Sales Day Book						
Date	Details	Inv No.	F	Net €	VAT €	Total €

OR

(B) Outline **two** reasons for Sales Returns:

(i) ____________________

____

(ii) ____________________

____

5. Explain the term **Utmost Good Faith** in relation to insurance:

____

____

6. **Column 1** is a list of legal documents. **Column 2** is a list of statements which can be matched to these documents. *(One statement does not refer to any of the documents.)*

Column 1 – Documents	**Column 2 – Statements**
1. Certificate of Incorporation	**A.** A document declaring that the tax situation in a company is in order
2. Articles of Association	**B.** A document stating that the directors agree to follow the rules of company law
3. Memorandum of Association	**C.** A document setting out the internal rules of a company
4. Declaration of Compliance	**D.** A document setting out the external rules of a company
	E. A document known as the birth certificate of a company

Match the two lists by placing the letter of the most appropriate statement under the relevant number below:

1.	**2.**	**3.**	**4.**

7. Explain the term **Chain of Distribution**:

____

____

8. **(i)** What do the initials **GNP** stand for?

____

(ii) GNP in 2005 was €900 million. In 2006, it was €954 million.

Calculate the rate of economic growth from 2005 to 2006:
(Show your workings.)

Answer:

Workings:

9. Complete and balance the Creditors Control Account on 30 April 2007 from the following information:

	€
Opening balance on 1 April 2007	400
Total credit purchases for April	8,600
Total payments to creditors during April	6,600

Dr		**Creditors Control Account**			Cr
Date	Details	€	Date	Details	€

OR (Alternative Format)

	Creditors Control Account			
Date	Details	Dr	Cr	Balance
		€	€	€

10. Use your knowledge of Industrial Relations to complete the following sentences:

A ______________________ is an organisation set up by employees to improve their interests. The employees elect a ______________________ to represent them.

11. Complete the Profit & Loss Appropriation Account by filling in the **three** unshaded areas, numbered **(i)** to **(iii)**, from the following information:

Authorised Share Capital	€600,000
Issued Share Capital	€400,000
Dividends declared	10%

Profit & Loss Appropriation Account for year ending 31–05–2007		
		€
Net Profit		150,000
Less Dividends		**(i)**
(ii)		**(iii)**

12. Distinguish between a **post-dated cheque** and a **stale cheque**:

____

____

13. Kevin purchases an item on eBay for £36 Sterling. He goes to the bank to change his euro into a sterling draft and sees the following rates quoted on a display board:

CURRENCY	BANK SELLS	BANK BUYS
Sterling	0.64	0.72

Calculate the total amount in euro that Kevin will pay for £36 Sterling: (Show your workings.)

Answer:
€

Workings:

14. List **two** factors that a company would take into account before deciding on a suitable delivery system for goods:

(i) ____________________

(ii) ____________________

15. (i) Enter the following balances in the partially completed General Journal of Finner Ltd:

1 January 2007	Premises	€120,000
	Creditor: Power Ltd	€8,000

(ii) Calculate the Ordinary Share Capital:

Finner Ltd – General Journal				
Date	Details	F	Dr	Cr
			€	€
	Bank	CB1	13,000	
	Premises	GL1		
	Creditor: Power Ltd	CL1		
	Ordinary Share Capital	GL2		
	Assets, Liabilities and Share Capital of Finner Ltd on this date.			

16. Complete the following Balance Sheet extract by filling in the **four** unshaded areas, numbered **(i)** to **(iv)**:

Balance Sheet (extract) as on 31–12–2006			
Fixed Assets	**Cost**	**Depreciation**	**Net Book Value**
	€	€	€
Vehicles	30,000	2,000	(i)
Buildings	(ii)	7,900	132,100
	(iii)	9,900	(iv)

17. Complete the following extract from a credit note:

	€
Total (excluding VAT)	
Trade Discount **25%**	
Subtotal	300.00
VAT **12.5%**	
Total (including VAT)	

18. Complete the sentence below by selecting the **two** correct terms from the following list:

Debtor	**Creditor**	**Delivery Note**	**Credit Note**	**Statement**

A firm purchases goods on credit from a ____________________ and receives a document at the end of the month called a ____________________.

19. Answer *either* **(A)** *or* **(B)**:

(A) (i) Calculate the unit price for **each** of the following boxes of cereal:

SIZE	PRICE	WEIGHT	UNIT PRICE
SMALL	€1.58	400 g	
MEDIUM	€2.70	750 g	
LARGE	€3.90	1 kg	

Workings:

(ii) Which size represents the best value for money? [ ]

OR

(B) Explain the term **False Economy**:

____

____

20. On 17 February 2007, Margaret Burke bought goods on credit from Ann Harte for €2,100. There was no VAT chargeable on these goods.

Complete the following ledger accounts of Margaret Burke showing the names of the accounts and the relevant details, numbered **(i)** to **(iv)**:

Dr **(i)** ____________________ **A/c** Cr

Date	Details	€	Date	Details	€
2007 Feb 17	**(ii)**	2,100			

Dr **(iii)** ____________________ **A/c** Cr

Date	Details	€	Date	Details	€
			2007 Feb 17	**(iv)**	2,100

For use with Section B – Question 1 (A)

GALVIN HOUSEHOLD	ORIGINAL BUDGET				REVISED BUDGET			
	JULY	AUG	SEPT	TOTAL	JULY	AUG	SEPT	TOTAL
PLANNED INCOME	€	€	€	€	€	€	€	€
Mr Galvin – Salary	1,500	1,500	1,500	4,500				
Ms Galvin	1,120	1,120	1,120	3,360				
Child Benefit	160	160	160	480				
Other								
TOTAL INCOME	2,780	2,780	2,780	8,340				
PLANNED EXPENDITURE								
Fixed								
Mortgage	800	800	800	2,400				
Loan Repayments	400	400	400	1,200				
Car Insurance	65	65	65	195				
Subtotal	1,265	1,265	1,265	3,795				
Irregular								
Household Costs	750	750	750	2,250				
Car Costs	150	150	150	450				
Light & Heat Costs	245		190	435				
Telephone Costs	50	50	140	240				
Subtotal	1,195	950	1,230	3,375				
Discretionary								
Entertainment Costs	200	200	200	600				
Presents	300		250	550				
Holiday			5,000	5,000				
Subtotal	500	200	5,450	6,150				
TOTAL EXPENDITURE	2,960	2,415	7,945	13,320				
Net Cash	(180)	365	(5,165)	(4,980)				
Opening Cash	500	320	685	500				
Closing Cash	320	685	(4,480)	(4,480)				

For use in answering Section B – Question 1 (B)

	For Office Use Only	
(i) In the Original Budget, name a month in which planned income is greater than planned expenditure.		
Answer:		

(ii) In the Original Budget, by how much did the Galvin household expect to overspend in the three months?		
Answer: €		

(iii) Give **one** reason why the repayments on the mortgage might increase.		
Reason:		

(iv) Is the Revised Budget a good one?	YES		*(Please tick appropriate box.)*		
	NO				
Give **two** reasons for your answer.					
Reason 1:					
Reason 2:					

For use with Section B – Question 5 (A) (i)

Bank of Ireland

CURRENT ACCOUNT APPLICATION FORM

PERSONAL DETAILS

Surname		Mr, Mrs, Ms.			
First Name		Male/Female			
Home Address					
Date of Birth		*Please tick appropriate box.* ➡	Married		
Country of Birth			Single		

EMPLOYMENT DETAILS

Occupation	
Employer's Name & Address	

Gross salary per month			
Length of time in your present employment			
Will your income be paid into your bank account?	YES		*(Please tick appropriate box.)*
	NO		

CONTACT DETAILS

Home Telephone Number	
Mobile Phone Number	
e-mail address	

Please open a Current Account in my name.
I certify the accuracy of the information given above.

SIGNATURE		DATE	

JUNIOR CERTIFICATE EXAMINATION, 2007

BUSINESS STUDIES – HIGHER LEVEL – PAPER I

WEDNESDAY, 13 JUNE 2007 – MORNING, 9.30 to 12.00 noon

SECTION B
(160 Marks)

- All questions carry equal marks.
- Attempt any **FOUR** questions.
- Marks will be awarded for layout and presentation including, where appropriate, folios and dates.
- Dates should show the day, month and year.
- Calculators may be used.

This is a Household Budget Question.

Answer all parts of this question:

(A) See an Original Budget and a Revised Budget form for the Galvin household from July to September 2007 at the end of Section A. After preparing the Original Budget, Mr Galvin changed jobs and his salary increased. However, Ms Galvin lost her job in the local factory after it closed down in June. The Galvin household decided to revise their Budget due to the changed circumstances.

You are required to complete the Revised Budget, taking the following into account:

- Mr Galvin's annual salary will be €25,800 net payable monthly. He also expects to receive a bonus of €1,000 net in September.
- Ms Galvin will receive €660 net monthly in unemployment benefit.
- The Galvins will sell one of their two cars and expect to receive €6,800 for it in August.
- Mortgage repayments will increase by 8% from 1 September 2007.
- The Galvin household will make one loan repayment in July and will repay the balance of the loan, €3,500, in August.
- Car insurance will reduce by €30 per month from 1 August 2007.
- Household costs will reduce by 12% per month from 1 July 2007.
- Car costs will reduce to €70 per month from 1 August 2007.
- Entertainment costs will be reduced by 50%.
- Due to their changed circumstances, the holiday planned for September will be postponed.
- All other income and expenditure will remain the same. (28)

(B) **(i)** In the Original Budget, name a month in which planned income is greater than planned expenditure.

(ii) In the Original Budget, by how much did the Galvin household expect to overspend in the three months?

(iii) Give **one** reason why the repayments on the mortgage might increase.

(iv) Is the Revised Budget a good one?
Give **two** reasons for your answer. (12)

Answer (i)–(iv) above in the space provided in Section A. **(40 marks)**

2. This is a Club Account Question.

Answer all parts of this question:

On 1 June 2006, Greenfield Golf Club had an Accumulated Fund of €305,770.

The following is a summary of the Club's financial transactions for the year ended 31 May 2007:

Receipts:	**€**
Competition Fees	34,400
Subscriptions	89,550
Annual Sponsorship	17,650
Payments:	**€**
Repairs	1,850
Stationery	2,460
Wages	27,800
Competition Expenses	6,200
Insurance	1,440
General Expenses	25,000

Additional information at 31 May 2007:

(i) Subscriptions prepaid €1,450
(ii) Stationery on hand €240
(iii) Wages due €2,400
(iv) Cash at Bank €15,620
(v) Depreciation:
Clubhouse 2% of €252,000
Equipment 15% of €115,000

(A) Prepare:

(i) An Income and Expenditure Account for the year ended 31 May 2007.
(ii) A Balance Sheet as at 31 May 2007. (31)

(B) Explain **three** functions of a club treasurer. (9)
(40 marks)

3. **This is a National Budget and Economic Awareness Question.**

Answer all parts of this question:

(A) The following figures were produced by the Government on Budget Day for the year 2007:

Summary of Revenue and Expenditure	**Projected Figures in millions €**
Capital Income	5,961
Capital Expenditure	5,812
Current Income	2,621
Current Expenditure	1,910

(i) From the above information, draft the National Budget for 2007, clearly indicating whether it is a Surplus or Deficit Budget. Show your workings.
(ii) Identify **two** examples of Current Income for the Government.
(iii) Identify **one** example of Capital Income for the Government. (18)

(B)(i) It is Government policy to increase spending on motorways throughout the country.
Explain **two** economic benefits and **one** economic drawback of this policy.

(ii) During 2007, many households will have to decide what will be done with money saved under the Government's SSIA (Special Savings Incentive Account) scheme.
(a) Household 'X' plans to invest the money for their five-year-old child's third level education.
Identify **two** types of financial institution where the household may invest the money.
(b) Household 'Y' plans either to buy a new car or build a house extension.
Explain the opportunity cost of deciding to buy the car.
(c) Household 'Z' plans to spend the money on a foreign holiday.
Outline **one** effect that this would have on the Balance of Payments.
(18)

(C) 'Ireland has a mixed economic system.'
Explain the above statement. (4)

(40 marks)

4. This is a Consumer Question.

Answer all parts of this question:

John and Laura Ryan live at 16 Allen View, Rahan, Co. Offaly. They booked a family holiday costing €1,200 with Sunshine Travel Ltd, Newtown Road, Tullamore, Co. Offaly for a week in Greece from 1 June 2007 to 8 June 2007. The holiday brochure clearly stated that the beach was five minutes walk from their apartment.

On arrival at their apartment, the Ryans discovered that the closest beach was five kilometres away. They were very disappointed.

(A) **(i)** Name the consumer law that applies in this situation.

(ii) State the relevant principle of consumer law that has been broken.

(6)

(B) **(i)** On 11 June 2007, after they returned home, Laura Ryan wrote a letter of complaint to the Manager of Sunshine Travel Ltd requesting suitable redress.

Write the letter that Laura Ryan sent to Sunshine Travel Ltd.

(ii) On 12 June 2007, Sunshine Travel Ltd contacted Laura requesting proof of payment for the holiday.

Give **two** methods that the Ryans could have used in paying for the holiday.

(24)

(C) If the Ryans are dissatisfied with the response, there are agencies who can assist them.

Name **two** such agencies and explain **one** service offered by each.

(10)

(40 marks)

5. **This is a Personal Banking Question.**

Answer all parts of this question:

Andy Mullen, who will be 25 years of age on 28 August 2007, lives at 28 Finbarr Road, Newbridge, Co. Kildare (his native county). His home telephone number is 045-633712 and his mobile phone number is 087-7867855. His e-mail address is andymullen@matteng.ie. He is not married.

On 1 June 2007, Andy commenced full-time employment as an engineer with Matthews Engineering Ltd, Main Street, Newbridge, Co. Kildare. His gross salary is €36,000 per year, payable monthly. His PPSN (Personal Public Service Number) is 3967892F.

As his new employer wants to pay his salary by Paypath, he has decided to open a Current Account. On 8 June 2007, he calls into the local branch of Bank of Ireland and completes an application form.

(A) **(i)** Complete the blank application form *at the end of Section A.*
(ii) Name **three** legal requirements that must be satisfied when opening a bank account.
(iii) Outline **two** differences between a current account and a deposit account.
(iv) Andy has been informed that he can request an overdraft.

(a) Explain what an overdraft means.
(b) Identify **three** requirements that Andy must satisfy before the bank will grant him an overdraft.

(30)

(B) Andy is considering borrowing money to buy a car.

(i) Identify **two** suitable sources of finance available to him for this purpose.
(ii) Outline **two** rights he would have as a borrower.

(10)
(40 marks)

6. **This is a People at Work Question.**

Answer all parts of this question:

Margaret Farrell has recently become self-employed as an accountant. She has employed Anne Power who has an expertise in ICT (Information and Communications Technology). Anne has recommended the purchase of suitable hardware and software for use in the business and by clients.

(A) **(i)** Outline **two** rewards for Margaret of being self-employed.
(ii) Explain **two** risks of being self-employed.
(iii) Outline **three** responsibilities Anne Power has to her employer.
(iv) Explain the difference between hardware and software. Identify **two** examples of each.

(30)

(B) The following information is available about Anne Power's earnings:

- Her basic wage is €792 for a 36-hour week.
- Overtime is paid at time-and-a-half for the first ten hours and double-time for work in excess of that.
- She pays income tax (PAYE) at the rate of 41% and PRSI at 8%.
- Her annual tax credits are €3,640.

Anne worked a total of 48 hours in the week ending 8 June 2007.

Calculate her net wage for that week. Show your workings.

(10)

(40 marks)

JUNIOR CERTIFICATE EXAMINATION, 2007

BUSINESS STUDIES – HIGHER LEVEL – PAPER II
(160 Marks)

WEDNESDAY, 13 JUNE – AFTERNOON, 2.00 p.m. to 4.00 p.m.

- All questions carry equal marks.
- Attempt any **FOUR** questions.
- Marks will be awarded for layout and presentation including, where appropriate, folios and dates.
- Dates should show the day, month and year.
- Calculators may be used.

1. **This is a Book of First Entry, Ledger and Trial Balance Question.**

Answer all parts of this question:

LONG Ltd had the following balances on 1 May 2007.

	€
Buildings	148,000
Debtor: SHORT Ltd	42,000

(A) Enter these balances in the GENERAL JOURNAL, find the ORDINARY SHARE CAPITAL balance and post these balances to the relevant Ledger Accounts. (8)

(B) Post the relevant figures from the Purchases and Purchases Returns Books below to the Ledger Accounts. (7)

PURCHASES BOOK

Date	Details	Invoice No.	F	Net €	VAT €	Total €
9/5/2007	SMYTH Ltd	97	CL	12,000	1,620	13,620
				GL	**GL**	

PURCHASES RETURNS BOOK

Date	Details	Credit Note No.	F	Net €	VAT €	Total €
18/5/2007	SMYTH Ltd	16	CL	4,000	540	4,540
				GL	**GL**	

(C) Record the following Bank Transactions for the month of May. Post relevant figures to the Ledger Accounts.

Note: Analyse the Bank Transactions using the following money column headings:

Debit (Receipts) Side: Bank; Sales; VAT; Debtor; Share Capital

Credit (Payments) Side: Bank; Purchases; VAT; Wages

1/5/2007	Shareholder invested €40,000 and this was lodged.		Receipt No. 14
6/5/2007	Cash Sales lodged	€68,100 (€60,000 + VAT €8,100)	
12/5/2007	SHORT Ltd paid its account in full and this was lodged.		Receipt No. 15
17/5/2007	Purchases for resale	(Cheque No. 26)	€24,000 + VAT 13.5%
30/5/2007	Paid Wages	(Cheque No. 27)	€14,000

(17)

(D) Balance the accounts on 31 May 2007 and extract a Trial Balance as at that date.

(8)

(40 marks)

2. This a Credit Sales, Business Document and Bookkeeping Question.

Answer all parts of this question:

The following Quotation was received by Martin Banner, Purchasing Manager, of HOMEFIT Ltd on 12 May 2007.

DOORS FOR ALL OCCASIONS Ltd **QUOTATION No. 456**
Wood Lane, Limerick

Telephone: 061 345672 VAT Reg. No. IE 4567123L

Date: 8 May 2007

The Purchasing Manager
HOMEFIT Ltd
Kilkee
Co. Clare

Dear Mr. Banner

Thanks for your enquiry of 2 May 2007. I enclose the following Quotation which I hope will be to your satisfaction.

50 Exterior Teak Doors @ €200 each
100 Interior Pine Doors @ €60 each

Terms: Trade Discount 20%
The above goods are subject to VAT at 21%.

I look forward to receiving your Order.

Yours sincerely
Joan Shannon
Sales Manager

(A) (i) Explain each of the following terms: VAT, Trade Discount.
(ii) What procedures would you recommend to DOORS FOR ALL OCCASIONS Ltd when preparing and processing quotations?
(iii) Martin Banner considers himself to be an effective purchasing manager. What does effective purchasing involve? (17)

Martin Banner completed an Order (No. 100) for 50 Exterior Teak Doors and 100 Interior Pine Doors. These were delivered on 18 May 2007.
When Martin examined the doors, he found that five of the Exterior Teak Doors were badly scratched. His complaint to Joan Shannon, Sales Manager, was accepted and she sent him a Credit Note No. 23 for the five Exterior Teak Doors on 1 June 2007.

(B) (i) State **two** other reasons why Martin Banner might have cause to complain to Joan Shannon.
(ii) Complete the blank Credit Note No. 23 *on the sheet supplied with this paper.*
(iii) Record the Credit Note issued in the Sales Returns Book of DOORS FOR ALL OCCASIONS Ltd *on the sheet supplied with this paper.* (23)

(40 marks)

3. **This a Cash Flow Forecast Question.**

Answer all parts of this question:

(A) *On the separate sheet supplied with this paper* is a partially completed Cash Flow Forecast for HARP Ltd. You are required to complete the forecast for the months of April, May, June and July 2008 together with the total column.

The following information should be taken into account:

- Monthly Cash Sales are expected to increase by 25% beginning in July;
- HARP Ltd expects to receive a loan of €150,000 in May;
- Monthly Cash Purchases are expected to increase by 15% beginning in July;
- Light and Heat is expected to decrease by 25% in the months of May and July;
- Wages are expected to remain the same, except in May, where an additional bonus of €8,000 will be paid;
- New motor vehicles will be purchased in May for €155,000;
- Shareholders will be paid a dividend of €15,000 in July;
- Rent is expected to remain the same every month.

(28)

(B) (i) Name **two** items, other than Cash Sales and loans, that could be entered in the 'Receipts' section of a Cash Flow Forecast.

(ii) List **two** possible ways a business could deal with a Net Cash deficit in a particular month.

(iii) Explain a difference between a Cash Flow Forecast and an Analysed Cash Book.

(12)

(40 marks)

4. This a Final Accounts and Balance Sheet Question.

Answer all parts of this question:

The following Trial Balance was extracted from the books of KENNY Ltd on 30 April 2007.

The Authorised Share Capital is 450,000 €1 ordinary shares.

TRIAL BALANCE OF KENNY Ltd as on 30 April 2007	Dr €	Cr €
Purchases and Sales	110,000	300,000
Sales Returns	15,000	
Opening Stock 1/5/2006	8,000	
Carriage Inwards	4,000	
Debtors and Creditors	18,000	32,000
Advertising	6,000	
Rent Receivable		15,000
Bank Overdraft		10,000
Wages	30,000	
Buildings	465,000	
Motor Vehicles	84,000	
Bad Debts	2,000	
Machinery	120,000	
Reserves (Profit and Loss Balance)		55,000
Issued Share Capital: 380,000 €1 Ordinary Shares		380,000
20 Year Loan		70,000
	862,000	862,000

(A) You are required to prepare the company's **Trading, Profit and Loss Appropriation Account** for the year ending 30 April 2007 and a **Balance Sheet** as on that date.

You are given the following information as on 30 April 2007.

(i) Closing Stock €17,000
(ii) Advertising due €5,000
(iii) Rent Receivable due €4,000
(iv) Dividends declared 14%
(v) Depreciation: Motor Vehicles 20%; Machinery 12%. (35)

(B) Explain the term 'depreciation'. (5)

(40 marks)

5. **This a Marketing and Business Plan Question.**

Answer all parts of this question:

(A) PJM Ltd, a clothing manufacturer, is considering the introduction of a new range of hoodies for teenagers. It intends to carry out market research to find out the following information: colour(s) to be used; price to be charged; retail outlets to sell in.
It will use a questionnaire with 200 teenagers throughout Ireland.

On the separate sheet supplied with this paper, construct **three** suitable questions to provide PJM Ltd with the information it requires.
Note: Question 1 has been completed as an example. (9)

(B) Paula and John Murphy are the directors of PJM Ltd. The company plans to produce hoodies for the Irish market. The company is located at 14 Claremorris Road, Balla, Co. Mayo. Mary Carey is the Marketing Manager and Finbarr Ward is the Production Manager. PJM Ltd has its bank account with the Ulster Bank.

There are 800,000 potential customers in the target market.
The two main competitors in the Irish market are COVERMEUP Ltd and HOODWINK Ltd.

PJM Ltd provided the following details for the year ended 31/7/2008:

- Expected cost of producing hoodies is €4,000,000;
- Forecasted sales of hoodies in 2007/8 is 200,000;
- Mark-up is cost plus 30%.

PJM Ltd requires €1,500,000 to go into full production. Paula and John will invest share capital of €500,000. PJM Ltd expects to receive a grant of €450,000 and will borrow the remainder from its bank.

(i) Calculate the selling price per hoody and insert your answer *in the relevant section of the Business Plan supplied with this paper.*

(ii) Name **three** suitable methods of promoting hoodies in the Irish market and insert these methods *in the relevant section of the Business Plan supplied with this paper.*

(iii) Complete, in full, the remainder of the *Business Plan* using today's date. (31)

(40 marks)

6. **This a question on Report Writing and Assessing a Business.**

Answer all parts of this question:

(A) The following **four** ratios are used by JACK Ltd, Tralee Road, Limerick, to assess the performance of its business:

(i) Rate of Stock Turnover;
(ii) Rate of Dividend;
(iii) Return on Capital Employed;
(iv) Current Ratio.

The directors of JACK Ltd supplied the following information for the year 2006.

	€
Average Stock	17,500
Net Profit	60,000
Cost of Sales	70,000
Dividend Paid	30,000
Current Liabilities	30,000
Current Assets	45,000
Issued Share Capital	300,000
Capital Employed	400,000

Using this information, calculate the **four** ratios for the year 2006. (16)

(B) The relevant figures for 2005 were:

Rate of Stock Turnover	3 times;
Rate of Dividend	20%;
Return on Capital Employed	5%;
Current Ratio	2 : 1.

Assume you are Michael Moran, Financial Adviser, Golf View, Limerick. Prepare a report, on today's date, for the directors of JACK Ltd comparing and commenting on the performance of the company for 2005 and 2006. (24)

(40 marks)

BUSINESS STUDIES – PAPER II, 2007

For use with QUESTION 5 (A)

1.	In your opinion, is there a market for a new range of hoodies for teenagers? Yes ☐ No ☐ No Opinion ☐ (Please tick one option.)
2.	
3.	
4.	

For use with QUESTION 5 (B)

BUSINESS PLAN

COMPANY DETAILS Name of Company		
Address of Company		
Directors	**(i)**	**(ii)**
Marketing Manager		
Production Manager		
Company Bank		
PRODUCT Description of New Product		
MARKET RESEARCH Size of Target Market		
Main Competitors	**(i)**	**(ii)**
Selling Price per hoody	€	
SALES PROMOTION Three Suitable Methods	**(i)**	
	(ii)	
	(iii)	
FINANCE Total Amount Required	€	
Amount of Finance Available	€	
Loan Required	€	
DIRECTORS' SIGNATURES	**(i)**	**(ii)**
DATE		

BUSINESS STUDIES – PAPER II, 2007

For use with QUESTION 2 (B) (ii)

DOORS FOR ALL OCCASIONS Ltd **Wood Lane, Limerick**		**CREDIT NOTE No. 23**	
Telephone: 061 345672		VAT Reg. No. IE 4567123L	
To: ______ ______ ______ ______		Date: ______ Order No. ______	
QUANTITY	**DESCRIPTION**	**UNIT PRICE €**	**TOTAL (EX VAT) €**
		Total (Ex. VAT)	
		Trade Discount	
		VAT	
E & OE		Total (Incl. VAT)	

For use with QUESTION 2 (B) (iii)

Sales Returns Book of DOORS FOR ALL OCCASIONS Ltd						
Date	**Details**	**Credit Note No.**	**F**	**NET €**	**VAT €**	**Total €**

For use with QUESTION 3 (A)

CASH FLOW FORECAST OF HARP Ltd FOR THE PERIOD FEBRUARY TO JULY 2008

	Feb. €	**March €**	**April €**	**May €**	**June €**	**July €**	**Total Feb.–July €**
RECEIPTS							
Cash Sales	85,000	85,000					
Loan							
A. TOTAL RECEIPTS	85,000	85,000					
PAYMENTS							
Cash Purchases	40,000	40,000					
Light and Heat		8,000					
Wages	30,000	30,000					
Motor Vehicles							
Dividend							
Rent	4,000	4,000					
B. TOTAL PAYMENTS	74,000	82,000					
Net Cash (A–B)	11,000	3,000					
Opening Cash	1,000	12,000	15,000				
Closing Cash	12,000	15,000					

Coimisiún na Scrúduithe Stáit
State Examinations Commission

JUNIOR CERTIFICATE EXAMINATION, 2008

BUSINESS STUDIES – HIGHER LEVEL – PAPER I

TUESDAY, 10 JUNE 2008 – MORNING, 9.30–12.00 p.m.

SECTION A
(80 Marks)

Answer all 20 questions. Each question carries 4 marks. Calculators may be used.

1. The following initials relate to Information Technology. What do they stand for?

VDU	
PC	
WWW	
RAM	

2. The share of profit which each shareholder in a company receives is called a

(i) Bonus. ☐

(ii) Dividend. ☐

(iii) Commission. ☐

(iv) Premium. ☐

Tick (√) the most appropriate box.

3. **Answer A or B.**
Complete the Balance Sheet (extract) below by filling in the **four** unshaded areas, numbered **(i)** to **(iv)**:

A.	**Balance Sheet (extract) as on 31-12-2007**	
	€	€
(i)		
	(ii)	250,000
	110,000	
(iii)		**(iv)**
Total Net Assets		420,000

OR

B.	**Balance Sheet (extract) as on 31-12-2007**	
	€	€
Financed by		
(i)		150,000
Reserves		**(iii)**
		310,000
Long-Term Liabilities		**(iv)**
(ii)		420,000

4. **(i)** The cost of living in a country in 2006 was €8,000. In 2007, it was €8,260.

Calculate the rate of inflation. (Show your workings.)

Workings:

Answer:

(ii) In Ireland, what is the official measure of inflation called?

___

5. On 9 June 2008, T. Magee, a supermarket owner, purchased goods for €32,000 by cheque. There was no VAT on these goods.

Complete the ledger accounts of T. Magee showing the names of the accounts and the relevant details, numbered **(i)** to **(iv)**:

(i) ____________________ **A/c**

Dr Cr

Date	Details	€	Date	Details	€
2008 June 9	**(ii)**	32,000			

(iii) ____________________ **A/c**

Dr Cr

Date	Details	€	Date	Details	€
			2008 June 9	**(iv)**	32,000

6. List **two** statutory deductions from wages.

(i) ______________________________

(ii) ______________________________

7. **Column 1** is a list of insurance terms. **Column 2** is a list of statements which can be matched to these terms. *(One statement does not refer to any of the insurance terms.)*

Column 1 – Insurance Terms	Column 2 – Statements
1. Actuary	**A.** Additional premium due to increased risk
2. Assessor	**B.** Calculates the amount of compensation
3. Principle of Contribution	**C.** Applies in the case of under-insurance and partial loss
4. Average Clause	**D.** Calculates the amount of premium
	E. Applies in the case where there are two or more Insurers

Match the two lists by placing the letter of the most appropriate statement under the relevant number below:

1.	2.	3.	4.

8. Fill in the names of the drawer, drawee and payee from the following transaction in the appropriate spaces below:

On 3 June 2008, John Ryan, who has a current account in Ulster Bank, Galway, paid €200 by cheque to Sarah Curran.

DRAWER	
DRAWEE	
PAYEE	

9. Explain the difference between a **grant** and a **loan**.

10. From the following list, calculate the total amount of Current Expenditure for a farm. (Show your workings.)

Vet Fees €14,000 **Land €56,000** **Machinery Repairs €18,000** **Sale of Hay €4,000**

Answer:
€

Workings:

11. Explain **two** reasons why stocktaking is essential in any business:

(i)

(ii)

12. Identify **two** rewards of self-employment:

(i) ____

____

(ii) ____

____

13. Complete and balance the Debtors Control Account on 31 May 2008 from the following information:

	€
Debtors balance on 1 May 2008	1,400
Total credit sales for May	8,500
Total cash received from debtors in May	6,300

Dr			**Debtors Control Account**		Cr
Date	Details	€	Date	Details	€

OR (Alternative Format)

Debtors Control Account				
Date	Details	Dr	Cr	Balance
		€	€	€

14. The following figures appear in a firm's Final Accounts:

Opening Stock €35,000 **Closing Stock €45,000** **Cost of Sales €300,000**

Calculate the Stock Turnover:
(Show your workings.)

Answer:
________________ times

Workings:

15. Name **two** headings in a Business Plan.

(i) ______________________________

(ii) ______________________________

16. Tick (√) the appropriate columns to indicate where in the final accounts the following items should be entered on 31/12/2007:

	Trading A/c	Profit & Loss A/c	Balance Sheet
Issued Share Capital			
Carriage Outwards			
Stock (31/12/2007)			

17. Complete the sentences below by selecting the **two** correct terms from the following list:

Visible Exports	**Invisible Exports**	**Visible Imports**	**Invisible Imports**

(i) Irish people taking a holiday in a foreign country is shown under

______________ ______________.

(ii) Winnings by Irish horses racing in foreign countries are shown under

______________ ______________.

18. **(i)** Enter the following balances in the partially completed General Journal of Power Ltd:

1 January 2008	Stock	€22,000
	Bank Overdraft	€5,000

(ii) Calculate the Ordinary Share Capital:

Power Ltd – General Journal				
Date	Details	F	Dr	Cr
			€	€
	Buildings	GL1	100,000	
	Stock	GL2		
	Bank Overdraft	CB1		
	Ordinary Share Capital	GL3		
	Assets, Liabilities and Share Capital of Power Ltd on this date.			

19. Explain **two** reasons why a business would prepare a cash flow statement:

(i) ______________________________

____

(ii) ______________________________

____

20. Enter the following transaction in the Sales Returns Book of McGrath Ltd:

On 12 May 2008, Roche Ltd returned goods €5,400 to McGrath Ltd (Credit Note No. 9). The VAT rate on these goods is 21%.

McGrath Ltd – Sales Returns Book						
Date	Details	C N No.	F	Net €	VAT €	Total €

For use with Section B - Question 1(A)

Budget Comparison Statement for the Burke household for the year 2007

INCOME	Budget Jan – Dec €	Actual €	Difference €
Salaries	21,000		
Child benefit	720		
Interest	250		
Other			
TOTAL INCOME	21,970		
EXPENDITURE			
Fixed			
Mortgage	4,080		
Car insurance	560		
House insurance	235		
Subtotal	4,875		
Irregular			
Household costs	7,800		
Car costs	1,550		
Clothing and footwear costs	2,000		
Light and heat costs	1,600		
Medical expenses	400		
Subtotal	13,350		
Discretionary			
Entertainment costs	1,560		
Presents	300		
Holidays	1,800		
Subtotal	3,660		
TOTAL EXPENDITURE	21,885		
Net Cash	85		
Opening Cash	1,400		
Closing Cash	1,485		

Note: *Do not complete the shaded boxes*

For use in answering Section B – Question 1(B and C)

1. (B)

(i)	What was the budgeted closing cash at the end of 2007?	**Answer:**	€
(ii)	How much had the Burke household budgeted to save during 2007?	**Answer:**	€
(iii)	What was the actual closing cash at the end of 2007?	**Answer:**	€
(iv)	State by how much the Burke household exceeded their budgeted total expenditure.	**Answer:**	€

(v) Explain **one** possible reason why the 'Actual' interest was less than the 'Budget' interest.

____

____

____

1. (C)

(i) Explain the term 'discretionary expenditure'.

____

____

____

(ii) Explain the term 'health insurance'.

____

____

____

(iii) Give **two** examples of companies offering health insurance to the public in Ireland.

1 ______________________________

2 ______________________________

For use with Section B – Question 4(A)

ESB Direct Debit Instruction											
Your Electricity Account Number:				-				-			
I wish to pay my electricity bill every two months.											
To	The Manager										
Bank											
Bank Address											
I give permission to ESB to charge variable amounts to my bank account.											
Name of Bank Account to be debited											
Account type											
Bank Account Number											
Branch Sorting Code			-			-					
Contact Telephone Number											
Signature											
Date											

**PLEASE REMEMBER TO RETURN THIS SECTION 'A'
WITH YOUR ANSWER BOOK**

Coimisiún na Scrúduithe Stáit
State Examinations Commission

JUNIOR CERTIFICATE EXAMINATION, 2008
BUSINESS STUDIES – HIGHER LEVEL – PAPER I

TUESDAY, 10 JUNE 2008 – MORNING, 9.30 a.m.–12.00 p.m.

SECTION B
(160 marks)

- All questions carry equal marks.
- Attempt any **FOUR** questions.
- Marks will be awarded for layout and presentation including, where appropriate, folios and dates.
- Dates should show the day, month and year.
- Calculators may be used.

1. **This is a Household Budget Question.**

Answer all parts of this question:

When the Burke household checked their Analysed Cash Book at the end of December 2007, they discovered that their actual income and expenditure for the 12 months differed from the budgeted figures (contained in the Budget Comparison Statement *on page 8 of Section A*) due to the following:

- The salaries of the Burke household increased by 4%.
- There are two children in the household. The monthly child benefit increased by €20 per child from 1 September 2007.
- The actual interest received for the year was €180.
- The Burke household received €400 from the sale of old furniture.
- Mortgage payments increased by €15 per month from 1 March 2007.
- The Burke household have a no claims bonus, so their car insurance was 15% less than budgeted.
- The house insurance was €325 for the year.
- Household costs were 7.5% greater than budgeted.
- Car costs were €375 greater than budgeted.
- Clothing and footwear costs were €300 less than budgeted.
- Light and heat costs were 6% less than budgeted.

- Medical expenses of €2,500 were incurred due to a serious illness to one of the children.
- Entertainment costs averaged €100 per month except for the three months of June, July and December, which averaged €170.
- Due to a wedding, presents cost an additional €190.
- Holidays were cancelled due to child's illness.

(A) Using the Budget Comparison Statement *on page 8 of Section A*, enter the appropriate figures into the **'Actual'** column.

Show the differences between the **'Actual'** and **'Budget'** figures by completing the column marked **'Difference'**. Use a **plus** or **minus** sign in front of each figure in that column.

Note: Use **'plus'** sign if **'Actual'** is GREATER than the **'Budget'** figure.
Use **'minus'** sign if **'Actual'** is LESS than the **'Budget'** figure.
Example:

	Budget	Actual	Difference
	260	200	– 60
	470	490	+ 20
Total	730	690	– 40

(22)

Answer the following parts **(B)** and **(C)** in the spaces provided *on page 9 of Section A.*

(B) **(i)** What was the budgeted closing cash at the of 2007?

(ii) How much had the Burke household budgeted to save during 2007?

(iii) What was the actual closing cash at the end of 2007?

(iv) State by how much the Burke household exceeded their budgeted total expenditure.

(v) Explain **one** possible reason why the 'Actual' interest was less than the 'Budget' interest. (10)

(C) **(i)** Explain the term 'discretionary expenditure'.

(ii) Explain the term 'health insurance'.

(iii) Give **two** examples of companies offering health insurance to the public in Ireland. (8)

(40 marks)

2. This is a Club Account Question.

Answer all parts of this question:

City Football Club had an opening stock of €12,000 in the bar on 1 May 2007.

The following is a summary of the Club's financial transactions for the year ending 30 April 2008:

Receipts:	€
Club Lotto	24,400
Bar Sales	47,600
Subscriptions	52,000
Payments:	€
Groundsman's Wages	22,100
Light and Heat	5,960
Purchase of Tractor	25,000
Bar Purchases	30,960
Insurance	11,200
Club Lotto Prizes	8,140
Telephone	1,655
Repairs and Maintenance	17,895

Additional information on 30 April 2008:

(i) Bar Stock €14,400
(ii) Light and Heat due €345
(iii) Subscriptions prepaid €2,500
(iv) Insurance prepaid €2,800
(v) Tractor to be depreciated by 20%.

(A) Prepare:
(i) A Bar Trading Account for the year ending 30 April 2008.
(ii) An Income and Expenditure Account for the year ending 30 April 2008.
(28)

(B) At the AGM, Mary Casey, the club officer who prepares the accounts, stated in her annual report that the Bar's gross profit percentage (gross margin) had improved this year.

(i) Identify the officer who prepares the accounts in a club.
(ii) Calculate the Bar's gross profit percentage.
(iii) Explain **two other** reasons why Mary Casey would prepare an annual report. (12)

(40 marks)

3. **This is a question on Factors of Production, National Budget and Opportunity Cost.**

Answer all parts of this question:

(A) State and explain the **four** Factors of Production, giving one example in **each** case. (12)

(B) The following figures were presented on Budget Day as projections for the year 2008:

Main items of Revenue and Expenditure	**Estimated Figures in Millions** €
Debt Servicing	290
PAYE	2,850
VAT	1,930
Health Services	1,960
Social Welfare	1,360
Education	1,490
Corporation Tax	260
Excise Duties	215
Agriculture	285

(i) Draft the National Budget for 2008 from the above information. State whether it is a 'surplus' or 'deficit' Budget.
(ii) Identify the Government Department responsible for preparing Ireland's National Budget.
(iii) Distinguish between Capital Expenditure and Current Expenditure for the Government. Use **one** example of **each** type of expenditure to explain your answer.
(iv) Explain, with an example, the term 'excise duties'. (24)

(C) Explain, with an example, the term 'opportunity cost'. (4)

(40 marks)

4. This is a Banking Question.

Answer all parts of this question:

John Murphy, Ashfield Park, Westport, Co. Mayo, has a Current Account Number 17940832 with AIB Bank, The Mall, Westport. The Branch Sorting Code Number is 93-26-05.

(A) In the past, John has paid his electricity bills by Laser Card (Debit Card). He has decided to pay future bills by Direct Debit.

His ESB Account Number is 753-889-462. His contact telephone number is 087-4536281.

On 5 June 2008, he completed a Direct Debit Instruction for the ESB.

(i) Complete the Direct Debit Instruction using the blank document in Section A, on page 369.

(ii) Explain **two** differences between Direct Debit and Standing Order.

(iii) Explain how a Laser Card (Debit Card) operates. (17)

(B) John is applying to his bank for a loan of €3,000 to finance new furniture.

(i) Give **three** examples of relevant questions which the bank manager would ask John before granting the loan.

(ii) Apart from Commercial Banks, name **two** other types of financial institution that offer loans to customers. (13)

(C) John is going on holiday to Canada. He goes to his bank to change €850 into Canadian Dollars and sees the following rates quoted:

CURRENCY	BANK SELLS	BANK BUYS
Canadian Dollar	1.50	1.60

(i) Calculate the total amount in Canadian Dollars that John will receive for his €850. Show your workings.

(ii) Explain **two** suitable methods of payment, other than cash, that John could use while shopping in Canada. (10)

(40 marks)

5. This is a Consumer Question.

Answer all parts of this question:

On 5 April 2008, Margaret Greally, High Street, Ballymote, Co. Sligo, bought a new microwave oven for €450 from Electric World Ltd, Port Road, Sligo. It was delivered the following day and while using it she discovered that it did not heat the food.

On 7 April 2008, Margaret wrote to the Sales Manager of Electric World Ltd outlining the problem, enclosing evidence of purchase and seeking **one** form of immediate redress.

(A) Write the letter that Margaret sent to Electric World Ltd on 7 April 2008. (19)

(B) **(i)** Explain **two other** forms of redress available to Margaret.

(ii) Name the consumer law which applies in this case.

(iii) State **two** relevant principles of consumer law which have been broken in this case.

(13)

(C) **(i)** Explain, with an example, the term 'impulse buying'.

(ii) Identify **two** characteristics of a good consumer. (8)

(40 marks)

6. This is a People at Work and Information Technology Question.

Answer all parts of this question:

The following advertisement appeared in a newspaper.

Roy Ltd
Main Road
Carlow

Staff required for Sales Department
Basic Pay: €425.50 for 37-hour week
Overtime and Flexitime available
IT skills required
Spreadsheet experience essential
Apply in writing *or* by e-mail to royltd@sipmail.com

Roy Ltd is an equal opportunities employer

(A) (i) Explain the **six** underlined terms in the above advertisement.

(ii) John Maguire applied for the position and forwarded his Curriculum Vitae (CV). List **three** pieces of information which John would give on his CV other than his name, address and telephone number.

(24)

(B) John's application for a job in Roy Ltd was successful. As an employee in the Sales Department, he may be entitled to commission. Experienced staff members often receive a benefit-in-kind from the company.

(i) Explain, with an example in **each** case, the terms 'benefit-in kind' **and** 'commission'.

(ii) Explain, with an example, how 'work' differs from 'employment'.

(10)

(C) Roy Ltd pays overtime on the basis that the first five hours are paid at time-and-a-half with double-time thereafter.

Calculate John's gross wage if he works 49 hours in a week. Show your workings.

(6)
(40 marks)

REMEMBER TO INCLUDE SECTION 'A' WITH YOUR ANSWER BOOK

Coimisiún na Scrúduithe Stáit
State Examinations Commission

JUNIOR CERTIFICATE EXAMINATION, 2008
BUSINESS STUDIES – HIGHER LEVEL – PAPER II
(160 marks)

TUESDAY, 10 JUNE – AFTERNOON, 2.00 p.m.–4.00 p.m.

- All questions carry equal marks.
- Attempt any **FOUR** questions.
- Marks will be awarded for layout and presentation including, where appropriate, folios and dates.
- Dates should show the day, month and year.
- Calculators may be used.

1. **This is a Book of First Entry, Ledger and Trial Balance Question.**

Answer all parts of this question:

KELLY Ltd is a retail store.

(A) Record the following Credit Transactions in the Purchases and Purchases Returns Books of KELLY Ltd for the month of April 2008. Post relevant figures from the books to the Ledger Accounts.

3/4/2008	Purchased goods on credit from NEE Ltd	Invoice No. 12	€16,000 + VAT 13.5%
9/4/2008	Purchased goods on credit from HAY Ltd	Invoice No. 67	€22,600 + VAT 13.5%
15/4/2008	Returned goods to NEE Ltd	Credit Note No. 5	€7,000 + VAT 13.5%

(16)

(B) Record the following Bank Transactions for the month of April in the Analysed Cash Book of KELLY Ltd. Post relevant figures to the Ledger Accounts.

Note: Analyse the Bank Transactions using the following money headings:

Debit (Receipts) Side:	Bank	Sales	VAT	Share Capital	
Credit (Payments) Side:	Bank	Purchases	VAT	Light and Heat	Creditors

1/4/2008	Shareholder invested €150,000 and this was lodged			Receipt No. 24
2/4/2008	Purchases for resale	(Cheque No. 45)	€70,000 + VAT 13.5%	
13/4/2008	Paid electricity bill	(Cheque No. 46)	€1,700	
19/4/2008	Cash Sales lodged		€90,800	(€80,000 + VAT €10,800)
28/4/2008	Paid HAY Ltd	(Cheque No. 47)	€17,500	

(15)

(C) Balance the accounts on 30 April 2008 and extract a Trial Balance as at that date.

(9)

(40 marks)

2. **This is a Sales, Business Documents and Bookkeeping Question.**

Answer all parts of this question:

(A) **(i)** State **three** methods of communication that a business could use to make enquiries about goods and services.

(ii) CARO Ltd purchased goods for €24,000. The mark-up on the goods when sold is 55%. All the goods were sold.

Calculate the Total Income to be made from the sale of all the goods. (Show your workings). (8)

(B) On 28 May 2008, BRIGHT PAINTS Ltd received an Order No. 3 from MARTIN Ltd, 10 Green Valley, Loughrea, Co. Galway for the following goods:

50	Ten litre drums of white paint	@	€60 per drum
50	Five litre drums of cream paint	@	€80 per drum
15	Five litre drums of wood preservative	@	€50 per drum

All the goods ordered were in stock, except for the wood preservative.

BRIGHT PAINT Ltd issued Invoice No. 42 for the goods in stock on 1 June 2008. The Invoice included the following terms: Trade Discount 30% and VAT 21%.

On receiving the goods and Invoice No. 42 on 4 June 2008, MARTIN Ltd paid the amount due in full.

BRIGHT PAINT Ltd issued Receipt No. 67 signed by Molly Bright, on today's date.

(i) What procedures would you recommend to BRIGHT PAINTS Ltd when preparing and processing receipts?

(ii) Complete Invoice No. 42 and Receipt No. 67 issued by BRIGHT PAINTS Ltd.

(iii) Record the issue of the Invoice and Receipt in the Sales Book and Analysed Cash Book of BRIGHT PAINTS Ltd *on the sheet supplied with this paper.* (32)

(40 marks)

3. This is a question on Employment and Industrial Relations.

Answer all parts of this question:

(A) State **three** rights and **three** responsibilities of employers. (6)

(B) Study the newspaper extract below and answer the questions that follow.

> Unions at Eircom are expected to serve strike notice on the company today after discussions to resolve a pay dispute collapsed. The unions must provide a week's notice of industrial action to management. The biggest union at the firm, the CWU, believes that the issue will go to the Labour Relations Commission when the notice is served. The CWU voted overwhelmingly in favour of industrial action after Eircom refused to pay workers a 2% increase due to them under the National Wage Agreement until they agreed to change their work practises.

(i) Name the **two** parties involved in the dispute.

(ii) What form of industrial action is being proposed?

(iii) Identify the third party who might help solve the dispute.

(10)

(C) **(i)** Other than pay, explain **three** possible reasons for industrial disputes.

(ii) Explain **three** of the following terms:

Arbitration

Conciliation

Shop Steward

Human Resource Manager.

(24)

(40 marks)

4. This is a Final Accounts and Balance Sheet Question.

Answer all parts of this question:

The following Trial Balance was extracted from the books of SCOTT Ltd on 31 May 2008. The Authorised Share Capital is 550,000 €1 ordinary shares.

TRIAL BALANCE OF SCOTT Ltd as on 31 May 2008	**Dr** €	**Cr** €
Purchases and Sales	175,000	273,500
Opening Stock 1/6/2007	12,000	
Import Duty	6,700	
Carriage Outwards	4,000	
Debtors and Creditors	60,000	30,000
Insurance	2,900	
Interest Receivable		6,500
Wages	44,000	
Machinery	120,000	
Buildings	300,000	
Bank	5,000	
25 Year Loan		140,000
Cash	1,400	
Land	230,000	
Reserves (Profit and Loss Balance)		111,000
Issued Share Capital: 400,000 €1 Ordinary Shares		400,000
	961,000	961,000

(A) You are required to prepare the company's **Trading, Profit and Loss Appropriation Account** for the year ending 31 May 2008 and a **Balance Sheet** as on that date.
You are given the following information as on 31 May 2008.

(i) Closing Stock €17,500
(ii) Import Duty due € 1,300
(iii) Interest Receivable due € 600
(iv) Insurance prepaid € 700
(v) Depreciation: Machinery 15%
(vi) Dividends declared 5% (35)

(B) Identify **two** suitable assets in the above TRIAL BALANCE which could be used as collateral for the 25 Year Loan. (5)

(40 marks)

5. **This is an Integrated Delivery Systems Question.**

Answer all parts of this question:

(A) Toll roads are being used more and more in Ireland.
State **one** advantage and **one** disadvantage for businesses that use them.
(4)

(B) Explain **two** reasons why a business might provide a delivery service for its customers.
(6)

(C) Calculate the cost of transport for **one day** from the following details provided by FAHY Ltd, a fruit distributor: (Show your workings.)

FAHY Ltd operates 330 working days per year

The diesel van used can do 33 kilometres per litre

The distance travelled per day is 660 kilometres

The cost of diesel is €1.10 per litre

Gross wage of driver €240 per day

Employer's PRSI is 12.5%

Annual Motor Tax is €1,320

Annual Motor Insurance is €2,640

Annual Motor Repairs is €1,650

Toll charges are €30 per day.

(16)

(D) On 25 May 2008, FAHY Ltd purchased a new delivery van on credit from COX MOTORS Ltd for €56,000.

Record the purchase of the delivery van in the General Journal and appropriate Ledger accounts of FAHY Ltd *on the sheet supplied with this paper.*

(14)
(40 marks)

6. This is an Analysed Cash Book and Monitoring of Overheads Question.

Answer all parts of this question:

(A) Identify **three** procedures a business should have in place to monitor its overheads. (6)

(B) Prepare the Analysed Cash Book of LP PLUMBERS Ltd from the data set out below.
Note: Use the following money column headings:

Debit (Receipts) Side: Bank

Credit (Payments) Side: Bank Wages Advertising Van Telephone Interest

			€
1/5/2008	Owed to the bank		1,200
2/5/2008	Paid for advertising	Cheque No. 1	3,000
4/5/2008	Received from WALSHE Ltd	Receipt No. 1	4,300
7/5/2008	Paid Eircom	Cheque No. 2	800
9/5/2008	Paid wages	Cheque No. 3	700
11/5/2008	Received from JONES Ltd	Receipt No. 2	6,700
14/5/2008	Paid diesel bill	Cheque No. 4	480
16/5/2008	Paid interest on loan	Cheque No. 5	500
18/5/2008	Paid wages	Cheque No. 6	550
22/5/2008	Received from St. Mary's GAA Club	Receipt No. 3	1,600
24/5/2008	Paid for advertising	Cheque No. 7	4,500
27/5/2008	Paid road tax for van	Cheque No. 8	800
29/5/2008	Paid insurance for van	Cheque No. 9	3,200
31/5/2008	Received from KELLY Ltd	Receipt No. 4	8,500

(17)

(C) *On the sheet supplied with this paper* you will find a partially completed table showing Budgeted Overheads for May 2008.

(i) Complete the **Actual** Column using the totals from the Analysed Cash Book.

(ii) List the overheads whose actual figures are **greater than** the budgeted figures and give **one** possible reason for the difference in each case *in the relevant section of the sheet supplied with this paper.*

(iii) List the overheads whose actual figures are **less than** the budgeted figures and give **one** possible reason for the difference in each case *in the relevant section of the sheet supplied with this paper.*

(17)

(40 marks)

Index